# European Monetary Integration

## The Euro

## George K. Zestos

## THOMSON

## SOUTH-WESTERN

THE ROBERT GORDON UNIVERSITY

Australia · Canada · Me — · United States

0060018288

**THOMSON**

**SOUTH-WESTERN**

European Monetary Integration: The Euro
George K. Zestos

**VP/Editorial Director:** *Jack W. Calhoun*

**VP/Editor-in-Chief:** *Dave Shaut*

**Developmental Editor:**
*Michael Guendelsberger*

**Sr. Marketing Manager:** *John Carey*

**Production Editor:** *Cliff Kallemeyn*

**Sr. Manufacturing Coordinator:**
*Sandee Milewski*

**Art Director:** *Michelle Kunkler*

**Production House:**
*Interactive Composition Corporation*

**Printer:** *RR Donnelley*
*Crawfordsville, IN*

For more information about our products,
contact us at:

Thomson Learning Academic Resource
Center

1-800-423-0563

**Thomson Higher Education**
5191 Natorp Boulevard
Mason, OH 45040
USA

**Asia (including India)**
Thomson Learning
5 Shenton Way
#01-01 UIC Building
Singapore 068808

**Australia/New Zealand**
Thomson Learning Australia
102 Dodds Street
Southbank, Victoria 3006
Australia

**Canada**
Thomson Nelson
1120 Birchmount Road
Toronto, Ontario
M1K 5G4
Canada

**Latin America**
Thomson Learning
Seneca, 53
Colonia Polanco
11560 Mexico
D.F. Mexico

**UK/Europe/Middle East/Africa**
Thomson Learning
High Holborn House
50/51 Bedford Row
London WC1R 4LR
United Kingdom

**Spain (including Portugal)**
Thomson Paraninfo
Calle Magallanes, 25
28015 Madrid, Spain

# Acronyms

| | |
|---|---|
| CA | Current account |
| CEECs | Central and Eastern European countries |
| CPI | Consumer price index |
| CV | Coefficient of variation |
| EC | European Community |
| ECB | European Central Bank |
| ECOFIN | Council of Ministers of Economics and Finance |
| ECSC | European Coal and Steel Community |
| ECU | European Currency Unit |
| EEC | European Economic Community |
| EMCF | European Monetary Cooperation Fund |
| EMI | European Monetary Institute |
| EMS | European Monetary System |
| EMU | Economic and Monetary Union |
| EONIA | Euro Overnight Index Average |
| EPU | European Payments Union |
| ERM | Exchange Rate Mechanism |
| ESCB | European System of Central Banks |
| EU | European Union |
| EUA | European Unit of Account |
| EURATOM | European Atomic Energy Community |
| FA | Financial account |
| FDI | Foreign direct investment |
| FE | Forward exchange rate |
| GDP | Gross domestic product |
| HICP | Harmonized Indices of Consumer Prices |
| IBRD | International Bank for Reconstruction and Development |
| IGC | Intergovernmental conference |
| IMF | International Monetary Fund |
| IT | Information technology |
| LDC | Less developed country |
| MAER | Monetary approach to the exchange rate determination |
| NCB | National Central Banks |
| NE | Nominal exchange rate |
| NEER | Nominal effective exchange rate |
| OCA | Optimum Currency Area |
| OECD | Organization of Economic Cooperation and Development |
| OEEC | Organization for European Economic Cooperation |
| PBAER | Portfolio balance approach to the exchange rate determination |
| PI | Portfolio investment |
| PPI | Producer price index |
| PPP | Purchasing power parity |
| RE | Real exchange rate |
| REER | Real effective exchange rate |
| SEA | Single European Act |
| SEM | Single European Market |
| SGP | Stability and Growth Pact |
| TARGET | Trans-European Automated Real Time Gross Settlement Express Transfer |
| TEU | Treaty on the European Union |

*To My Parents*
*Konstantinos and Vasiliki Zestos*

George K. Zestos is presently an Associate Professor of Economics at Christopher Newport University in Newport News, Virginia. Dr. Zestos was born in a small town in Thessaly, Greece at the foot of Mount Olympus. He began his university studies at the Aristotelian University of Thessaloniki Greece, where he studied economics and political science for two years. He continued his college education in the US at Saginaw Valley State University in Michigan where he received a B.A. degree in economics and business. He received his M.A. in economics from Michigan State University and his Ph.D. from Indiana University (Bloomington).

His fields of specialization are international economics and public finance. In addition to economic principles, Professor Zestos also teaches international economics, research methods in economics, public finance, managerial economics, business forecasting, money and banking, and European economic integration. Dr. Zestos taught at Depauw University and Ball State University for six years before he started teaching at Christopher Newport University.

His research interests are on international economics, and particularly in the European economic integration, a topic in which he wrote his Ph.D. dissertation, publishes, teaches, and often gives lectures. His research has appeared in journals and edited books in the US and in other countries. His articles have appeared in a variety of journals, including: *Journal of Economic Integration* (Korea), *Southern Economic Journal* (US), *Journal of International Economic Studies* (Japan), *Review of International Economics* (US), *Atlantic Economic Journal* (US), *Economia Internazionale* (Italy), *Journal of Business and Society* (Cyprus), and *Journal of Economic Asymmetries* (Canada). He involves several students in his research and collaborates with scholars from the US and other countries, such as China, Canada, and Greece. His hobbies are traveling, fishing, soccer, and reading.

# Contents

# Preface

Writing a book on European monetary integration and the euro is a true challenge since significant changes in this area occur so frequently. These changes are introduced by any of the European Union (EU) governing institutions or by the Economic and Monetary Union (EMU) authorities.

Currency markets can also affect the European monetary integration process and international monetary and financial conditions. On December 24, 2004, the euro hit an all-time record high against the dollar. Following this record, any plausible forecast would have suggested that this would have been the end of a further euro appreciation. The euro, however, surprised everyone by attaining record highs for four consecutive trading days before and after Christmas on December 23, 24, 27, and 28, 2004, reaching its last record high against the US dollar at $1.3641.

European integration, and more specifically, European monetary integration, is a unique and unprecedented phenomenon in the world's economic and monetary history. Never before have such a large number of sovereign states voluntarily given up their monetary, exchange rate, and to a large extent, their fiscal policies to a supranational authority. EU countries have derived benefits above their costs from joining the EU. This started with the Treaty of Rome in 1957, when the EU established a customs union and a common market.

The formation of the EMU and the adoption of the euro by 12 EU countries, which became known as the Euro Area (Eurozone) countries according to many authors, resulted in benefits exceeding costs. This claim is supported since no Euro Area country has ever left the EMU and since other EU countries are interested in joining the EMU. The greatest tangible benefit of the EMU is the established price stability in the Euro Area countries.

The Mercado Comun del Cono Sur (MERCOSUR or Southern Cone Common Market), which is a Latin American trading bloc, recently proposed to include more countries and to launch a monetary union like the EU did. This proposal constitutes further evidence of the EMU's success. The euro has been around for more than six years (since its introduction) and trades against the dollar and most other major currencies above its introductory values. This provides strong evidence that the euro will survive and will perform well as a world currency. Economic and monetary integration in Europe is now recognized to have benefitted all member countries. The greatest benefit derived from European integration, however, may be the establishment of permanent peace and prosperity in Europe.

## Chapter Sequence of the Text

Students and reviewers who read the chapters of the manuscript expressed surprise in discovering that so much had occurred prior to the introduction of the euro. Indeed, important events contributed to the establishment of the EU and the formation of the EMU. This explains why Chapter 1 begins with a historical perspective highlighting the most important events (causes) that created the appropriate environment for the formation of the EU and the EMU. Since this book focuses on European monetary integration and the euro, the text moves quickly to examine whether the EU countries were likely to profit from the formation of a monetary union.

The introduction of a common currency by the Euro Area countries was a huge step beyond the established customs union and the common market. To study whether a monetary union was an appropriate choice, economists invoked the Optimum Currency Area (OCA) theory. The OCA theory identifies the necessary characteristics of candidate countries to form a successful monetary union. In Chapter 2, the book examines whether EU countries have the necessary characteristics for the formation of a successful monetary union. A monetary union can be exposed to great risk caused by asymmetric shocks. If business fluctuations (business cycles) differ among member countries, a common monetary policy will be ineffective. Accordingly, Chapter 2 examines the effect of EU policies in transforming the EU to an OCA.

A number of agreements among the EU countries following the Treaty of Rome, motivated by the Werner Plan and the Delors Report, led to the formation of the EMU and the adoption of the euro on January 1, 1999. The launching of the euro occurred after the required nominal convergence of the candidate member countries was attained. Nominal convergence was explicitly stated in the Maastricht Treaty, which required candidate EMU countries to achieve price stability. To achieve price stability, candidate countries were required to meet five convergence criteria. These became known as Maastricht Convergence Criteria and involved the following macroeconomic variables: inflation, long-term interest rates, government deficit and debt to GDP ratios, and exchange rates. Through severe austerity measures, the EU countries achieved price stability that allowed the EMU to become reality on January 1, 1999.

Meeting the Maastricht Convergence Criteria required monetary and fiscal discipline. To safeguard the euro, the Stability and Growth Pact (SGP) was adopted. The main goal of the SGP was to restrain countries from excessive spending. This was an area where some EU countries made promises they could not keep; several have violated the SGP. As a result, the "mechanics" of the SGP were frozen temporarily. The Maastricht criteria and the SGP are discussed in Chapter 3.

The Euro Area countries created the necessary institutions to allow them to conduct a single monetary policy. Indeed, the National System of Central Banks (NSCB) was established and is comprised of the European Central Bank (ECB) and the member countries' National Central Banks (NCBs).

The ECB is an independent central bank free of influence from the 12 member Euro Area countries' governments or any other EU institution. The ECB is responsible for exercising monetary policy in the Eurozone. During its first six years, the ECB attained and maintained price stability. However, several political leaders and economists accused the ECB that its contractionary monetary policy since 2002 delayed the Euro Area recovery. In Chapter 4, the ECB's single monetary policy is discussed. Throughout this chapter, the ECB monetary policy is compared with the US Federal Reserve (the Fed) monetary policy.

Chapters 5, 6, and 7 primarily deal with the performance of the euro versus a few major world currencies. Various exchange rate theories are empirically tested in Chapter 7, examining how accurately they predict exchange rates. Since the dominant world currency is the US dollar, most of the discussion and analysis pertains to the dollar-euro exchange rate.

Chapter 5 presents and discusses six years of data on the nominal exchange rates of the euro with respect to several major world currencies. In addition to the nominal exchange rate, the real dollar-euro exchange rate is discussed. To evaluate the overall performance of a currency, the trade-weighted or nominal effective exchange rate was constructed. The nominal effective and real effective exchange rates for the euro, the US dollar, the Japanese yen, and the Swiss franc are constructed and illustrated in the same graphs for comparison purposes.

In Chapter 6, a supply and demand model of euros is developed to explain movements in the dollar-euro exchange rate. Knowledge of the US and EU economies starting in the early 1990s is necessary for an in-depth understanding of changes in the dollar-euro exchange rate. In the same chapter, an analysis of the balance of payments of the US, the Euro Area, Japan, and China sheds further light on the dollar-euro exchange rate. Large US current account deficits, accompanied with the pegging of the Chinese yuan and other South-East Asian currencies to the US dollar, contributed significantly to the continuous depreciation of the dollar versus the euro after 2001. This analysis supports the view that the value of the US dollar depends on the willingness of foreign investors and foreign central banks to invest in the US by buying US government bonds.

In Chapter 7, established exchange rate theories are employed to explain the performance of the euro versus the US dollar, the UK pound sterling, and the Japanese yen. Considering that the euro has been in existence for only a few years, exchange rate theories designed to explain exchange rate movements in the long-run are not expected to be useful in predicting the value of the euro exchange rate. Indeed, this is the case for the Purchasing Power Parity (PPP) theory (absolute and relative versions). These two theories, however, predict the direction of the dollar-euro exchange rate, allowing one to correctly forecast appreciation or depreciation of the euro over longer periods of time. Similar results were obtained by the uncovered interest rate parity theory.

The covered interest rate parity theory, however, was found to hold closely thanks to the existence of the forward exchange rate markets that eliminate exchange rate risk. Combining the term structure of interest rates with the interest rate parity theory yields accurate results in predicting exchange rate changes. This is useful information, especially in light of the volatility and uncertainty in the dollar-euro exchange rate starting in the fall of 2004.

Chapter 8 deals with the 10 new countries that joined the EU on May 1, 2004. It examines whether these ten new countries' economies achieved sufficient real and nominal convergence to qualify for membership to the EMU. For this purpose, the countries' performances are evaluated with respect to the five Maastricht Convergence Criteria. While substantial progress has been made, more work has to be done to attain price and fiscal stability to qualify for EMU membership and adoption of the euro. Fiscal stability will become a major problem for these countries in the next few years as they will have to meet the Maastricht Convergence Criteria prior to adopting the euro. The book concludes by considering prospects for future developments in the dollar-euro exchange rate and visions for the EU and the EMU.

# To Users of the Text

This textbook was written in a language accessible and useful to many readers. The reader-friendly approach of the text was adopted without a need to compromise the rigorous or in-depth analysis. Many people who are interested in the EMU and the euro, which is frequently making the front page of many newspapers and magazines, will find the book challenging and useful.

The highest mathematics utilized by the text is algebra, used only in Chapter 7. The two appendices that utilize a diagrammatic analysis are purposefully placed at the ends of the chapters. Readers who are not interested in the graphical analysis may skip the appendices and go to the next chapters without a loss of continuity.

Chapter 6 utilizes a demand-supply diagram to explain the dollar-euro exchange rate. Even those readers with no formal background in introductory economics should understand this analysis as the requisite demand-supply economic tools are explained there.

The book can be used for various courses and by different departments. It can be used as the single text for an undergraduate course or for a seminar on European monetary integration and the euro. It can be used as a second text in courses on European integration along with another general text. The book can be used as a second textbook or as a supplement in a variety of undergraduate courses including international economics, international finance, and money and banking. Business schools offering courses or seminars on international business with an emphasis on Europe can adopt this book as a second text or as a supplement for undergraduate or Masters level courses. International relations departments offering courses on Europe at the undergraduate or graduate level may adopt the text. Political science and government departments that offer courses on contemporary Europe will find the text appropriate for several courses.

The book can be used by those interested in the European monetary integration and wish to go beyond the coverage in magazines and newspapers. Business people who are interested in Europe and the Euro Area will find this text provides logical and plausible explanations for the formation of the EMU and the dollar-euro exchange rate.

Financial investors, including individual and corporate financial officers, who may wish to consider a more international portfolio that includes foreign currencies will find this text interesting and informative. For such investors, the euro should be considered as a serious candidate currency for a diversified portfolio. The book can be an important aid to international financial investors.

Readers will enhance their knowledge on contemporary economic and monetary affairs of Europe and the euro. Readers may access Power-Point software at the author's website: http://www.cnu.edu/busn/faculty/g_zestos.html. This software includes all the tables and graphs from the chapters of the text.

## Acknowledgments

I would like to express my gratitude to the economics editor at South-Western, Mr. Peter Adams, to the Developmental Editor, Mr. Michael Guendelsberger, and the Production Editor, Cliff Kallemeyn, who made the writing of this book a pleasant journey by being such great professionals to work with from the beginning to the end of the project. I thank my European Economic Integration students at Indiana University and at Christopher Newport University, who enthusiastically received these courses, participated in meaningful discussions, and asked many thorough and penetrating questions. Mark Tyndal, Richard Hofler, Lambis Filis, and John Dahlgren are a few of these students. I thank Professor Norman Furniss from Indiana University. As chairman of the department of West European Studies, Dr. Furniss, along with his colleagues, selected me from many qualified applicants to teach a seminar on West European Integration. This occurred when I was a graduate student in economics at Indiana University. This appointment was an intellectual challenge to me. Dr. Furniss recommended me for a generous grant from the US Department of Education that I was awarded and helped me complete my dissertation.

I express my gratitude to two of my colleagues and friends from Christopher Newport University, Dr. Robert Winder and Dr. Roark Mulligan, who read the entire manuscript and provided help, encouragement, constructive criticism, and editing. Professor Michele Fratianni, chair of the Business Economics Department of the Business School at Indiana University and family friend, read the entire manuscript and provided constructive criticism and useful recommendations that have improved the text. Dr. Georgios Chortareas, of the Central Bank of England, read and commented on some of the chapters as did Professors Travis Taylor and Gemma Kotula from Christopher Newport University. Thank you one and all.

I am grateful to Christopher Newport University for continuous support and for awarding me a sabbatical to write this text and for providing me with a sequence of Faculty Development Research Grants. A few students from my International Economics and European Integration courses read the chapters and helped me with useful suggestions and editing. I would like to thank my students, Lucas Edwards, Hamilton Pham and John Branton. My student research assistants helped me with the book and other research projects at different times. Gregory Zimonopoulos, Claire Neaves, Jeannie Chung, John McCleary and James Crippen were exceptionally helpful. Lastly I would like to thank my family, my wife Eva and my son Kostis for their patience, and particularly my son, Alexander Zestos. Alexander and my research assistant, John McCleary, were dedicated and helped me finalize the manuscript. I would like to thank the European Central Bank for granting permission to publish the Glossary and Table 4.1 (The Eurosystem Monetary Operation).

# W e b s i t e s

http://www.bankofengland.co.uk/Links/setframe.html

http://www.bea.gov

http://www.bloomberg.com

http://www.economist.com/markets/Bigmac/Index.cfm

http://europa.eu.int/comm/eurostat/newcronos/reference/sdds/en/exint/
ermfluc_sm.htm

http://www.ecb.int

http://www.ecb.int/bc/intro/html/map.en.html

http://europa.eu.int/comm/economy_finance/euro/transition/conversion_
rates.htm

http://dailynews.yahoo.com/h/nm/20011231/wl/euro_dc_5.html

http://www.euractiv.com

http://www.oanda.com

http://fx.sauders.ubc.ca

http://www.nationmaster.com

http://english.people.com.cn/200403/08/eng20040308_136818.shtml

http://news.muzi.com/ll/English/1344873.shtml

# chapter 1

# A Historical Review of European Monetary Integration

## Introduction

On March 1, 2002, the euro became the sole legal tender in the Euro Area (Eurozone), a group consisting of twelve European Union (EU) countries: Austria, Belgium, Finland, France, Germany, Greece, Ireland, Italy, Luxembourg, the Netherlands, Portugal and Spain.[1] The massive withdrawal of the national paper currencies and coins and their replacement with euros during the period of January 1, 2002 through February 28, 2003, was reported as exceptionally smooth. The adoption of the common currency by the Euro Area countries is an event of extraordinary importance without a precedent in world history, and this adoption has already had a major impact on the international financial system.

The twelve Euro Area (EU12) countries presently constitute the largest and most economically integrated group of countries in the world with a population of over 300 million people. The adoption of the euro in the long run is expected to facilitate trade among countries, encourage foreign investment, promote price stability, and boost economic growth in the world economy. The introduction of the euro and the establishment of the European Central Bank (ECB), which is responsible for monetary policy in the Euro Area, is not a surprise to anyone who has closely followed the historical, economic, and political developments in Europe. The Economic and Monetary Union (EMU) was created by the historical and celebrated Maastricht Treaty (1992). This treaty paved the way for the arrival of the euro as a result of more than 50 years of economic and monetary integration on the European continent.

## The Early Years of Reconstruction and Reconciliation in Europe

At the end of World War II, Europe was left devastated and divided. The European people became fearful, uncertain of the future, and distrusting of humanity. Out of human despair and ruins, hope was born for a new beginning and peace. The United States (US) demonstrated its strong will and determination to assist in the reconstruction of Western Europe with the historical Marshall Plan through massive aid distributed to these countries. Americans and Europeans quickly realized that the division of Western Europe into small independent nation-states that followed protective trade policies hindered economic development. High trade barriers and the immobility of factors of production (capital and labor) between regions and countries became bottlenecks to development and economic growth. To overcome this problem, it became evident that Western Europe could substantially benefit from integrating economically.

In the 18th century, a few authors and intellectuals proposed European unification; no political group or party, however, had ever pursued these ideas. It was only after the two World Wars that some Europeans visualized a unified Europe as the only safe way to prevent future conflicts. The Pan-European Union Movement, initiated by the Austrian Count Richard Coudenhove-Kallergi, succeeded in mobilizing some people for the unification of Europe. A Pan-European Congress was organized in 1926, but despite some initial successes, the movement died out quickly. More than anyone else, Jean Monnet, a French businessman and politician who served as the minister of planning and industrial development in the General de Gaulle government (1946–1955), laid the foundation and plans for the long road to European integration. Monnet proposed to the German government that coal and steel production should be organized in both countries into a single market, regulated by a joint supranational authority and not separately by the national governments. The Germans were receptive to the proposal, as were the BENELUX countries, and Italy expressed its interest to participate in the common market for coal and steel.[2]

The six countries approved a plan to establish the European Coal and Steel Community (ECSC), a common market in the two commodities to be achieved by eliminating tariffs and quotas between member countries. This plan, announced by the French Foreign Minister Robert Shuman, became known as the Shuman Declaration. In April 1951, with the Treaty of Paris, six European countries (Belgium, France, Germany, Italy, Luxembourg, and the Netherlands) established the ECSC. The objectives of this historical treaty were to create an efficient European market for coal and steel and, more importantly, to safeguard peace in the European continent by controlling coal and steel, i.e., the means to war.

The ECSC was administered mainly by institutions independent of their national governments. These institutions were the High Authority, the Court of Justice, and the European Assembly. The

Council of Ministers was a governing institution of the ECSC but was comprised of cabinet members (ministers) of the national governments that represented the interests of their own countries. The ECSC was a unique organization, since it was delegated authority by the member states beyond their own power in areas involving production, distribution, and competition of steel and coal. The ECSC turned out to be a great success and marked the beginning of the long road to European economic integration. For this reason, Jean Monnet is considered the founding father of European unification.

## The European Economic Community (EEC) and the European Atomic Energy Community (EURATOM)

Because the ECSC turned out to be beneficial to all its member states, the leaders of the six countries decided to expand the ECSC's success to new horizons. In June 1955, the foreign ministers of the six ECSC member countries held a conference in Messina, Sicily, chaired by the Prime Minister of Belgium, Paul Henri Spaak, to study the possibility of establishing a customs union. The following year, at the ECSC foreign ministers' meeting in Venice, a proposal was introduced announcing the intention of creating a customs union and a common market.[3] In March 1957 in Rome, the six ECSC countries signed two more treaties, which created the European Economic Community (EEC) and the European Atomic Energy Community (EURATOM). The EURATOM created a common market for atomic energy, and the EEC established a common market and a customs union for all other commodities. In addition, the EEC provided for common policies among all member states aiming to correct market deficiencies in the three common markets.[4]

The visionaries who wrote the Treaty of Rome (1957) set high and noble objectives aiming to "promote harmonious and balanced economic growth to all members and regions for the purpose of raising the standards of living in all member countries."[5] With the 1967 merger treaty, the three communities began sharing the same governing institutions: the Commission, the European Court of Justice, the European Parliament, and the Council of Ministers.[6] After the 1967 merger treaty, the three communities (ECSC, EURATOM, and EEC) became known as the European Community (EC). By the end of 1968, the customs union was complete, three years ahead of its schedule and, as a result, all tariffs and quotas were eliminated. According to many empirical studies, the rapid trade liberalization within the EC boosted economic growth and development in the six EC member countries.

In 1973, Ireland, the UK, and Denmark joined the EC, and Greece became the tenth member in 1981. Portugal and Spain joined in 1986. The EC gradually became a vital economic entity with competencies in several areas. The Commission is the sole representative for all the EC countries in international forums, such as the World Trade Organization (WTO), for trade negotiations. In addition, the EC Commission solely exercises its authority and signs bilateral and multilateral trade agreements.

The decision-making process within the EC is rather cumbersome and complex. The EC countries chose a unique way to integrate their economies. Two distinct and opposite approaches to economic integration exist that continue to be influential in the shaping of the EC. The first approach is known as federalism. According to this approach, the EC should evolve similarly to the US as an entity with a powerful federal European central government, i.e., the EC should develop into the United States of Europe. According to the other approach (intergovernmentalism), the EC countries should integrate their economies through intergovernmental negotiations by adopting and undertaking only those policies and programs that are jointly agreed upon by all member state governments. Intergovermentalism requires the EC member states to reserve all sovereign powers to themselves and not delegate authority to the EC institutions. The EC followed a middle of the road solution by adopting some aspects from both approaches.

## The Single European Market (SEM)

Due to the diminishing benefits from trade liberalization and the 1973–1974 and the 1979–1980 oil crises, many EC economies began revealing signs of weakness and a tendency for stagnation. "Eurosclerosis" was a term used to describe this new economic phenomenon, which was making inroads in Europe. Economists and politicians soon realized that the EC needed a new impetus to stimulate its economies and redirect them to a more rapid economic growth path. Such an impetus was initiated in a 1985 white paper by the EC Commission that outlined a plan for the creation of the SEM. Existing differences and requirements in product safety, health standards, non-tariff trade barriers, and tax rates on commodities and factors of production were a few of the hindrances that kept the EC from becoming a true common market.

In 1985, the Commission presented a white paper that listed all the crucial areas requiring harmonization in the EC countries. According to the 1985 white paper, harmonization was to be completed by 1992 by all member countries to create a true SEM in the EU. For this reason, the Single Market Program is often referred to as "Europe 1992." The Single Market Program was adopted in 1987 when the EC member countries signed the Single European Act (SEA). By the end of 1992, the EC member states introduced approximately 300 EC directives into national legislation. These became national laws complying with the SEA and intended to create a SEM without internal frontiers for goods, services, capital, and labor. The SEM is considered a great success and the most important program after the treaties of Paris and Rome that promoted European integration in the 1980s and 1990s.

As the EC countries began to benefit from the implementation of the SEM program, it was quickly realized that the EC currencies were exposed to an increased exchange rate risk. This increased exchange rate risk was the result of the free capital mobility introduced to the EC countries as was required by the SEA. Free capital mobility conflicted with the fixed exchange rate system that had essentially prevailed for several years in the EC and was the foundation of the European Monetary System (EMS).

# The Early Years of European Monetary Integration: The Post World War II Period

## The Bretton Woods International Monetary System

At the end of World War II, a new international monetary system was established. This system became known as the Bretton Woods International Monetary System (or the Bretton Woods System), named after the small town in New Hampshire, US, where the representatives of 44 countries met in 1944. The Bretton Woods System was a fixed exchange rate system with the US dollar as its anchor (key) currency. The US, according to the Bretton Woods System, was obligated to keep the price of gold fixed at $35 per ounce. All other countries fixed the price of their currency in relation to the dollar and indirectly, in terms of the gold. The central banks of all member countries were obligated to intervene and support their exchange rates, maintaining them within a specified band of $\pm 1$ percent.

The Bretton Woods agreement, besides establishing the new International Monetary System, set up two sister international organizations: the International Monetary Fund (IMF) and the International Bank for Reconstruction and Development (IBRD), or the World Bank, as it is popularly known.[7] The IMF was designed to assist member countries with short-term balance of payment difficulties and thus facilitate international trade and finance. The World Bank was established to provide subsidized low interest rate loans to less developed countries (LDCs) for the purpose of fostering economic growth and development. All the Western European countries became members of the Bretton Woods System.

## The European Payments Union (EPU)

In April 1948, the Organization for European Economic Cooperation (OEEC) was established as an intergovernmental organization to oversee the effective allocation of the US Marshall Plan aid to Europe. The OEEC was entrusted with the task of assuring that US aid was distributed according to the donor country's conditions. These conditions were the coordination of economic policies among aid recipient countries and the reduction of tariffs and quotas. Furthermore, to minimize balance of payments problems among West European countries, the European Payments Union (EPU) was established in 1950 by pooling together the West European countries' international reserves.

As discussed, under the Bretton Woods System, all West European countries, as members, were required to keep their exchange rates fixed relative to the dollar and, by implication, fixed in relation to each other's currencies. During the years of reconstruction in Europe following World War II, all European countries were in great need of US dollars. This resulted in an excess demand for US currency. Such a situation prevailed in Europe for several years. The cause of this problem was the constraint of European countries that could only pay for their imports with US dollars since their currencies were not accepted for international payments.

According to the EPU, exporting countries could receive half of the payments in dollars and half in the currency of the importing (debtor) countries. This arrangement alleviated the dollar scarcity problem to a certain degree. Nonetheless, it was unanimously agreed in 1958 to dissolve the EPU. By that time, the West European currencies had all become convertible for international payment. The OEEC fulfilled its mission and was renamed the Organization of Economic Cooperation and Development (OECD), a well-known international organization that exists today with new objectives. It is now mainly an economics research institution, and is often referred to as the "Paris Club" or the "Club of the Rich Nations" since most of its members are the wealthiest countries in the world.

## The Werner Plan

The Treaty of Rome did not explicitly address monetary integration though it included two small chapters on national economic policy coordination. As early as 1958, the EC established the Monetary Committee as an advisory body to the Council of Ministers of Economics and Finance (ECOFIN). In 1964, the Committee of the Central Bank Governors was formed by the EC as part of a grandiose plan proposed by the Commission aiming to achieve the formation of a complete monetary union by 1971. The Committee of the Central Bank Governors, however, did not become functional before the 1970s. In 1969, at the Hague Summit, the EC heads of states appointed a committee headed by the Prime Minister of Luxembourg, Pierre Werner, to study the feasibility of the formation of a European monetary union.[8] In the following year (1970), the Werner Committee presented its report recommending the formation of a European Monetary Union within ten years, by 1980. The Werner report envisaged the formation of a monetary union in three chronological stages.

In the first stage that was to last three years, the EC governments were to begin coordinating monetary and fiscal policies on a voluntary basis and, thus, reduce exchange rate variability to a smaller range than the ±1 percent authorized by the IMF under the Bretton Woods System. In the second stage, the European Monetary Cooperation Fund (EMCF) was to be created to assist governments in stabilizing the foreign exchange markets. In the third stage, the EMCF was going to evolve into the Central European Bank, which would be responsible for monetary policy. In this final stage, exchange rates would become irrevocably fixed. Lastly, the EC countries would coordinate their fiscal national policies, and the EC budget would increase substantially.

Three important events worked against the Werner Plan and the establishment of a European Monetary Union by 1980. The first event was the collapse of the Bretton Woods System in August 1971. The principal reason for this collapse was a major structural change in international monetary conditions. Specifically, the supply of dollars increased outside the US in comparison to the early years of the Bretton Woods System. This structural change shook the foundation of the Bretton Woods system of fixed exchange rates because the market fundamentals for its key currency, the dollar, had changed radically. The second event was the entrance of the UK, Ireland, and Denmark in the EC, which made exchange rate agreements even more difficult. The third event that worked against the Werner Plan was the October 1973 oil crisis that affected EC countries differently and forced them to abandon the coordination of macroeconomic policies. During the 1973–1974 recession, each EC country was compelled to focus on its own battle against domestic macroeconomic problems and on the fight against national unemployment.

Despite the abandonment of the Werner Plan, not all of the plan's provisions were lost. Several of its recommendations found their way to the EMS (1979), to the Delors Report in December 1989, and to the Maastricht Treaty in 1992.[9] One of the recommendations of the Werner Plan was the reduction of the band margins of the exchange rates for the EC countries to a narrower range than the ±1 percent allowed by the Bretton Woods System. The exchange rate fluctuation band, however, became irrelevant after August 1971 due to the collapse of the Bretton Woods System and the suspension of the dollar convertibility to gold announced by US President Nixon.

## The Breakup of the Bretton Woods System

According to the Smithsonian Agreement, which was characterized as the last effort to save the Bretton Woods System, the EC currencies were allowed to fluctuate within a range of ±2.25 percent against any of the G10 major developed countries' currencies and another ±2.25 percent against each other.[10] In March 1972, the EC countries decided to reduce the band margins and let their currencies fluctuate within a ±1.125 percent range or within a total range of 2.25 percent against each other. This narrow band of exchange rate fluctuation of the EU currencies was called "the snake." The EC countries, however, maintained the old margins of ±2.25 percent or a total of 4.5 percent against any other currency of the G10 countries, such as the US dollar. This wider band of fluctuation for the EC currencies versus G10 countries' currencies and the dollar was called "the tunnel." This entire exchange rate arrangement became known as the "snake inside the tunnel."

The snake in the tunnel did not last long. In March 1973, the Bretton Woods System was replaced by the floating exchange rate system for most major industrialized countries. Many developing countries, however, pegged their currencies to one of the major industrial countries' currencies. As the tunnel broke down, a few EC countries decided to respect the snake margins. The countries that participated in the joint float were Belgium, Denmark, Germany, the Netherlands, and Luxembourg. These countries demonstrated a high degree of price stability by generally following the monetary policy of the German Central Bank, the Bundesbank.

These five countries, along with a few other EC countries that joined the snake in 1979, embarked on a new program of monetary integration. This program became known as the EMS and has played a crucial role in European monetary integration. The EMS was developed as a result of the political will and determination of the French President Valery Giscard D'Estaing and the German Chancellor Helmut Schmidt, who were committed to creating a zone of monetary and exchange rate stability in the EC. Thus, while the Werner Plan was forever shelved, monetary integration continued with a new and important but less ambitious program of European monetary integration, the EMS.

# The European Monetary System (EMS)

While economists were divided on how to achieve monetary integration in Europe after the failure of the Werner Plan, politicians took the leading role in designing a new program to pursue monetary integration. The German chancellor Helmut Schmidt, French president Valery Giscard D'Estaing, and the EC Commission were the driving force for this new program for monetary integration in the EC. During the last fifty years of European integration, politicians and some EC governments were visionaries and initiators of new ideas promoting further integration. They have been ahead of their people, who often were hesitant and unconvinced of the merits of economic integration because they were unwilling to surrender their national sovereign rights for uncertain benefits. Unlike the ultimate objective of the Werner Plan for a complete monetary union, the purpose of the EMS was monetary and exchange rate stability in the EC. This was not as ambitious an objective as the formation of a complete monetary union, but the EMS was a necessary monetary program to stabilize prices and exchange rates to boost intra-EC trade and economic growth.

The EMS was first proposed in 1977 by Roy Jenkins, the president of the Commission, and it was negotiated at the European Council meeting in Bremen, Germany, in July 1978. An agreement was reached at the European Council meeting in Brussels, in December 1978, and as a result, the EMS became effective on March 13, 1979. The EMS was designed to expand the success of the "joint float" by including France, Italy, and the UK in this group of European countries that respected the snake after the collapse of the Bretton Woods System. The three main components of the EMS were the following:

1. The Exchange Rate Mechanism (ERM)
2. The European Currency Unit (ECU)
3. The European Monetary Cooperation Fund (EMCF)

As it turned out, the ERM proved to be the most significant of the three main EMS components. The principal objective of the EMS was the permanent reduction of the exchange rate variability. According to the EMS, the EC countries had to maintain their exchange rates versus the ECU (central rates) within band margins of ±2.25 percent. Belgium, Denmark, France, Germany, Ireland, and the Netherlands were the countries that entered the EMS with these narrow band margins. The ECU was a weighted average of all EMU countries with the weights chosen according to the importance of the country in terms of the relative size of its economy and its trade share in the EC. Though every EC currency was included in the ECU, not every EC currency was participating at all times in the ERM.

Not all countries participating in the ERM were required to respect the narrow bands of ±2.25 percent. Italy for example entered originally with a wider band of ±6 percent but in 1990, decided to adhere to the narrower band margin of ±2.25 percent. Spain joined in 1989 with the wider band of ±6 percent and the UK followed the next year (1990) with the wider band of ±6 percent as well. Portugal joined in 1992 using the wider band, before the major 1992–1993 EMS crisis. Greece was the last country to join the EMS in March 1998. Greece entered the EMS only after a 14.5 percent devaluation of the Greek drachma in relation to all other ERM currencies. Greece agreed to adhere to the wider band of ±15 percent, which was decided upon by the EC Council of Ministers, in August 1993, in response to the 1992–1993 exchange rate crisis. The ±15 percent is known as the wider band; in contrast, the narrower band of ±2.25 percent is often referred to as the normal band.

High-inflation countries have trouble maintaining their exchange rates within narrow bands in relation to low-inflation countries' currencies. This is why EC countries accustomed to high inflation chose to enter the ERM with wider margin bands.

## The European Currency Unit (ECU)

The ECU was a basket of all EC members' currencies with the weights assigned according to the size of the economy and the intra-EC trade shares of each country. The ECU replaced the European Unit of Account (EUA).[11] The exact amount of each member currency units per ECU is shown in the first column in Table 1.1; this is the exchange rate versus the ECU for March 1979 and is called the central rate. In the second column, the number of currency units in one ECU is shown. The third column shows the percentage of each currency in one ECU as of March 1979.

According to Table 1.1, the most important currencies in the ECU were the Deutsche mark and the French franc, which comprised 33 percent and 19.8 percent of the ECU's value, respectively. These percentages are justifiable because these were the currencies of the two major EC economies committed to European integration. The weights of the currencies in the ECU were fixed but were subject to review every five years. Once the weights were assigned, the value of each currency in terms of the ECU was determined; this exchange rate of each EC currency versus the ECU was known as the central rate. Lastly, the bilateral exchange rates between two EC currencies could be easily obtained by

Table 1.1

## Exchange Rates per ECU and Composition of ECU in March 1979

| Name of Currency | | Number of Currency Units/ECU | National Currency Units in 1 ECU | % Share |
|---|---|---|---|---|
| Belgian franc | BFK | 39.46 | 3.66 | 9.3 |
| Danish krone | DKR | 7.09 | 0.22 | 3.1 |
| Deutsche mark | DM | 2.51 | 0.83 | 33.0 |
| French franc | FF | 5.80 | 1.15 | 19.8 |
| Italian lira | ITL | 1148.15 | 109.00 | 9.5 |
| Irish pound | IRL | 0.66 | 0.01 | 1.1 |
| Dutch guilder | HFL | 2.72 | 0.29 | 10.5 |
| Luxembourg franc | LFR | 39.50 | 0.14 | 0.4 |
| UK pound | UKL | 0.66 | 0.09 | 13.3 |
| Total | | | | 100.0 |

## National Currency Units in 1 ECU

| Name of Currency | | Sept. 17, 1984 | Sept. 21, 1989 |
|---|---|---|---|
| Belgian franc | BFK | 3.71 | 3.30 |
| Danish krone | DKR | 0.22 | 0.20 |
| Deutsche mark | DM | 0.72 | 0.62 |
| Greek drachma | GRD | 1.15 | 1.44 |
| Spanish peseta | ESP | — | 6.89 |
| French franc | FF | 1.31 | 1.33 |
| Irish pound | IRL | 0.01 | 0.01 |
| Italian lira | ITL | 140.00 | 151.80 |
| Luxembourg franc | LFR | 0.14 | 0.13 |
| Dutch guilder | HFL | 0.26 | 0.22 |
| Portuguese escudo | PTE | — | 1.39 |
| UK pound | UKL | 0.09 | 0.09 |

Sources: "*Texts Concerning the European Monetary System.*" By the Committee of Governors of the Central Banks of the Member States of the European Economic Community, 1979. Also, http://europa.eu.int/comm/eurostat/newcronos/reference/sdds/en/exint/ermfluc_sm.htm

dividing the ECU exchange rates of the two currencies.[12] The composition of the ECU for two other dates is shown in the lower part of Table 1.1. These dates are September 17, 1984, and September 21, 1989. The Greek drachma became part of the ECU on September 17, 1984. Similarly, on September 21, 1989, two more currencies, the Spanish peseta and the Portuguese escudo, became part of the ECU.

The ECU was never a legal tender; this means that no paper currency or coins were ever circulated in ECUs. The ECU was, however, employed for other purposes besides its use in the official EC accounts. EC member nations' private banks utilized the ECU for transactions between businesses and other organizations or even individuals. Lastly, the ECU was traded daily in the foreign exchange markets.

## The European Monetary Cooperation Fund (EMCF)

To support weak currencies, the EMS member countries established the EMCF. Each country contributed 20 percent of its gold and foreign exchange reserves, mostly in US dollars, to the EMCF in exchange for ECUs. Countries with troubled currencies could borrow from these reserves for the purpose of intervening in the foreign exchange market by buying back their own currencies. This was carried out directly by the central banks of the two countries whose bilateral exchange rate required correction.

The EMS member countries' central banks could also borrow from the very short-term financing facility for up to 45 days, or they could borrow from the mid-term financing facility for a period of two to five years. The latter provided loans to assist countries with structural problems in the balance of payments. It should be mentioned that although the ECU reserves were available, they were only used when the exchange rates reached the limits of the bands. For all other cases, when exchange rates were within the bands, the central banks intervened in the foreign exchange markets using national currencies or US dollars but not ECUs.[13]

## The Exchange Rate Mechanism (ERM)

The EMS prevailed for a period of approximately two decades from March 13, 1979, to December 31, 1998. This had a profound impact on European monetary integration. The most important component of the EMS was the ERM. The total fluctuation of the exchange rate allowed under the Bretton Woods System was 2 percent. In contrast, the exchange rate fluctuation under the EMS was 4.5 percent; this band is more than 100 percent wider than the corresponding permissible fluctuation under the Bretton Woods System. Clearly, the EMS was designed to be a more flexible exchange rate system.

Under the Bretton Woods System, the central bank of the weak currency was alone obligated to intervene in the foreign exchange market. This occurred when its currency reached the bottom limit of a fluctuation band. In contrast to the Bretton Woods System, under the EMS, the central banks of both countries were obligated to intervene in the foreign exchange market and support the weak currency. If, for example, the French franc (FF) per Deutsche mark (DM) exchange rate moved to the limit of the exchange rate band versus the FF, then both central banks were responsible to intervene and rescue the French franc. This was accomplished when the French central bank bought back its own currency and the Bundesbank bought French francs with Deutsche marks.

It was customary for the central banks to rely on the short-term credit facility of the EMCF. Central banks theoretically had an unlimited access to any EC country's currency.[14] For this reason, the EMS was a symmetric system, while the Bretton Woods was an asymmetric one. Both systems, however, were vulnerable and became victims to speculators. Once speculators identified a weak currency, they engaged in one-way selling until they forced a devaluation, i.e., an official realignment of a currency's value versus another currency. This usually occurred when the central bank of the weak currency ran out of reserves and could no longer support its currency.

It was a relatively low risk and profitable activity for speculators, who were involved in a one-way selling of a weak currency that was targeted for devaluation. The currency was sold to the central bank, which was ready to repurchase it. After the devaluation, the speculators bought back the same currency realizing extraordinarily large profits in a short period. Under the EMS, which was a symmetric system, it was theoretically possible for a currency to be defended by the two central banks. Under the Bretton Woods System, a currency was defended by only one central bank. The 1992–1993 crisis demonstrated that neither system was immune to speculative attacks.

Under the EMS System, the central banks did not wait for the exchange rates to reach the lower limit of their parity grid before intervening to support a currency. There were built-in warning signals known as divergence indicators that signaled early warnings as soon as an exchange rate deviated significantly from the parity rate based on thresholds that were approximately 75 percent of the bands. Such an early warning system usually allowed sufficient time for central bankers to respond and prevent a potential exchange rate crisis.

Permanent cost and price disparities had developed among EC countries during the EMS period. Such disparities were developed because the EC economies were affected and responded differently to the 1979–1980 oil crisis. During periods of severe cost and price disparity, the EMS allowed exchange rate realignments. Countries could devalue or revalue their currencies against any other country or against all other EC countries simultaneously upon mutual agreement. Most of the realignments occurred during the early years of the EMS. There were seven realignments in the first five years from 1979–1983 and five realignments during the period 1984–1991. In the latter period of the EMS, fewer exchange rate realignments with smaller percentage changes were made, indicating exchange rate stability.

During the 1987–1992 period, the EMS was transformed into a fixed exchange rate regime. By 1990–1991, according to many economists and politicians, the EMS proved to be a great success. Exchange rate variability was halved in the years 1979–1985 from what it was during the five years prior to the establishment of the EMS. In the next four years, the exchange rate variability was halved again. Exchange rate stability brought substantial benefits to member countries' economies.

As a result of the elimination of capital controls and the increased financial integration that occurred during this period, many new opportunities were developed within the larger market for banks and insurance companies. The joint intervention in the exchange rate markets and the interest rate management produced positive economic results, such as convergence in inflation rates and a favorable climate that encouraged further monetary integration. Despite this progress, no formal coordination of policies was agreed upon since countries were unwilling to formally give up their sovereignty in monetary and economic policy.[15]

# The Economic and Monetary Union (EMU)

## The Delors Report

In June 1988, another committee was appointed by the European Council to study the feasibility of a complete monetary union in the EC. The President of the EC Commission Jacques Delors, a charismatic and committed federalist, chaired this committee. The work of the Delors' Committee was completed in December 1989 and became known as the "Delors Report." The Delors Committee recommended the formation of an EMU for the EC in three stages. The recommendations by the Delors Committee were accepted by the Madrid Summit in June 1990. Lastly, in December 1991, at the Maastricht Summit in the Netherlands, the heads of the state governments approved the formation of the EMU for the EC.

## The Role of the Bundesbank in the EMS

The witnessed price and exchange rate stability by the EMS countries was considered to have resulted from the alignment of the monetary policies in the EMS countries with the monetary policy chosen by Germany's central bank, the Bundesbank.[16]

The EMS countries discovered that to maintain stable exchange rates, they had to follow the Bundesbank's monetary policy. This allowed them to peg their exchange rates to the Deutsche mark (DM). The question arises, how did the Bundesbank evolve to be the dominant central bank among the EMS countries and the DM to be the anchor currency? The answer to this question lies in what is known as the n-1 currency problem of the fixed exchange rate systems.[17]

In a fixed exchange rate system of n countries and n currencies, n-1 exchange rates (i.e., values of n-1 currencies) must be fixed in relation to the value of an anchor or key currency. In the EMS, this anchor currency was the DM. The reason the DM evolved into this role is the earned credibility of the Bundesbank in fighting inflation and maintaining price stability over several years. Another factor that contributed in the emergence of the DM as the dominant currency and the transformation of the EMS into a DM zone was the German economy, which was the largest and strongest in Europe.

The Bundesbank earned its credibility in fighting inflation because of its independence from the executive branch of the government established in the German Constitution. Such independence allowed the Bundesbank to exercise monetary policy in pursuing its main objective, price stability, free from any constraints from the German government. The only other major central bank that was independent of the executive branch of the government during those years was the central bank of the US, the Federal Reserve System (also called the "Fed").

A related question arises: Why didn't the ECU become the anchor currency in the EMS since all other currencies were expressed in terms of ECU? The primary reason is that the ECU was a basket currency, a weighted average of all EMS currencies, and as such, it was a dependent currency. Because of this dependence, the ECU could not have taken the role of the numeraire (the unit of account) of all currencies and become the anchor due to the n-1 currency problem of the fixed exchange rate regimes.

## The 1992–1993 EMS Exchange Rate Crisis

In the early 1990s, the EMS was considered a successful exchange rate system. Inflation rates were reduced significantly and converged due to measures undertaken by high inflation countries in the ERM to adhere to the Bundesbank's policies. The Maastricht Treaty was approved by the heads of the government of the states in December 1991, paving the way for a complete EMU near the end of the millennium. After the approval of the Maastricht Treaty in December 1991, several events occurred that reversed the prevalent optimism developed during the favorable monetary and economic conditions of the previous five years. First, the Bundesbank, to curtail inflation immediately after the approval of the Maastricht Treaty, raised its target rate (repo) even though most EC countries were entering a recession. On September 20, 1992, Denmark held an unsuccessful referendum for the ratification of the Maastricht Treaty. The failure to ratify the Maastricht Treaty by Denmark was a huge disappointment for the formation of the EMU that eroded the trust in the EMS, which was considered an important preliminary phase to the EMU.

In August 1992, the most turbulent period of the EMS began. At the beginning of this exchange rate crisis, the EMS consisted of ten members, with the UK, Spain, and Portugal in the wider band of ±6 percent. Speculators realized that politics in the UK and Italy were such that it would have been difficult for them to follow the high interest rate policy pursued by the Bundesbank.[18] The exchange rate crisis started early in September in two countries, which were not members of the EMS or the EC, but had declared their intentions to join the EC. The Finnish markka was pegged to the DM, but speculative attacks forced the Finnish government to float its currency. Speculative attacks on the Swedish krona forced the Riksbank, the central bank of Sweden, to raise interest rates to unprecedented high levels of 500 percent to defend its currency.

On September 14, 1992, the next speculative attack was directed against the Italian lira, which, in response, was devalued by 7 percent. It soon became evident that a 7 percent devaluation of the lira was insufficient to stabilize the exchange rate. On Wednesday, September 16, 1992, massive interference from the Bank of England could not keep the pound within the band limits; this forced the UK to withdraw the pound from the ERM. Subsequently, the Italian lira followed, and both currencies floated. In the meantime, Ireland raised interest rates by 1,000 percent to protect its currency, the punt, and France lost half of its reserves to protect its franc. These events constituted nothing short of a disaster for the ERM; thus, Wednesday, September 16, is remembered as "Black Wednesday." In the aftermath, all currencies were tested one after the other. The Spanish peseta was devalued twice by a total of 11 percent and the Portuguese escudo by 6 percent. In November 1992, these two currencies were devalued for a third time. Spain and Ireland decided to apply capital controls to thwart further attacks on their currencies.

The next year, 1993, was also a turbulent time for the ERM. First, the Irish pound was forced to a 10 percent devaluation, and in May, the peseta and the escudo were devalued for a fourth time. Other currencies, including the French franc, were earmarked for speculative attacks.

The Central Bank of France, Banque de France, held steadfast against devaluation of the franc by following what became known as the "franc fort policy." Such a policy of pegging the French franc to the Deutsche mark gained credibility for France's monetary policy. In the summer of 1993, France found itself in the middle of a recession and could no longer keep raising interest rates by following a monetary policy compatible with that of the Bundesbank.

The worst day in the history of the ERM took place on July 30, 1993. This date is now remembered as "Black Friday." Speculative attacks on many currencies, and particularly on the French franc, forced the devaluation of the franc, but this devaluation was different from all other devaluations. On August 1, 1993, it was announced by the EC Commission that the exchange rate band was widened to ±15 percent, a total range of fluctuation of 30 percent, for all currencies except the Deutsche mark and the Dutch guilder. As a practical matter, this decision made the ERM band non-binding since the permissible limits of the bands were too wide to have any effect in restricting the exchange rates.

## Causes of the 1992–1993 Exchange Rate Crisis

Many explanations were offered for the 1992–1993 exchange rate crisis. Some of these explanations, however, are invalid. One such unsound explanation is that the crisis was created by greedy speculators who ought to have acted more responsibly toward entire nations. This cannot be a legitimate explanation since speculators' objective is the pursuit of profit. A sound exchange rate system should not be vulnerable to speculators, nor can its success depend on expectations of altruistic and socially responsible behavior. A few people thought that the 1992–1993 crisis was the result of an Anglo-Saxon conspiracy, who would have preferred the EMS and EMU bankrupt at their inception. Such an explanation, however, lacks any logical basis even though European integration in the UK was never popular among the British people and their government.

The primary causes of the EMS crisis can be explained by the inherent deficiencies in the design of the EMS and the fundamental structural changes, which occurred prior and during the 1992–1993 exchange rate crisis. Two flaws in the original design of the EMS, which are possible explanations of the 1992–1993 exchange rate crisis, are the absence of an agreement among the EMS member countries for an official coordination of monetary and economic policies and the existence of the n-1 currency problem for every fixed exchange rate system.[19] Regarding the second flaw, the emergence of the DM as the anchor currency was problematic because the Bundesbank has pursued German interests when those conflicted with the wider interests of the EC. What the EMS needed, according to the critics of the Bundesbank, was a European central bank committed in pursuing European interests.

However, this problem of conflicting interests between Germany and the rest of the EC members appeared when the two were experiencing asymmetric shocks. Asymmetric shocks are rare events: the reunification of Germany was such a rare event. To finance the German reunification, the West German government relied on expansionary fiscal policy and incurred huge deficits every year starting in 1989. Government deficits tended to raise prices and wages. These deficits were financed with continuous increases in national debt as the German government sold bonds to the public.

Such actions taken by the German government along with the refusal of the Bundesbank to increase the German money supply by monetizing the debt (increase the money supply by an amount equal to the new debt) resulted in higher interest rates. Higher interest rates attracted massive capital inflows to Germany from other EC member countries.

The completion of the single market program at the end of 1992 promoted financial integration and freed capital mobility. Capital outflows from EMS countries to Germany put pressure on all exchange rates in relation to the DM. To avoid devaluations, most EC countries tried to match the Bundesbank's interest rate increases. The Bundesbank's dictated high interest rate policy turned out to be detrimental to other EC economies, which were in desperate need of expansionary monetary policy to lower interest rates to combat unemployment and recession. The end result of this policy were two currency withdrawals from the ERM (the pound and the lira) and several forced devaluations versus the DM and the ECU. Central banks experienced huge losses of their reserves reminiscent of the gold loss of the US, prior to the Bretton Woods System's collapse in 1973. In the meantime, speculators earned excessive amounts of profit at the expense of the central banks.

The last country to break away from the ERM was France, but this did not occur until the EMS was fully tested. First, the French appealed officially to the German government and the Bundesbank to reduce interest rates. This, however, fell on deaf ears. The Bundesbank, fearful of introducing inflation, refused to reduce interest rates by relaxing monetary policy. The French were determined to keep the franc strong, and by following the "franc fort policy," were compelled to intervene in the foreign exchange market repeatedly by buying back their own currency. This was carried out by utilizing the EMCF credit lines and by borrowing Deutsche marks from the Bundesbank. The Bundesbank, however, at this time, refused to lend additional Deutsche marks to the Central Bank of France because most loaned Deutsche marks were ultimately finding their way back home to Germany.

The Bundesbank was accustomed to neutralizing the effect of the repatriated loaned Deutsche marks on domestic money supply by selling bonds to the public. The buyers of the German bonds were paying the Bundesbank by checks drawn on a commercial bank, thus reducing German money supply. This phenomenon is called sterilization. During the 1992–1993 exchange rate crisis, the Bundesbank chose not to co-operate with the rest of the EMS countries' central banks.

Alternatively, cooperation with EMS member banks would have required the Bundesbank to keep lending Deutsche marks via the open credit lines of the EMCF and simultaneously abstain from sterilization. In such a case, the increased money supply in Germany due to the lending of Deutche marks to EMS member central banks would have reduced interest rates in Germany but increased inflation. This action would also have reduced the high interest rates in the EMS countries, enabling them to fight their way out of recession. These two policy options of the Bundesbank are demonstrated on a simple diagrammatic model in the appendix of this chapter. To simplify things, only the two-country case, Germany and France, is examined. The situations of all the other EMS countries, which were forced to maintain high interest rates, are identical to the French case.

Another suggested cause of the 1992–1993 exchange rate crisis was the free capital mobility, which was introduced as a requirement for the completion of the SEM. This argument is worth pursuing, especially if one considers that international currency markets have been consistently growing at a rapid pace. Robert Jones reported that over 1.7 trillion euros were traded daily back in 2001. This amount was equal to 2.5 times of the reserves of the 10 largest industrialized countries.[20] This implies that even a coordinated joint effort of several central banks cannot offset the effects of massive speculative attacks.

A counter argument to the last proposition suggests that sufficiency of the total reserves in the EMS to counteract market forces in the foreign exchange markets are unimportant. More relevant for the stabilization of the exchange rates, according to this argument, was the commitment of each central bank to lend its own currency in unlimited amounts to the other EMS central banks. Following this logic, Paul De Grauwe came to the conclusion that the 1992–1993 crisis was the result of the unwillingness of the Bundesbank to lend Deutsche marks to its EMS partners.[21]

According to the West German constitution, the Bundesbank was solely responsible for monetary policy. The Bundesbank pursued monetary policy with price stability as its ultimate objective. The German government, however, made inconsistent commitments to the EMS partners and the Bundesbank. It promised its EMS partners open credit lines of its own currency according to the Basle-Nyborg Agreement (1987) and promised the Bundesbank it could pursue a totally independent monetary policy. In a letter written by the President of the Bundesbank Otmar Emminger addressed to the German government, in 1986, the Bundesbank was seeking assurances it would be allowed to perform its own constitutional obligations to pursue price stability in the event that "conflict under the rules of the EMS" may arise in the future.[22]

Lastly, the vulnerability of the EMS after the removal of capital controls was colorfully and successfully portrayed by Tommaso Padoa-Schioppa (1988), a member of the executive board of the ECB. Padoa-Schioppa compared the EMS of the late 1980s after the removal of capital controls to an "inconsistent quartet" of four policy objectives: free trade, full capital mobility, fixed exchange rates, and independent national monetary policies. He continued by stating that the only long-run solution to the SEM was the adoption of a common currency by all member countries.

Many criticized Padoa-Schioppa's view that the SEM needed to be complemented by a monetary union, but no one had any doubts that major inconsistencies existed in his four stated EMS policies.[23] Padoa-Schioppa correctly predicted the future of the EMS. Many economists pointed out that the 1992–1993 exchange rate crisis was caused by the lack of coordination of monetary and exchange rate policies and the non-cooperative policy of the dominant currency central bank, the Bundesbank. Despite this, early realignments of the exchange rates could have prevented the exchange rate crisis; thus, EMS member countries other than Germany were responsible for the ERM crisis.

## Some Basic Statistics and Information of the Euro Area

Table 1.2 provides some information and basic macroeconomic statistics on the twelve Euro Area countries that adopted the euro and formed the EMU. Information and statistics are provided for the entire Euro Area, the former EU15, and the EU25, which was created by the May 1, 2004, expansion of the EU. The Euro Area countries comprise a large area spanning from Lappland (Finland) to the Mediterranean Sea (Greece).

The country with the largest area in the Euro Area is France, and the one with the smallest area is Luxembourg. This should not be a

Table 1.2

| | | | | | |
|---|---|---|---|---|---|
| **Data for the Euro Area Countries 2003 and 1999–2003 Averages** | | | | | |
| | **Austria** | **Belgium** | **Finland** | **France** | **Germany** |
| **Area** (thous. sq. km.) | 84 | 33 | 338 | 552 | 357 |
| **Population** (millions) | 8.1 | 10.3 | 5.2 | 59.9 | 82.4 |
| **GDP per Capita** (PPP $) | $29,600 | $28,730 | $27,740 | $27,840 | $27,060 |
| **GDP** (PPP, billions $) | $240.1 | $295.9 | $144.3 | $1,666.2 | $2,230.0 |
| **Real GDP Growth (%)** | 0.8 [2.0] | 1.1 [1.9] | 1.4 [2.7] | 0.2 [2.2] | −0.1 [1.2] |
| **Unemployment Rate (%)** | 7.0 [5.5] | 12.3 [9.9] | 10.6 [10.7] | 9.5 [9.4] | 11.7 [9.8] |
| **Inflation Rate (%)** | 1.3 [1.6] | 1.5 [1.9] | 1.3 [2.1] | 2.2 [1.7] | 1.0 [1.2] |
| **Capital City** | Vienna | Brussels | Helsinki | Paris | Berlin |
| | **Greece** | **Ireland** | **Italy** | **Luxembourg** | **Netherlands** |
| **Area** (thous. sq. km.) | 132 | 70 | 301 | 2.5 | 41 |
| **Population** (millions) | 10.97 | 3.9 | 57.5 | 0.5 | 16.1 |
| **GDP per Capita** (PPP $) | $18,340 | $33,120 | $27,010 | $48,221 | $29,580 |
| **GDP** (PPP, billions $) | $201.2 | $129.5 | $1,552.5 | $21.7 | $475.4 |
| **Real GDP Growth (%)** | 4.0 [3.9] | 2.2 [7.3] | 0.3 [1.5] | 0.4 [4.1] | −0.8 [1.6] |
| **Unemployment Rate (%)** | 9.3 [10.5] | 4.7 [4.6] | 8.7 [9.8] | 3.8 [2.8] | 3.4 [2.7] |
| **Inflation Rate (%)** | 3.4 [3.2] | 4.0 [4.1] | 2.8 [2.4] | 2.5 [2.4] | 2.2 [3.1] |
| **Capital City** | Athens | Dublin | Rome | Luxembourg | Amsterdam |

*(continued)*

Table 1.2   *Continued*

|  | Portugal | Spain | Euro Area | EU15 | EU25 |
|---|---|---|---|---|---|
| Area (thous. sq. km.) | 92 | 506 | 2,509 | 3,246.5 | 3,985.1 |
| Population (millions) | 10.1 | 41.0 | 305.8 | 379.1 | 455.0 |
| GDP per Capita (PPP $) | $18,990 | $21,450 | $26,250 | $26,529 | $24,213 |
| GDP (PPP, billions $) | $190.9 | $879.0 | $8,026.7 | $10,056.4 | $10,992.7 |
| Real GDP Growth (%) | −1.3 [1.7] | 2.4 [3.1] | 0.5 | 0.7 | 0.9 |
| Unemployment Rate (%) | 6.3 [4.8] | 8.8 [11.5] | 8.9 | 8.0 | 9.1 |
| Inflation Rate (%) | 3.3 [3.3] | 3.1 [3.0] | 2.1 | 2.0 | 1.9 |
| Capital City | Lisbon | Madrid | — | — | — |

Source: IFS cd-rom, www.nationmaster.com, *World Development Report, ECB*

Figures in brackets are the 1999–2003 averages.

surprise since Luxembourg has the smallest population of approximately half a million people. Spain, Germany, Italy, and Finland are the other large countries in terms of area. With the exception of Finland, which has a relatively small population (5.2 million), Germany, France, Italy, and Spain are large in terms of population and Gross Domestic Product (GDP). For example, Germany constitutes about 27 percent of the GDP and population of the Euro Area. France ranks second to Germany in terms of GDP and population at about 20 percent of each. Italy follows France with approximately 19 percent in GDP and population. Another large Euro Area country is Spain, which comprises 11 percent of the Euro Area GDP and 13.4 percent of the total Euro Area population. These four large Euro Area countries constitute approximately 77 percent of the Euro Area GDP and 79.4 percent of the population.

Luxembourg, the smallest Euro Area country, has attained the highest standard of living. Luxembourg's per capita GDP in 2003 was $48,221. Next to Luxembourg, the country that attained the second highest standard of living is Ireland, which happened to be the second smallest country in the Euro Area in terms of population. Ireland's per capita GDP in 2003 was $33,120, higher than the corresponding Euro Area average per capita GDP of $28,140. The Euro Area countries with the lowest per capita GDPs are three Mediterranean countries:

Greece, Portugal, and Spain. These countries were the last to join the EU15 before the 1995 northern EU enlargement that included Sweden, Finland, and Austria.

In Table 1.2, the growth of the real GDP for all the Euro Area countries is reported along with the real GDP growth rates of the Euro Area, the EU15, and the EU25. The real GDP growth rate in 2003 for the Euro Area was relatively low at only half of one percent. This rate of growth was slightly lower than the real GDP growth of the EU15 and the EU25. Three Euro Area countries, Germany, the Netherlands, and Portugal have even experienced negative growth rates in 2003.

Next to the 2003 real GDP growth rate figures of the Euro Area countries in Table 1.2, the average real GDP growth rates for the period 1999–2003 are shown in brackets. This period covers the first five years of the EMU. By comparing the average 1999–2003 real GDP growth of the Euro Area countries with the 2003 real GDP growth, the Euro Area countries, in 2003, grew at a slower rate.

Similarly, by comparing the 2003 unemployment rates of the Euro Area countries with the 1999–2003 average unemployment rates (shown in brackets next to the 2003 values), the 2003 unemployment rates were higher for most countries. This finding is consistent with the poor performance of the Euro Area countries' real GDP growth in 2003. A notable exception is Spain, which reduced its unemployment rate by more than 2.5 percent in 2003 from its five-year average.

According to Table 1.2, the Euro Area performed relatively well in reference to price stability. The inflation rate of the Euro Area in 2003 was 2.1 percent; the European Central Bank's target rate for the year was 2 percent. There is, however, some variability in the inflation rates among the Euro Area countries. Generally, rapid growth countries experience higher inflation rates than slow growth countries. Regarding the 2003 inflation rates of the Euro Area countries in relation to their 1999–2003 average, shown in brackets, some countries reduced their inflation rates; whereas, others experienced higher inflation rates. Nonetheless, all Euro Area countries performed relatively well in terms of price stability. Inflation does not seem to be a current threat to these economies.

In Table 1.3, the Euro Area (EU12) countries are compared with the US and Japan, the world's largest (number one and two) developed market economies in terms of key macroeconomic statistics. The Euro Area is the most populous of the three, closely followed by the US. Japan's population is less than half of the Euro Area or the US populations.

Table 1.3

| Macroeconomic Statistics: 1999–2003 Period Average | | | |
|---|---|---|---|
| | **Euro Area** | **US** | **Japan** |
| **Real GDP Growth (%)** | 1.78 | 2.72 | 1.22 |
| **Unemployment Rate (%)** | 8.76 | 4.96 | 5.02 |
| **Inflation Rate (%)** | 1.94 | 2.46 | −0.58 |
| **Area (thous. sq. km.)** | 2,509 | 9,631 | 377 |
| **Population (millions)** | 308.7 | 291.1 | 127.6 |
| | | | Source: ECB |

## Comparative Statistics of the Euro Area, US, and Japan

In terms of area, the US is more than three times the size of the Euro Area and is more than 25 times larger than Japan. As a result, the Euro Area and Japan are much more densely populated than the US.

The Euro Area average unemployment rate of 8.76 percent for the period 1999–2003 was nearly four percent above the unemployment rates of the US and Japan. High unemployment is a major macroeconomic problem of the Euro Area countries.

Lastly, the US experienced the highest average inflation rate of 2.46 percent, followed by the Euro Area rate, which had an average inflation of 2 percent. Japan however, experienced deflation during the same period (1999–2003) that many economists believe caused a low real GDP growth rate in this country. According to Table 1.3, the Euro Area's real GDP growth and inflation rates were both lower than those of the US, but higher than those of Japan.

## A Diagrammatic History of the EMU

The timeline path "The Path to the euro," Figure 1.1, shows the chronological order of some of the most important events that played a significant role in the formation of the EMU.

1. The Treaty of Rome (1957) did not provide any explicit reference to monetary integration. The Treaty of Rome, however, made possible the occurrence of certain events and EC decisions that played a crucial role for further developments in the European monetary integration.

2. In 1958, only one year after the establishment of the EEC, the Monetary Committee was formed as an advisory body to the Economics and Finance Council (ECOFIN) of the EEC.

Figure 1.1

# The Path to the Euro

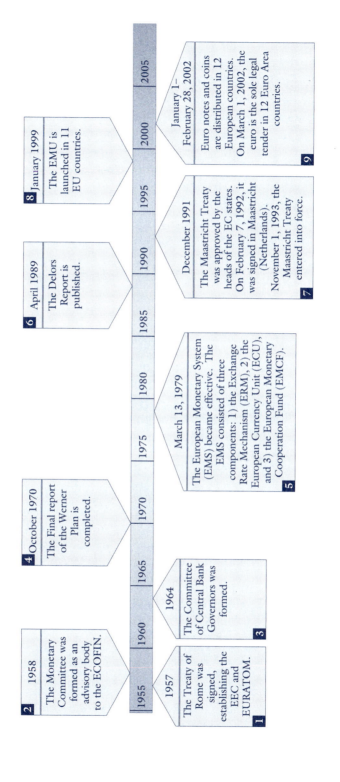

3. In 1964, the Committee of the Central Bank Governors was formed. This committee, however, became fully functional in the 1970s.

4. In October 1970, a committee headed by the Prime Minister of Luxembourg, Pierre Werner, completed its report on the formation of a European monetary union. The Werner Plan recommended the establishment of a European monetary union within ten years and in three stages. Though the Werner Plan, per se, was never approved, most of the plan's recommendations were adopted by other EC monetary programs and made their way to the EMU. For this reason, Pierre Werner was given the title "the Father of the euro."

5. On March 13, 1979, nine EC countries adopted the European Monetary System (EMS). The EMS was an EC monetary program (1979–1999) with an immense impact on European monetary integration that lasted about 20 years. The EMS fell short of becoming a complete economic and monetary union, but it paved the way for further integration and was replaced by the EMU in January 1999.

6. A committee appointed by the European Council and headed by the President of the EC Commission, Jacques Delors, was appointed to study the feasibility of creating a monetary union in the EC. In April 1989, the Delors Report recommended the formation of an EMU in three stages. The recommendation of the Delors Committee was accepted and the EMU was established in the EC, in January 1999, 10 years after the Delors Report.

7. In December 1991, the Maastricht Treaty for the formation of an EMU was approved by the heads of the government states. This Treaty cemented the will of the member countries for a closer European union among the European people who were committed to the formation of an EMU.

8. On January 1, 1999, the EMU was launched and the euro became the official currency of 11 EU countries. The euro, however, only existed in the form of demand deposits (checking accounts). Two years later, Greece joined the EMU. As a result, on January 1, 2001, the EMU consisted of 12 countries.

9. From January 1, 2002, to February 28, 2002, the euro circulated in 12 countries as currency and coins, along with the national currencies of all the 12 Euro Area countries. On March 1, 2002, the euro became the sole legal tender that circulated in the 12 Euro Area countries: Austria, Belgium, Finland, France, Germany, Greece, Ireland, Italy, Luxembourg, Netherlands, Portugal, and Spain.

# Euro Area Countries

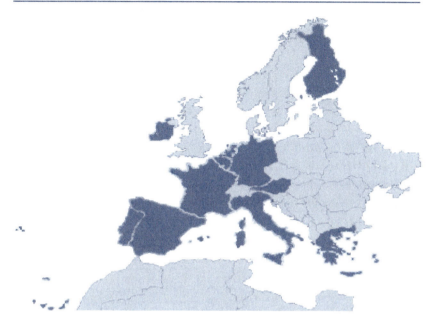

Source: ECB: http://www.ecb.int/bc/intro/html/map.en.html

## Countries That Have Adopted the Euro

| | | |
|---|---|---|
| Austria | Germany | Luxembourg |
| Belgium | Greece | Netherlands |
| Finland | Ireland | Portugal |
| France | Italy | Spain |

## SUMMARY

This chapter provided a historical review of the economic and monetary developments in Western Europe from the end of World War II to the Maastricht Treaty in 1993. The end of the Second World War left Western Europe devastated. Efforts to distribute US aid from the Marshall Plan for the reconstruction and development of Europe were hindered by protective trade policies among European nations. The OEEC was established to facilitate the distribution of the US aid to Europe under the Marshall Plan.

Two years later, in 1950, the EPU was established to assist its member countries with balance of payment problems. In 1951, with the Treaty of Paris, The ECSC was established. The purpose of this treaty was to create a common market for steel and coal among six West European countries (Belgium, France, Italy, Germany, Luxembourg, and the Netherlands). The ultimate goal of the ECSC was to safeguard peace in Europe. The member states delegated authority to the institutions of the ECSC on all issues regarding the production and distribution of coal and steel.

The success of the ECSC was repeated with the creation of two more communities in 1957 by the Treaty of Rome. The first was the EEC and the second was the EURATOM. The EEC was a customs union and a common market for all commodities other than coal and steel. EURATOM was a common market in atomic energy. In 1967, the three communities merged into one entity, referred to as the EC.

The EC contributed significantly to the integration of Western Europe. Although substantial progress in economic integration among EC member countries occurred in the early 1980s, the EC was far from being a complete market. A program to achieve a true European market in the EC began in 1986 and was completed in 1992. This program became known as the SEM. The SEM program harmonized several aspects of the EC economies and removed, to a large extent, capital controls among EC member countries.

The EC countries strived to promote exchange rate stability. In the early 1970s, these countries agreed to float their currencies within a ±2.25 percent band of fluctuation (the snake), while they let their currencies float jointly against the dollar (the tunnel) within another ±2.25 percent fluctuation band. This arrangement, however, did not last long. The tunnel was discontinued, but a few EC countries maintained the snake. The EC countries subsequently pegged their currencies against the DM in an effort to stabilize exchange rates.

A committee chaired by the Prime Minister of Luxembourg, Pierre Werner, was appointed by the EC to study the possibility of creating a monetary union. Pierre Werner's committee recommended the formation of a monetary union in three stages by 1980. The Werner Plan was never implemented due to the 1973–1974 oil crisis. Most of the Werner Plan's recommendations, however, reappeared under new plans and proposals, including the Maastricht Treaty in which the EC countries laid the foundation of the EMU, launched on March 1, 2002.

Prior to the formation of the EMU, the EC countries established the EMS, in 1979, to create a region of monetary and exchange rate stability. According to the EMS, countries decided to restrain their exchange rates within a narrow parity grid or exchange rate band of ±2.25 percent margin limits. The EMS consisted of three components:

the ERM, the ECU, and the EMCF. The most important of the three was the ERM, which established a process for maintaining exchange rate stability. The ECU was a weighted-average basket currency destined to become the currency of the EC (the euro).

The EMS suffered a major crisis from speculative attacks in 1992–1993. In response to these attacks, the parity grid was widened to an extreme ±15 percent, rendering the band non-binding and meaningless.

Many explanations were offered for the 1992–1993 EMS crisis. The most significant one was the lack of policy coordination among member countries, and in particular, the unwillingness of the Bundesbank to follow a monetary policy serving the interest of the entire EC. The sources of the crisis were the uncooperative position of the Bundesbank and the refusal of some member countries to devalue their currencies.

The chapter concludes with a presentation of some basic statistics of the 12 Euro Area countries. Similarly, some comparative macroeconomic statistics of the Euro Area, the US, and Japan are presented to demonstrate the relative size of the Euro Area economy in relation to the US and Japan.

## Essay Questions

1. Explain why, when, where, and by whom the ECSC was established. In which way is the ECSC different from any other international organization? Identify the governing institutions of the ECSC and describe their role in the decision-making process.

2. Name two different approaches to economic integration and describe how, under each of these two approaches, integration is pursued and achieved. Which approach was adopted by the EC countries? Evaluate these two approaches by discussing the characteristics of each approach and the implications to these countries.

3. Explain the significance of the Treaty of Rome (1957) to the unification (integration) of Western Europe. What were the main objectives of the Treaty of Rome and how were these objectives to be attained?

4. Discuss the Werner Plan. What is the significance of the Werner Plan for the European monetary integration?

5. For approximately 20 years, the EMS was the monetary and exchange rate system of the EC. Thoroughly discuss this monetary system from its inception to its end. What are the three principal components of the EMS? Has the EMS always

functioned smoothly or were there period(s) that the EMS became unstable? Explain.

6. What was the significance of the Delors Report? Thoroughly discuss the Delors Report and its importance to the European monetary integration and the adoption of the euro.

7. The 1992–1993 exchange rate crisis of the EMS threatened the EC economies and, for a short period, stalled any further monetary and economic integration. What were the causes of this exchange rate crisis? How was the EC able to overcome such a devastating exchange rate crisis?

8. Write out the full name of the following acronyms:

EEC, ECSC, EURATOM, CAP, SEM, ERM, EMS, ECU, EUA, OEEC, EPU, EMCF.

# APPENDIX

## Hegemonic (Uncooperative Solution) to an Assymetric Shock on the Leader Country

Figure 1.2

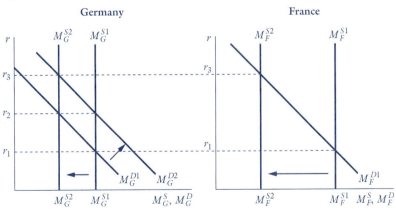

The above graphs illustrate the money markets in Germany (the leader) and France. $M^D$ and $M^S$ represent the money demand and supply functions of the two countries, the subscripts $G$ and $F$ signify the two countries and $r$ is the nominal interest rate. The Bundesbank determines the initial money supply, which is given by $M_G^{S1}$, in Germany. Similarly, the initial money demand function for Germany is given by the $M_G^{D1}$ curve. $M_F^{S1}$ and $M_F^{D1}$ are the money supply and money demand functions for France. Once the Bundesbank (the leader) decides on the level of its money supply $M_G^{S1}$, given the German money demand $M_G^{D1}$, the nominal interest rate $r_1$ is determined in Germany. The Central Bank of France has no choice but to set its money supply to the level that will result in the same nominal interest rate $r_1$, forcing France to sacrifice its monetary policy. If the Central Bank of France had set its money supply greater than $M_F^{S1}$, this would have resulted in a lower interest rate than $r_1$. The lower interest rate in France would have caused a capital outflow to Germany and a reduction of the French money supply back to $M_F^{S1}$ with the same interest rate $r_1$ as in Germany.[24]

The initial situation above characterizes the money markets in the two countries at the end of 1988, just before the reunification of Germany. After the collapse of the Berlin Wall, the German government applied expansionary fiscal policy by running large deficits starting in 1989. Expansionary fiscal policy can be indicated by an increase in aggregate demand, which raised prices, wages, and national income. The higher national income caused an increase in money demand (see the left graph in Figure 1.2). The increase in money demand in Germany resulted in an increase in the German interest rate to $r_2$. To thwart increases in prices and wages, the Bundesbank applied contractionary monetary policy by selling bonds to the public, causing a reduction in money supply to $M_G^{S2}$ and a further increase in the interest rate to $r_3$. Higher German interest rates attracted capital inflows from France and a reduction in the French money supply to $M_F^{S2}$, until French interest rates were equated to the German interest rates $r_3$.

Capital outflows from France to Germany, assuming everything else held constant, would have reduced the interest rates in Germany. This, however, did not happen because the increase in the money supply caused by capital inflows was sterilized by the Bundesbank, i.e., it was offset by equal reduction in money supply through bond sales to the German public. This is the reason this solution is called the hegemonic, asymmetric, or uncooperative solution. Paul De Grauwe, who introduced this model, examined both the hegemonic (uncooperative) and cooperative solutions of the n-1 problem of the fixed exchange rate regimes. The cooperative case is not examined here. If the Bundesbank abstained from sterilizing the increase in the money supply caused by the French capital outflow to Germany, this would have resulted in lower interest rates in both countries. This latter solution is symmetric or cooperative and would have saved the EMS from the 1992–1993 exchange rate crisis at a cost of higher inflation in both countries.

# chapter 2

# An Optimum Currency Area (OCA)

## Introduction

The creation of the European Monetary System (EMS) was only an intermediate step prior to the completion of a European monetary union. Starting in the early 1990s, the idea of European monetary integration became popular and gained many supporters in all EU member countries. The increased popularity of monetary integration among the Europeans is well demonstrated by the two EU proposed monetary programs, the Werner Plan and the Delors Report. Based on these two programs, the EU embarked on a long monetary integration campaign that led most of its member countries to a complete monetary union. The EU countries officially agreed to the formation of the Economic and Monetary Union (EMU) with the signing of the celebrated 1992 Maastricht Treaty. The EMU was launched on January 1, 1999, when eleven countries irrevocably fixed their exchange rates and the European Central Bank (ECB) became responsible for the monetary policy of these countries. Complete monetary integration was established on March 1, 2002, when twelve EU countries successfully adopted a new common currency, the euro, as their only legal tender.

In this chapter, all major arguments for and against the formation of a monetary union will be discussed. Starting with the Werner Plan, a long and fervent debate began in many forums among economists, labor leaders, business people, politicians, as well as numerous concerned citizens of the candidate EMU countries.

The economic theory examining the necessary and desirable characteristics of countries' economies for membership qualification to a monetary union is known as the theory of the Optimum Currency Area (OCA). This theory was introduced and popularized by Robert Mundell (1961, 1973a, 1973b), Ronald McKinnon (1963, 2004), and Peter Kenen (1969). Robert Mundell received the Nobel Prize in economics in 2000 for this contribution. The necessary characteristics of these candidate member countries' economies for the formation of a successful monetary union were pointed out in the early literature of the OCA by the authors. It was suggested that the costs and benefits should be weighed against each other to determine whether a monetary union membership was beneficial to a candidate country. The effects of the candidate member country on the existing members' economies must also be considered since existing members will not agree to expand membership if their expected costs from enlargement exceed expected benefits. The expected costs and benefits from the candidate country's point of view are important and must be examined, evaluated, and compared. These expected costs and benefits ought to be the determining factors for each candidate country in its decision to seek membership in a monetary union.

The decision to join a monetary union is difficult since the relevant costs and benefits are not always quantifiable. The accurate costs and benefits include those that will arise before and after the country joins the monetary union. In most cases, a substantial lapse of time occurs from the announcement of the country's candidacy to an existing monetary union and the effective date of the accession. In this transitional period, the candidate countries' governments adopt appropriate policies to prepare their economies for the monetary union. Such policies aiming to make the transition to the monetary union less costly and smoother often reverse the balance in favor of the benefits in relation to costs.[1] Many of the OCA's early authors erred when calculating the costs and benefits of joining a monetary union because they did not consider the positive effects of the adopted policies during the transition period.

## Expected Costs

To measure the expected costs and benefits of a candidate country applying for membership to a monetary union, certain macroeconomic perceptions regarding the state of the economy must be assumed. The results of the cost-benefit analysis will differ according to whether the economy of the candidate country is characterized by relatively stable or rising prices and wages. Since these two opposite assumptions regarding price and wage stability lead to different analytical results, it is helpful to understand how and why the two assumptions play a key role in the cost-benefit analysis.

The formation of a monetary union results in the loss of monetary and exchange rate policies; member countries that adopt a new common currency also adopt a common monetary policy.[2] Mundell (1961) and other authors of the OCA considered the loss of the two policies to be the most important cost of the formation of a monetary union because both policies are exceptionally useful to a country experiencing asymmetric shocks.[3] When a monetary union member country is confronted with an asymmetric shock that may cause recession, the country cannot depend on its monetary and exchange rate policies to fight the negative effects of the shock. If a country, however, is not a member of a monetary union, it may exercise expansionary monetary policy to reduce interest rates to increase domestic consumption and investment. Similarly, a country could devalue its currency to improve its trade balance, and this would increase the value of exports and reduce the value of its imports. Under a flexible exchange rate regime, a country's currency can depreciate to improve a trade imbalance and, thus, increase the country's GDP. Both policies can increase the country's aggregate demand and consequently raise employment and income. For the two policies to be effective, prices must remain stable, close to their pre-shock levels.

Robert Mundell's initial contribution on the OCA was developed within a constant price level framework of a Keynesian model. However, if the price level increases, it can then neutralize some or all of the favorable effects of the expansionary monetary policy or of the devaluation. The diagrammatic analysis (Figures 2.1 and 2.2) in the chapter's appendix demonstrates this point.

## Integration and Asymmetries

An exchange rate policy can be utilized by a non-member country of a monetary union to fight its way out of a recession caused by an asymmetric shock. Therefore, one must study the nature of all possible asymmetric shocks and their expected frequency of occurrence for the EU countries. Since most shocks are symmetric, monetary union countries can jointly combat these shocks. In this case, a country will not gain by remaining outside a monetary union. The reason for this is that the symmetric shock affects all countries in the same way; thus, a common monetary union policy can be as effective as an independent national monetary policy.

As mentioned previously, asymmetric shocks can be related to the demand side or to the supply side of the economy. Some asymmetric shocks may arise from differential growth rates among countries, and others may be caused by differing financial, legal, and tax systems. Other asymmetric shocks are caused by differences in the organizational structures of labor markets and institutions, such as labor unions and employers' organizations. Lastly, a few asymmetric shocks are the result of natural disasters affecting only one or a few member countries.

Many economists believe that increased intra-industry trade and further economic integration will substantially reduce country differences responsible for the occurrence of asymmetric shocks.[4] Empirical evidence suggests business cycles, i.e., economic activity fluctuations in all EU countries, became more synchronized after the 1980s.[5] Such increased synchronization of the business cycles according to these authors reduced the number of asymmetric shocks as a result of the EMS' success in reducing inflation rates in all EU countries. Despite this evidence, not all economists agree that economic integration reduces the number of asymmetric shocks. For example, Paul De Grauwe (2000) discussed two opposite views on this issue.

The first view is represented by a study undertaken by the EC Commission (1990), which supports the position that economic integration assimilates the participating economies and reduces the number of asymmetric shocks. An opposite view was presented by Paul Krugman (1993) who was convinced that economic deepening, i.e., increased economic integration, leads to regional concentration of industries. Krugman presented evidence on this issue from the US, which is a much more integrated economy than the EU economies. In the US, some industries have located only in certain regions of the country. A good example of this is the automobile industry, which has concentrated around Detroit, Michigan.

There are, however, serious reservations regarding Krugman's regional concentration theory when applied to the EU. Since most of the EU states are small, it is highly unlikely that any one of these small states will alone attract an entire industry. In addition, Krugman's automobile example is not convincing since Michigan was never the only host-state of the entire automobile industry. The neighboring Midwest states to Michigan and the Canadian province of Ontario were and still are hosts to several automobile plants. The Krugman argument is less convincing since several auto plants have moved to other states and countries. In addition, the rapid development of intra-industry trade in the auto parts industry complicates governmental investigations regarding the true country origin of manufactured automobiles. Automobile components are produced in different countries and states in the US, far from the locations where the automobiles are assembled. As a result, it is difficult to speak of the true location of the auto industry.

## Seigniorage

Some authors pose a third cost of the formation of a monetary union in addition to the loss of the monetary and exchange rate policies. This cost is the loss of seigniorage, i.e., the loss of the ability of governments to raise revenues through inflationary finance. Seigniorage is an undeclared tax on the money balances held by the people and businesses.

When governments print money and cause inflation, the money balances held by the public lose value (purchasing power). The loss in value of the outstanding money balances at any point in time is almost equivalent to the value of the newly printed money by the government. This is seigniorage. The term seigniorage is derived from the Spanish word seignior, or lord, implying that the government (the lord) has the first right to the people's money balances.

In the past, almost all governments relied on raising public revenues via seigniorage. After the end of World War II, most industrialized countries, however, introduced and adopted well-developed national tax systems. These tax systems functioned efficiently by making it feasible for governments to raise substantial revenues without significantly distorting the allocation of resources. The adoption of tax systems made it possible for most developed countries to stop relying on seigniorage in raising government revenue. Among those countries that introduced efficient tax systems were almost all the EU countries with the exception of the Southern European countries.

Southern EU countries consistently depended on seigniorage to extract governmental revenues. A few authors have argued that, for the Southern EU countries, the marginal cost of raising public revenue through taxation is higher than the marginal cost of raising public revenue through seigniorage. This was the result of the absence of well-developed tax systems in the Southern EU countries. Such a conviction has influenced these authors to support the position that the Southern European countries should remain outside the monetary union. This logic, however, is unconvincing since almost all economists are well aware of the detrimental effects of high inflation on an economy. Today, few, if any, economists will recommend that a country should rely on seigniorage; a well-developed tax system is a better option. An efficient tax system protects the country from the many negative effects of inflation, and it frees the central bank of the candidate country to pursue independent price-stability policies prior to becoming a full member of a monetary union.

The expected costs of the formation of a monetary union will be lower if labor markets are flexible and if free labor mobility within the regions of each country and between countries is possible. In case a region or an entire country is experiencing an asymmetric shock and unemployment begins to rise, then unemployed workers may be absorbed by other industries located in other regions of the country or by any other member states within the monetary union. Similarly, the expected costs of a monetary union will be lower if the budgetary process is centralized and the central authority of the monetary union is vested with fiscal powers, i.e., a substantial budget. Under these circumstances, a country hit by an asymmetric shock that results in high unemployment can receive transfers in the form of loans or aid to cope with the adverse effects of the asymmetric shock.

# Expected Benefits

The expected benefits, like the expected costs from the formation of a monetary union, cannot be accurately estimated since they are not always explicit and apparent. The most frequently mentioned benefits are those that arise from the elimination of transaction costs. These costs occur when businesses and consumers exchange currencies to purchase goods and services from other countries. They occur when businesses invest abroad by buying or building factories and when financial investors purchase foreign securities such as stocks and bonds.

A few authors have expressed doubts whether the elimination of the transaction costs from the adoption of a common currency produces any real benefits. The rationale for their skepticism arises because banks, which are in the business of exchanging currencies after the formation of the monetary union, will lose an amount of income equivalent to transaction cost savings. Economists, however, do not consider the banks' lost income as a true cost to the total economy. Their reasoning is that the banks' freed resources that were facilitating the exchange rate transactions can be absorbed by alternative economic activities after the adoption of the common currency.

Another major expected benefit from joining a monetary union is the increased trade among the monetary union member countries. The increase in trade volume is the result of the replacement of all national currencies by a common currency. Exchange rate variability often deters many firms from committing to long-term contracts with foreign companies. Firms, however, may eliminate exchange rate risk by arranging to receive the foreign currency at the time of the actual payment at an agreed exchange rate. Such an activity is known as hedging and is usually made available by large banks at a cost to the firms. Many financial contracts exist, providing these services at a certain cost to the firm. This cost can be avoided with the formation of the monetary union.

An additional benefit from the formation of a monetary union is the gained price transparency. Expressing prices in all countries in terms of only one currency allows consumers and businesses to compare prices more easily. This helps consumers become price-conscious buyers and forces firms to become more efficient competitors. Price transparency promotes competition, contributing to a downward convergence of prices among the monetary union member countries.

The formation of a monetary union frees a member country from its responsibility of holding reserves of other monetary union member countries' currencies that no longer exist. The elimination of these reserves is an additional benefit to each member country because the amounts of these reserves are a binding constraint in determining the maximum purchases of imports each country could afford to buy per period.

If the monetary union consists of a group of countries that established a large, successful, and stable economic entity, then the monetary union will probably generate additional benefits to its members. One benefit in this case arises because the currency of the monetary union will be accepted as an international medium of exchange along with other dominant hard currencies. The US dollar, the Japanese yen, and the UK pound are employed by other countries as a medium of exchange for foreign transactions. Some non-member countries of the monetary union may use the new common currency for international reserves. In such situations, the central bank of the monetary union will gain a new asset equal to the amount of its own currency borrowed and used by other countries.[6]

Lastly, a successful monetary union, which maintains low inflation rates, generates the greatest benefit of all for its members: It gains the credibility of price stability. An economic system characterized by price stability directs resources to the most productive sectors of the economy. Price stability induces people and businesses to commit resources for a long time, avoiding all necessary transactions that aim to protect them from losses due to unanticipated inflation.

## Is the EU15 an OCA?

An OCA, according to economic theory, must consist of only economically integrated countries.[7] Economic integration leads to the formation of a flexible common market for all factors of production and products. Economic theory dictates that the central authority of the monetary union must be empowered with significant fiscal powers. These two characteristics of an OCA are highly desirable and constitute necessary conditions for a monetary union's success for two main reasons. The first reason is to assure the occurrence of asymmetric shocks are highly improbable and the second reason is to enable countries to cope with such asymmetric shocks if they do occur.

The Single European Act (SEA), which became effective on January 7, 1993, contributed to the harmonization of many aspects of the EU economies. The aim of the SEA was to establish a true Single

European Market (SEM) or internal market without frontiers. Economic integration is an ongoing phenomenon in the EU countries; thus, many structural differences exist among these economies. These differences are found in the legal, taxation, and financial systems. Other remaining differences pertain to the organization and flexibility of labor markets, the real growth of the economies, and the unemployment rates.

One of the greatest differences, however, among the EU countries lies in the division between the Northern and Central European countries and the Southern Mediterranean European countries. The former group includes the more developed industrial countries, while the latter includes a small group of relatively less developed countries. The southern Mediterranean European countries employ a greater percentage of their labor force in agriculture than the northern and central Western European countries.[8] With the May 1, 2004, expansion of the EU to include ten new member countries, the same question of whether these countries meet the requirements of an OCA to become members of the EMU is posed (see Chapter 8). This question is more relevant for the new eight Central Eastern European countries which, in 1989, began undergoing major transformations of their planned communist economies to become free market economies.

The north-south division of the EU countries motivated several economists in the past to consider whether all former EU15 countries had constituted an OCA. One example of these studies is by Bayoumi and Eichengreen (1994), who estimated and compared permanent supply shocks among eight regions in the US and among eleven EU countries. The authors found that permanent supply shocks are not correlated in the eleven EU countries. The supply shocks in the EU were larger than those in the US regions, which in contrast were highly correlated. Their conclusion was that the eleven EU countries did not constitute an OCA. Similarly, other comparative studies found that the EU15 countries did not constitute an OCA.

Many of those studies, including the one by Bayoumi and Eichengreen, found that a smaller core of the EU countries comprised of Germany, France, Belgium, Netherlands, and possibly Denmark constituted a more homogeneous group and, therefore, qualified to be an OCA. These authors recommended the formation of a monetary union consisting of only the smaller core group of EU countries. As for the remaining countries, they could join if their economies met certain economic criteria. This was the idea for the "two-speed Europe" approach, which gained some popularity but was not adopted by the EU.

The reason the EU did not adopt the "two-speed Europe" approach was based on more recent studies including one published by the EC Commission in 1990, which found that some of the costs of forming a monetary union were exaggerated. The loss of the exchange rate policy, for example, was less important as it was initially perceived for different reasons. When an EU country employs the exchange rate as an instrument to improve its own trade balance and reduce its unemployment, it does so at the expense of some other countries. Such a phenomenon is known as a competitive devaluation, which can often trigger a reprisal by a country's trading partners.

Furthermore, for the exchange rate policy to be effective, prices and wages have to be assumed constant. This assumption was a realistic one prior to and during the 1960s, but starting in the early 1970s, both prices and wages had been volatile. This led to the conclusion that for a devaluation to be permanently effective, the real exchange rate must change.[9] It is, however, possible for an opposite proportional change to the nominal exchange rate to take place in the foreign to domestic price ratio after the devaluation. If this happens, no change in the real exchange rate will occur.

In the appendix of this chapter (Figure 2.2), it is demonstrated that a devaluation to cope with a supply-side shock can increase the price level of a country since a devaluation increases the foreign import prices and reduces the export prices. The increased price level will reduce the country's trade balance and, thus, the aggregate demand. Increases in the price level induce workers to demand higher nominal wages, which would trigger further price increases. The increased price level will have a negative impact on the country's output level as aggregate demand and supply decline (shifts left). As a result, the country may lose the obtained gains from the devaluation. In general, the more open an economy is, the less effective a devaluation will be. In the long run, the competitive advantage of a devaluation of a small open economy can be totally lost. The aggregate supply will not, however, decrease further unless nominal wages remain constant after the increase in the price level, i.e., when workers are fooled (money illusion) or when they knowingly accept lower real wages.[10]

Sometimes workers voluntarily accept lower wages usually during periods of recession by choosing to keep their jobs even if they have to work for lower wages.[11] Modern macroeconomists do not support the view that money illusion can continue for long periods; thus, changes in nominal exchange rates in general are expected to have temporary effects on the economy. The above analysis supports the view that a country's decision to join a monetary union is not as costly as was originally thought.

## External Benefits of European Monetary Integration

Critics of the EMU have usually claimed that the reduction in transaction costs, which was estimated to be about 1 percent of the EU15 countries' GDP, was insufficient to counterweigh the loss of the countries' economic policies. Countries joining the EMU must relinquish their autonomy of monetary and exchange rate policies and, to a large extent, fiscal policy to comply with the Maastricht Treaty's two fiscal criteria and the Stability and Growth Pact (SGP). Though the SGP has been violated by several EU countries, it is an EU law that will be revised and is expected to become more flexible.

The expected costs and benefits from the formation of the EMU, however, ought not to be calculated from the perspective of each country independent of the other candidate countries but jointly by the entire group of the EMU countries. Each country entering the EMU generates external benefits, which must also be included in the calculation of total benefits. If such external benefits were ignored, then total benefits would have been underestimated.

As the members of the monetary union increase, the benefits from monetary integration also increase, i.e., the optimum number of member countries of the EMU becomes endogenous to integration. This is an important reason explaining why the static method of measuring costs and benefits from monetary integration is incorrect. There is, however, a practical problem with the above analysis regarding the external EMU benefits. Since the EMU lacks a substantial budget power and cannot be involved in any meaningful income redistribution, candidate member countries will not expect to be compensated for their external benefits. As a result, individual candidate countries may ignore the external benefits in their decision to join the EMU.

Some of the benefits from monetary integration are directly related to the beneficial effects of the EMU on the completion of the Single European Market. From the EMU experience, it is now clear that the countries which benefited the most from the formation of the EMU are those that "imported price stability" by adopting the common currency, the euro. These are primarily the Southern European Mediterranean countries of Greece, Spain, Portugal, and Italy, along with Ireland (a northern European country). These countries, during the period prior to the adoption of the euro, attained high rates of growth above the EU average. This positive but limited experience of integration among the unequal partners has already favorably influenced the negotiations of the last enlargement, which resulted in the expansion of the EU to include 10 new members on May 1, 2004. It will also explain the eagerness of these countries to join the EMU and the hesitancy of the UK, Sweden, and Denmark, who have already established price stability, not to join the EMU.

## Labor Markets in the EU

It is widely known that labor markets in the EU and in Europe in general are rigid. Many European workers are unwilling or unable to relocate within their own country, let alone to other EU countries to secure employment. Labor immobility in the EU is attributed to a variety of reasons, such as language and cultural barriers as well as differences in climatic conditions. In addition to labor immobility, other structural problems in the EU labor markets include strict labor laws and labor market organizations that are responsible for wage rigidity. Many economists are convinced that labor market rigidity is one of the most important causes of the high unemployment rates in most EU countries.

Specifically, more problematic is the heavy centralization of trade unions and employers associations that often negotiate labor agreements at the national or regional levels. This type of organization of labor markets leaves little room for variation in wages to account for differences in labor productivity among companies. In the last few years, however, there has been a tendency for change. This issue, for example, surfaced in May 2002 with the strikes of Germany's largest industrial union, the IG Metall. Wage increases in the engineering sector were long ago set at the industry level between the trade union, IG Metall, and, Gesamtmetall, the engineering employer's association. Many small companies, however, left the employer's association to avoid paying the high wages.[12] These companies sought to obtain company-specific collective agreements to enhance their flexibility. Such types of agreements in 2002 were close to six thousand in Germany. This trend persisted in 2003 and 2004 and is expected to continue. If this trend continues, the entire system in this major sector of the German economy will become more flexible.

Since the late 1990s, many policies were adopted and several measures were taken in almost every EU state to introduce more flexibility in labor markets. The *Financial Times*, on May 7, 2002, reported that labor markets in the Euro Area (Eurozone) were becoming more flexible.[13] Numerous incentives were offered to firms to increase hiring and to unemployed workers to seek employment more aggressively. As a result of these new programs, gains in employment were achieved, but some of these gains came as increases in part-time employment and in terms of hiring temporary workers. From 1996 to 2001, employment in the countries that formed the Euro Area (in 1999) increased by 1.6 percent per year, yet employment for the US increased by

1.3 percent per year. Such progress in Euro Area employment occurred though the US economy during the same period grew at 3.5 percent per year. Still, the EU15 countries do not have the flexible markets of the US or the UK, and they did not match the tremendous increases in the US labor productivity during the 1990–2000 decade of the information technology boom.

Economic miracles, though, can occur everywhere and countries can leap forward to prosperity in a few years. A good example of this is Ireland, which not long ago was "an impoverished nation of emigrants." In 2001, Ireland attained the second highest per capita income in the EU ($28,500), which was behind Luxembourg's per capita income, the highest one in the EU. In 2003, Ireland's per capita GDP remained one of the highest in the EU ($33,120), second to that of Luxembourg and above the EU and the Euro Area averages. At the same time, Ireland has maintained the lowest corporate tax rate in the EU at 12.5 percent.[14]

Though labor market flexibility is undoubtedly beneficial to the success of the EMU, its absence according to Gros and Thygesen (1998) should not be a reason for a country to avoid the EMU. The formation of the EMU will have beneficial effects on all participating countries despite the absence of sufficient labor market flexibility. According to Gros and Thygesen, the reason for these positive effects is that the benefits from joining the EMU exceed the costs. Gros and Thygesen compared the expected benefits of the EMU to an iceberg, most of which is hidden under the ocean water with about one-eighth of it visible.

## The Lisbon Agenda

During the March 2000 EU Summit in Lisbon, Portugal, the EU heads of state and government agreed to transform the EU by the year 2010 to the most dynamic, knowledge-based, competitive economy in the world. To achieve such a high goal, the official representatives of the EU countries decided to pursue economic, social, and environmental policies that would lead to sustained development, high economic growth, and social cohesion.

The goals of the Lisbon Agenda were to be attained as the EU countries introduced the necessary structural reforms in their economies by investing in research and development, by entrepreneurial innovations, and by completing the internal market. A successful pursuit of the Lisbon Agenda by the EU countries was expected to contribute to the creation of more and better jobs. Attainment of macroeconomic and fiscal stability would support and sustain a social model without exclusions of any minority groups.

The successful implementation of the Lisbon Agenda aimed to make all the EU countries' economies more competitive and similar. As a consequence, all such EU competitive economies were to become a better fit group for an OCA.[15] Most EU countries began introducing reforms in their economies even before the adoption of the Lisbon Agenda in 2000 to help their business firms become more competitive. One of the most important, but difficult, reforms that the EU countries initiated was the introduction of flexibility in their labor markets. These reforms aimed to change labor laws to allow companies to respond more easily to business condition changes. In addition, during this period, EU businesses have been campaigning for reduced long-term unemployment benefits, reduced pension payments, more freedom in laying off workers, and increased working hours per week.

Many policies adopted to implement the Lisbon Agenda were perceived by EU workers and trade unions as a plan directed against workers' rights and benefits, introduced by neo-liberal economic thinking with the full support of businesses. Many European economists and politicians had accepted that the US economic system was more capable of promoting high-tech industries and employment through innovation.

For this reason, EU countries introduced massive deregulation in industries, including privatization programs and liberalization in product and input markets.

Most governments accepted, in principle, the Lisbon Agenda as a necessary program to help the EU economies recover from slow growth and high unemployment. Many believed the Lisbon Strategy was a necessary impetus to enable EU economies to withstand the enhanced competition from the US and the emerging developing countries. The revitalized EU economies would reverse the continuous and massive loss of jobs due to outsourcing or due to outflow of foreign direct investment. Similarly, most EU governments became convinced that the reforms and consolidation of the national pension programs were unavoidable due to the aging populations and increased life expectancy that rendered uncapped EU pension plans unsustainable.

### Defending the Lisbon Agenda in Germany

EU countries adopted different policies to carry out the Lisbon Agenda. Germany's Chancellor Gerhard Schröder convinced his own Social Democratic Party (SDP), the trade unions, and the German people that his proposed Agenda 2010 would be beneficial to the country in the long run. Despite the painful short-term effects, these policies were "objectively necessary," according to the German chancellor. After many bitter and long debates, he convinced his own party, the opposition, and some members of the trade unions to support the proposed reforms. As a result, some of the Agenda 2010 policies were enacted to laws. This success, however, came at a great cost to Chancellor Gerhard Schröder, who lost his popularity and the SDP leadership. The misfortunes of the chancellor passed to his party. The SDP sank in terms of popularity among the German voters and, for the first time, ranked third in the European elections of June 13, 2004, receiving only 21.5 percent of the popular vote.

France made some progress by pursuing policies introduced because of the Lisbon Agenda, e.g., a new labor law that allowed companies to enter into agreements with their own workforce at the plant level, independent of any other labor agreements at the national or regional level. Similarly, France began privatizing state enterprises, including the Electricité de France despite union resistance. These and other reforms were introduced by the French Finance Minister Nicolas Sarkozy prior to his resignation.

### A Little Help from Outside for France

Nicolas Sarkozy is a French politician who associated his political career with liberal economic reforms to revitalize the French economy. The popular politician consulted the former head of the International Monetary Fund (IMF), Michel Camdessus, and asked him for an explanation of the causes of the French economic slowdown. Sarkozy challenged Camdessus to recommend policies that would "reinvigorate" the French economy.

Camdessus, the former head of the IMF whose job for many years was to give policy recommendations to countries around the world, "prescribed some bitter pill for the ailing French economy" according to the *Financial Times*.* On October 19, 2004, the French native Camdessus published a 140-page report on his own country with the assistance of a 20-member team from France's finance department. Camdessus asserted that France was experiencing declining competitiveness because of its failure to respond to three major unprecedented challenges dealing with diffusion of new technologies, aging of the population, and globalization. The former head of the IMF reported that France was protected from further economic deterioration because of its relatively low interest rates and the introduction of the euro.

Camdessus's report recommended labor market liberalization, public debt reduction, and cooperation of universities with small companies to promote the desired knowledge economy. The Camdessus "prescription" to the ailing French economy is similar to the Lisbon Strategy for 2010. In addition to policy recommendations offered by Camdessus, the report pointed out that recovery of the French economy was feasible, as similar reforms were successful in four other European countries: Sweden, which restructured its state finance (pensions); Finland, which attained a high-level knowledge economy; Denmark, which was able to modernize the welfare state; and lastly, the UK, which liberalized its labor market.

Sarkozy, a declared candidate for the French presidency, made an interesting announcement as he stood beside Camdessus, who gave a press conference on the report of the French economy. Sarkozy contended that he was a firm believer that the French economy could be reinvigorated with the adoption of reform policies. On November 28, 2004, Sarkozy was elected as the leader of the right wing French ruling party, the Union for Popular Movement (UMP), with 85.1 percent of the votes. To assume this role, Sarkozy was forced to resign as the finance minister of France as President Chirac would not permit him to hold both posts.

It will be difficult to predict whether Sarkozy will win the elections and become the president of France in 2007. Even if he becomes the president of France, he may not be able to pass through all the necessary reforms to reinvigorate the French economy. The trade unions, and the socialist and the communist political parties that are interested in social equality will resist. Sarkozy's response to demands for social equality was that liberal economic reform will boost economic growth, and this will lead to increased social equality.

* Thornhill, J. "Camdessus prescribes bitter pills for ailing French economy" (2004), *Financial Times*. October 20.

A few studies (including the Camdessus report) have found that, for many years, GDP growth for the US exceeded the growth of France and other EU countries. The same studies revealed that labor productivity in the US is almost the same as labor productivity in France. Such a result implies that the problem of France and other EU countries catching up with the US in not competitiveness. European workers, by choice, work 20 percent fewer hours than the US workers.

The optimism of the former head of the IMF, Michel Camdessus, that France would be capable of stimulating its economy and return to periods of high growth, is supported by the annual "Competitiveness Report" for 2004, published by the World Economic Forum. In this report, Finland, a Euro Area member state, kept the number one spot in a group of 104 countries for the third time in four years, followed by the US. Interestingly, among the ten most competitive economies in the world, six of them were European: Finland, Sweden, Denmark, Norway, Switzerland, and Iceland. The first three of these six countries are EU members and five of them are Nordic European countries.

The World Economic Forum, the organization that ranks countries on international competitiveness, is basing its assessment on factors and criteria that determine the country's overall business environment, as each country pursues sustainable economic growth. The Nordic European countries' economies maintain excellent legal business environments, low levels of corruption, and respect for business contracts. Many of their business firms are world-wide leaders in technological innovation. A good example of this is Finland, which is the home country of the well-known international mobile phone corporation, Nokia. Finland maintained its number one spot because of its business friendly policies that encouraged technological innovation. Lastly, Nordic European countries maintained fiscal stability by generating government surpluses.

Sweden is an EU country considered successful in reforming its economy and making substantial progress in implementing the Lisbon Agenda ahead of the other EU member countries. Sweden introduced substantial labor market flexibility that has helped boost labor productivity, particularly in the manufacturing sector. Sweden, however, did not increase productivity in the services sector as the US did. Wages in Sweden are no longer set at the national level. Sectoral labor contracts are characterized by flexibility. The Lisbon Agenda was one of the factors that motivated Sweden to reform its pension system, a change that guarantees financial stability. This was accomplished by determining the pension income according to the real wages and to the longevity of the retiree and the growth of the economy. Such drastic reform implies that the guaranteed generous Swedish government pension was given up for the financial health of the entire system. This is an important and difficult step that other countries, such as France and Germany, have been hesitant to take. The above discussion means that the success of the Nordic European countries could be repeated by other EU countries.

## Evaluation of the Lisbon Agenda

The Lisbon Agenda was adopted by the EU Council during the March 2000 Summit in Lisbon. In February 2004, the EU Commission prepared the annual report "Delivering Lisbon Reforms for the Enlarged Union." This was the fourth annual report prepared by the Commission and was submitted to the Spring EU Summit meeting in Brussels on March 25–26, 2004.

The Commission report appraised certain achievements that EU countries attained as a result of implementing policies pursuing the Lisbon Strategy 2010 objectives. One such achievement is the employment rate in the EU, which increased from a 62.5 percent participation rate in 1999 to 64.3 percent in 2002. This rate is short of the 70 percent participation target of the Lisbon Strategy for 2010. This increase in employment resulted in the creation of more than six million jobs. Several markets have been liberalized; others are presently undergoing liberalization. Telecommunications, postal services, rail freight, electricity, and gas are a few of these markets. All these reforms reduced production costs, induced modernization of these markets, and improved product quality; thus, European firms became more competitive.

The Commission report indicated progress in the knowledge-based economy. A few EU countries have made progress in reforming pension programs, enabling them to cope with the aging of the population. Similarly, EU countries are more concerned with protecting the natural environment.

The Commission report pointed out that much work needed to be done to achieve the Lisbon goals by 2010. The Commission emphasized three priority areas upon which the governments should focus to achieve the Lisbon goals:

1. Investment in networks and knowledge.
2. Strengthening competitiveness in industry and services through the completion of the internal market.
3. Increased labor participation of older people by encouraging older workers to delay retirement.

On March 25–26, 2004, after reviewing the Commission report, the EU Council reaffirmed its commitment to the Lisbon Strategy. All

EU leaders pledged to accelerate the pace of the reforms. The EU Council appointed a former Dutch prime minister, Wim Kok, to head a high-level group to study the overall situation in the EU and prepare a report to revitalize the Lisbon Strategy for 2010.

The Kok Report was delivered to the EU Commission and Council on November 3–4, 2004. The progress of the Lisbon Agenda during the first four years was characterized in the Kok report as gloomy. The poor performance was attributed to an "overcrowded agenda, poor coordination, and conflicting priorities." However, most important was the lack of political commitment of the EU member states.

In the spring summit of 2005, the EU Council will assess the performance of the EU countries in meeting the Lisbon goals. Because the time of this assessment marks the halfway point designated by the Lisbon Council for the implementation of the goals, this report will be significant.

## SUMMARY

Most authors of the OCA emphasized the high costs a country may incur by joining a monetary union. These costs are directly related to the loss of monetary and exchange rate policies. Both policies are useful to a country experiencing asymmetric shocks. The country's cost during an asymmetric shock will be higher when labor markets are rigid, i.e., characterized by inflexible wage rates and labor immobility within the country and among the candidate monetary union countries. Labor markets are rigid when firm and labor organizations are centralized, which limits the freedom to negotiate wages and other benefits for workers at the firm level to take into consideration differing labor productivities among firms. Similarly, the cost of the formation of a monetary union will be higher when the central authority of the monetary union has limited spending power. If, however, the central authority of a monetary union has a relatively large budget, then it can rescue countries experiencing asymmetric shocks.

Recent contributions to the OCA theory point out that the costs of the formation of monetary unions in early studies were exaggerated and that total benefits were underestimated. Many authors investigated whether the EU15 countries constitute an OCA. Some studies found that the EU15 countries did not constitute an OCA. The main reason for this finding was the division of the EU between Northern-central and Southern countries, or rich and poor countries. Ireland was included in the second group. Many structural differences existed between these two groups of countries. The most important problem was that the two groups of countries were characterized by asynchronous business cycles. As a result, these authors recommended that the monetary union should begin with a small group of more homogeneous countries that included Germany, France, Belgium, Luxembourg, the Netherlands, and possibly Denmark. Some other authors supported the view that a wider European monetary union with a larger number of countries constituted an OCA. The 1990 EU Commission study advocated that with further economic integration, the optimum number of included countries in the EMU would be greater. These authors prevailed; and the EMU began with almost all EU countries willing to join the EMU.

The EMU, however, did not begin until all candidate countries met certain criteria. The principal purpose of these criteria was to ensure all candidate countries attained price stability before they became EMU members. These criteria are known as Maastricht convergence criteria that will be discussed in the next chapter where the formation of the EMU will be studied.

The EMU is already in place. Twelve countries since March 1, 2002, share the same currency, the euro. Prior to the adoption of the euro, all countries had attained price stability. The risk of asymmetric shocks, however, remains a threat, especially when one considers that the EU operates with a small budget of less than 1.5 percent of the EU GDP.

In March 2000, the EU leaders agreed in Lisbon, Portugal, to transform the EU by 2010 to the most competitive economy in the world. This objective was to be achieved by following the Lisbon Agenda. The Lisbon Agenda includes many programs that will liberalize the EU economies. Certain progress has been achieved, but the EU is far from implementing all policies recommended by the Lisbon Agenda. If EU countries are successful in implementing the Lisbon Agenda, the EU economies will become more integrated and, thus, more qualified for an OCA membership.

## Essay Questions

1. Discuss the most important costs of a country considering possible membership to a monetary union. Evaluate the importance of these costs. A few authors recently provided evidence that some of these costs are not as important as originally thought to be. Do you agree with this new evidence? Elaborate thoroughly.

2. Describe all the necessary characteristics of a group of countries that constitute an OCA. Once the monetary union is formed, are there any desired powers that the monetary union central authority must be vested with to remain successful?

3. Explain all the expected benefits to a country from joining a monetary union.

4. What are asymmetric shocks? Can asymmetric shocks negatively affect a monetary union? Explain. Is it possible for a monetary union to protect its members better from a symmetric shock than it can from an asymmetric shock? Explain thoroughly.

5. Do you think the former EU15 countries constituted an OCA prior to the formation of the EMU on January 1, 1999? Has anything changed since? Discuss thoroughly.

6. What is the Lisbon Agenda? Why was a strategy based on the Lisbon Agenda adopted by the EU member countries? Are the EU countries, so far, successful in pursuing policies motivated by the Lisbon Strategy?

7. Explain the concept of seigniorage. Is seigniorage an important cost to a country joining a monetary union?

# APPENDIX

## Exchange Rate Policy and Asymmetric Shocks

Many authors stressed the importance of the loss of the exchange rate policy to a country joining a monetary union. It will be interesting to examine how effective exchange rate policy is to a country inflicted by a recession caused by an asymmetric shock. In Figure 2.1 below, it is assumed that the price level remains constant while the country experiences a demand-side asymmetric shock, e.g., when

Figure 2.1

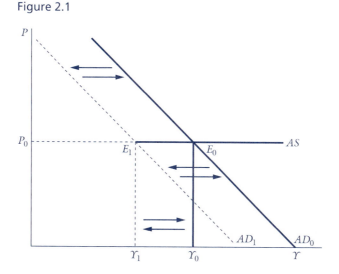

foreign consumers' tastes turn against certain products of one particular country.

On the horizontal axis of Figure 2.1 above, we measure real GDP or real national income denoted by $Y$, and on the vertical axis we measure the country's aggregate price level, $P$. The aggregate supply curve of this hypothetical economy is drawn as a horizontal line implying that prices in this economy are assumed to remain constant regardless of the level of output produced.

This assumption of the Keynesian model was employed by the authors who developed the theory of an OCA. These authors focused mainly on comparing expected costs and benefits of a country considering membership to a monetary union assuming prices in the economy remain constant.

Let us assume that a monetary union member country experiences a demand-side asymmetric shock; this is depicted in Figure 2.1 above by a reduction in the aggregate demand ($AD$) from $AD_0$ to $AD_1$ (a shift to the left). The reduction in $AD$ causes a decrease in the country's real GDP from $Y_0$ to $Y_1$. If the country was not a member of the monetary union, it could have devalued its currency against its trading partner's currencies. A currency devaluation reduces the country's export prices and increases the country's import prices. Under some plausible assumptions, a devaluation is expected to improve a country's trade balance ($X - M$), where $X$ is the value of the country's exports and $M$ is the value of the country's imports. An improvement in the trade balance will increase (shift to the right) the $AD$. By choosing the appropriate rate of devaluation, the $AD$ can shift back to its original position, $AD_0$. This $AD$ shift will raise real GDP from $Y_1$ back to its initial level, $Y_0$.

With this example, it is demonstrated that when the price level of a country remains constant, the country may gain from employing an active exchange rate policy and cope with a demand-side asymmetric shock. It is, therefore, costly for the country to join a monetary union.

Now assume the country experiences a supply-side asymmetric shock such as a reduction in the supply of an input to production, essential to a few home industries. Assume also that the aggregate supply ($AS$) curve is upward sloping. This implies that as output in this economy increases, the price level increases. Figure 2.2 demonstrates a possible scenario of a small open economy country that experiences a supply-side asymmetric shock. $AD_0$ and $AS_0$ are the original aggregate demand and aggregate supply curves of the hypothetical small open economy. The intersection of $AD_0$ and $AS_0$ at point $E_0$ determines the initial equilibrium real national income (real GDP) denoted by $Y_0$ and the initial price level denoted by $P_0$. Due to the supply-side shock that

Figure 2.2

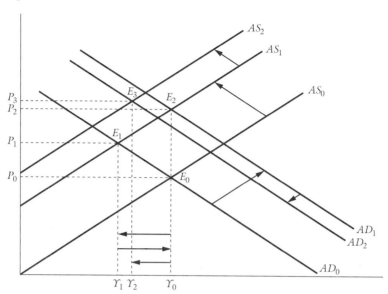

was inflicted on the country, the *AS* curve declines (shift to the left) from $AS_0$ to $AS_1$. As a result, the economy reached a new equilibrium at $E_1$ with a lower real GDP, $Y_1$, but a higher price level ($P_1$). If the country was not a member of a monetary union, it could have devalued its currency to increase its real GDP. Under a flexible exchange rate system, a depreciation of the currency could have achieved the same result. A devaluation under some plausible assumptions can increase a country's trade balance, $X - M$. If the country's currency is devaluated by the appropriate rate, the *AD* can increase (shift to the right to $AD_1$) to restore the initial higher equilibrium real GDP, $Y_0$. This can only take place at a higher price level, $P_2$ as seen in Figure 2.2. The increase in the country's price level is a consequence of the devaluation that raises import prices.

This can be seen if the aggregate price-level ($P$) is expressed as a weighted average of the domestic and foreign prices in the economy as shown below by Equation (1).

$$P = \alpha P^d + (1 - \alpha)P^f \qquad (1)$$

$P^d$ is an index of domestic prices and $P^f$ is an index of foreign prices, i.e., the prices of the country's imports, $\alpha$ is the share of the domestic goods in the price level $P$, and $1 - \alpha$ is the share of imports.[16]

A large value of $\alpha$ close to one indicates that the country is isolated from foreign markets. On the contrary, a small $\alpha$ close to zero implies that the country's price level is greatly affected by import prices. This is the assumption of a small open economy country.

The increase in the price level will affect the *AD* and the *AS*. A higher domestic price level will tend to reduce the country's exports as they become more expensive and increase the country's imports as they become cheaper. These two effects will deteriorate the country's trade balance $(X - M)$ and, thus, the *AD* curve will decrease to $AD_2$.

Higher prices will reduce the real wage, $W/P$, as workers find out when they cash their checks to purchase goods and services. As a result, workers will demand higher nominal wages $(W)$. Those businesses having to pay the higher nominal wages will respond by hiring fewer workers, causing a reduction in the number of workers hired. Consequently, the short-run aggregate supply curve will be further reduced as it shifts from $AS_1$ to $AS_2$.

The last shifts in the *AD* and *AS* result in a new equilibrium, $E_3$, the new equilibrium real GDP $Y_2$, is lower than the initial GDP, $Y_0$. As for the new price level, it will be above or below $P_2$ depending on the relative shifts of the *AD* and *AS* curves. In Figure 2.2, the new price level, $P_3$, is shown to be above $P_2$.

The reduction in real GDP demonstrates that a country's exchange rate policy is less effective when the country's price level increases after the devaluation. A country which consistently employs exchange rate policy to improve its trade balance in relation to its trading partners will be confronted with the risk of possible retaliation from its trading partners. An active exchange rate policy for the purpose of gaining competitive trade advantage is known as competitive devaluation. Competitive devaluations were criticized by many economists and some government officials as an unfair policy directed against the country's trading partners.

# chapter 3

# A New Currency for Europe: The Euro

## The Delors Report

As legislation for the completion of the Single European Market (SEM) was introduced during the second half of the 1980s, many Europeans became convinced that the EU also needed a common currency to complete the SEM. The new common currency was expected to eliminate the high exchange rate transaction costs and the exchange rate risk, which discourage international trade and foreign investment. To deal with this issue, the European Council at the Hanover Summit in June 1988, appointed Jacques Delors, the president of the EC Commission, as head of a committee to study and possibly draw a plan for further monetary integration in the EC. The Delors committee consisted of seventeen members including the governors of the twelve EU national central banks and five experts in monetary affairs.

In December 1989, the Delors Committee completed and submitted its work: "The Report on Economic and Monetary Union" or "The Delors Report" as it popularly became known. The Delors Report recommended a gradual approach to the formation of an economic and monetary union to allow sufficient time for all candidate countries to prepare their economies for monetary integration. The prerequisites for membership to the monetary union outlined in the Delors Report required the coordination and convergence of the economic and monetary policies by all candidate member countries. The Delors Report, like its predecessor, the Werner Plan, did not explicitly recommend the adoption of a common currency. The Delors Report, however, recommended that the candidate monetary union countries should irrevocably fix the exchange rates. The Delors Report was accepted by the European Council at the Madrid Summit in June 1990. The European Council decided to address and work on the European monetary integration project as recommended by the Delors Report at its next intergovernmental conference (IGC). This conference took place in December 1991 in the Dutch town of Maastricht, where the

European heads of state signed the historic Maastricht Treaty for the formation of the Economic and Monetary Union (EMU).[1] The Maastricht Treaty was destined to change the EC economies and the future of Europe.

# The Maastricht Treaty

The Maastricht Treaty, or Treaty on the European Union (TEU) in December 1991, complemented the Treaty of Rome that had established the EC in 1957. In Article B of the TEU, the objectives of the historic Maastricht Treaty are stated:

> To promote economic and social progress, which is balanced and sustainable, in particular through the creation of an area without internal frontiers, through the economic and social cohesion and through the establishment of economic and monetary union, ultimately including a single currency in accordance with the provisions of the Treaty.

Since the signing of the Maastricht Treaty, the EC has been commonly referred to as the European Union (EU), indicating a higher level of integration.[2] The main objective of the Maastricht Treaty was the formation of a complete EMU in which all member countries shared a new common currency that would eventually replace all national currencies in a few years.

According to the Maastricht Treaty, monetary integration would take place only after member countries had attained substantial convergence in certain macroeconomic variables. Candidate EMU countries were required to demonstrate a high degree of price stability and fiscal discipline to qualify for EMU membership. The performance of the candidate EMU countries was evaluated on five macroeconomic variables: inflation rates, long-term interest rates, government deficits, government debts, and the exchange rates. Only countries that met certain conditions or criteria based on these five macroeconomic variables were to qualify for EMU membership. These criteria, which are listed below, are known as the Maastricht convergence criteria.

## Maastricht Convergence Criteria

The first four Maastricht convergence criteria require that, in the year prior to the examination, a candidate EMU country must maintain:[3]

1. An inflation rate of no more than 1.5 percentage points above the average inflation rate of the three countries with the lowest inflation rates.

2. A long-term interest rate of no more than 2 percentage points above the average interest rate of the three countries with the lowest inflation rates.

3. A government budget deficit to Gross Domestic Product (GDP) ratio of no more than 3 percent.

4. A government debt to GDP ratio not exceeding 60 percent or rapidly approaching 60 percent.

The fifth Maastricht criterion regarding the exchange rate of each country involved a two-year examination period.

5. The exchange rate of each country should remain within the ±2.25 percent normal band of the Exchange Rate Mechanism (ERM) without a devaluation during the last two years prior to the examination.

Why did the candidate countries, in preparation for the EMU membership, agree to adopt these particular convergence criteria? According to the Optimum Currency Area (OCA) theory, such macroeconomic variables play no role in determining which countries qualify for an OCA membership. To understand where and how these criteria originated, one must be familiar with the history of all candidate member countries as well as the politics and process that led to the formation of the EMU.

The first and most significant of the Maastricht criteria, price stability, requires all candidate member countries to pursue and maintain low inflation rates. The remaining four convergence criteria were adopted as additional auxiliary measures to assure that the inflation criterion would not be violated. A few economists claimed that if the inflation criterion were the only required criterion by the Maastricht Treaty and if the candidate member countries satisfied this criterion, they would automatically have met the other four.

Germany, the most populous country in the EU, played a dominant role in the formation of the EMU. Once the Germans were convinced that the EMU would be a worthy project expected to strengthen the EU, they decided to support the EMU on the condition that they could decide the terms and preconditions to its formation. The rationale of selecting inflation as the most important precondition to the formation of the EMU is explained by Germany's strong preference for price stability. After experiencing the disastrous effects of hyperinflation during and between the First and Second World Wars, the German people were determined and committed to take all necessary measures to safeguard price stability in their own country.

Germany achieved price stability by constitutionally rendering independence to its central bank, the Bundesbank. The Bundesbank achieved price stability in the post-World War II period because the German government could not interfere with its monetary policy. During this period, Germany attained significant increases in productivity. Continuous economic growth and price stability in Germany were the primary reasons for the emergence of the Deutsche mark (DM) as the strongest currency in Europe. In fact, the DM became a dominant currency prior to the establishment of the European Monetary System (EMS) period. Price stability in Germany induced most EU countries to peg their currencies to the DM. The German people were adamantly opposed to giving up their "beloved" DM unless they were absolutely certain that it would be replaced by a currency that was going to be as strong or stronger than the DM. The Germans found many allies who had a clear vision and plans for monetary integration in the EU. This support came from the EMS countries, which had enjoyed price stability benefits by allowing their central banks to follow the Bundesbank's monetary policy.

Economists are great supporters of price stability since many empirical studies have shown that price stability leads countries to a steady path of economic growth. In contrast, high inflation is a source of many negative economic effects. Such negative effects include a persistent decline in the purchasing power of money, i.e., a reduction in the consumers' standard of living. Inflation also causes increased uncertainty, arbitrary redistribution of wealth, and distortionary effects in the allocation of resources, away from the most productive activities.

However, some economists have recommended that countries should accept low inflation, particularly during periods of recession. In their view, low inflation rates can have positive effects on the economy by increasing output and reducing unemployment.[4] Some economists criticized the Maastricht convergence criteria as being the cause of the EU recession in the early 1990s. Germany, however, had insisted that only countries demonstrating strong anti-inflation preferences should be allowed to join the EMU. For this reason, all candidate EMU countries adopted anti-inflationary policies. This indeed was a substantial policy change especially for a few countries that had not consistently pursued price stability in the past.

The Maastricht Treaty set out a schedule for the completion of the EMU. During this period, the European System of Central Banks (ESCB) was to be established. The ESCB consisted of a new institution, the European Central Bank (ECB) and the member countries' National Central Banks (NCBs), which became branches of the ECB. The Maastricht Treaty required the NCBs to gain total independence from the executive branch of their governments if candidate member countries were to qualify for EMU membership. Rendering independence to the NCBs prior to EMU membership required the introduction and adoption of the appropriate legislative changes. According to the Maastricht Treaty, the ECB is solely responsible for the monetary policy of all the EMU countries.

The EU Economics and Finance Council (ECOFIN) and the ECB are jointly responsible for the exchange rate policy of the new common currency. The ECOFIN has the authority to make decisions regarding exchange rate policies after consultation with the ECB, while the ECB is responsible for implementing these policies. The Maastricht Treaty specified the duration of each stage of the EMU and the expected preparations in each of these stages.

# The Three Stages of the EMU

## First Stage (July 1, 1990–December 31, 1993)

It was recognized in Maastricht that the first stage had already begun prior to the signing of the treaty. During this stage that started on July 1, 1990, capital controls were to be removed as a requirement for the completion of the SEM Program.

Candidate countries were required to coordinate their monetary and economic policies and to reduce exchange rate variability. All EMU candidate member countries were to join the ERM and limit the exchange rate fluctuation around the central parities against the ECU and the other ERM member countries' currencies within the normal band of ±2.25 percent.

## Second Stage (January 1, 1994–December 31, 1998)

During the second stage, the European Monetary Institute (EMI) was established in Frankfurt, Germany, as the precursor to the ECB. The main task of the EMI was the preparation of the groundwork for the completion of the EMU. The EMI was also responsible for the coordination of the monetary policies of the candidate EMU countries, which it achieved by issuing the appropriate recommendations to the candidate EMU countries. Starting in March 1994, coordination and convergence policies were monitored according to an elaborate surveillance based on economic reports on each country prepared by the EU Commission and submitted to the Council. If countries were found not to be making substantial progress toward convergence, they were to receive a recommendation from the Council to correct their economic policies. The country surveillance lasted throughout the second stage until the decision was taken to launch the EMU. During this stage, the EU Commission and the EMI were responsible for preparing and submitting economic convergence reports to the Council on all candidate countries. Upon receiving the country reports, the Council was to evaluate all candidate EMU countries' performances in reference to the Maastricht convergence criteria.

In addition to meeting the five Maastricht convergence criteria, during this stage, candidate EMU countries were required to enact the appropriate legislation to ensure the independence of their central banks from the executive branch of their governments. Such legal arrangements for the independence of the central banks were required by the Maastricht Treaty and are considered as important as the five Maastricht convergence criteria.[5] In addition to the five Maastricht convergence criteria and the independence of the central banks, other indicators were considered in evaluating the countries' EMU candidacy. These indicators included the balance of payments, unit labor costs, and other price indices.

According to Article 109 (J) of the TEU, the Commission and the EMI were to report to the Council their recommendations regarding the transition of the EU countries to the third stage of the EMU. The convergence reports were based on the performance of the countries in reference to the Maastricht convergence criteria. A decision by the European Council had to be made no later than December 1996. If, according to these reports, the majority of the candidate countries qualified for membership, then the EMU was to begin in 1997. According to the 1996 reports, the majority of the countries did not qualify for EMU membership. Therefore, the EMU could not begin in 1997. In accordance with the TEU, if the EMU did not begin in 1997, then it would begin on January 1, 1999, even if the majority of the countries did not qualify for membership.

In March 1998, the EU Commission and the EMI again submitted their reports on economic convergence of the candidate EMU countries to the EU Council. Based on these convergence reports, eleven countries met the Maastricht convergence criteria and, therefore, qualified for membership. After receiving the opinion of the European Parliament and acting by qualified majority, the Council recommended to the European Council (the Council in composition of the heads of state or of government) the establishment of the EMU on January 1, 1999, starting with eleven member countries.

The decision by the European Council was taken on May 2, 1998, in Brussels. The eleven countries were Austria, Belgium, Denmark, Finland, France, Italy, Ireland, Luxembourg, the Netherlands,

Portugal, and Spain. Two countries, Denmark and the UK, were given separate protocols that allowed them to exercise their choice on participation in the third stage of the EMU. Both of these countries opted out. Sweden purposefully remained outside the ERM to disqualify itself for membership and did not enact the appropriate legislation to render independence to its central bank. Greece, though wanting to join the EMU, failed all five Maastricht convergence criteria and, consequently, was disqualified for membership, but it continued to make progress. Greece's economy was later reevaluated, and it was then decided that the country met the Maastricht criteria. On January 1, 2001, Greece became the twelfth member of the EMU.

---

### UK Indecision About the Euro

In October 1997, the chancellor of the exchequer, Gordon Brown, set five tests to decide whether the UK should join the EMU:

1. Has sufficient convergence taken place between the UK and the Euro Area so the UK can permanently share the same monetary policy and interest rates?
2. Is the UK economy sufficiently flexible to deal with any asymmetric shocks?
3. Would Euro Area membership induce investment and increase employment in the UK?
4. How would the city of London be affected if Britain adopted the euro?
5. Lastly, would joining the euro promote higher growth?

On June 9, 2003, Mr. Brown announced to Parliament that the UK failed four of the five economic tests. The only test that the UK passed was the effect of the euro on the city of London. The results of the five economic tests were the same as in 1997. The chancellor mentioned that there were benefits from membership in the Euro Area. Whether the UK will adopt the euro is not certain.

Source: Champion, M. "U.K. rejects adopting euro this year but may revisit issue next year," (2003). *Wall Street Journal.* June 10.

---

## Third Stage (January 1, 1999–Present)

This third and final stage is divided into three sub-stages. During this period, the EMU was established by a group of 11 EU countries. A new currency, the euro, was introduced and accepted as the official currency of over 300 million people. The 11 EU countries that formed the EMU are called the Euro Area, Eurozone, or Euroland countries. The most important events that developed during each of these sub-periods are discussed below.

## January 1, 1999–December 31, 2002

The exchange rates of the EMU countries were irrevocably fixed during this period against the new common currency, the euro. The euro, however, existed only in the form of demand and saving deposits, i.e., checking and savings accounts. The euro was used for interbank transactions as well as for transactions between the ECB and commercial banks. National currencies coexisted with the euro, and individuals and businesses could keep bank accounts in euros or in national currencies. All newly issued government bonds (public debt) were denominated in euros. The ECB, which replaced the EMI on July 1, 1998, became exclusively responsible for monetary policy in the 11 EMU countries. The Council, however, has the responsibility for the exchange rate policy. On January 1, 1999, the 11 currencies of the EMU countries ceased to exist as independent currencies and were perceived and treated as denominations of the euro. The conversion rates of each national currency in relation to the euro became effective on January 1, 1999.

At the Madrid Council, in 1995, when the name of the new currency (the euro) was agreed upon, it was decided that one euro would be equal to one ECU. As a result, the irrevocably fixed conversion rates of the national currencies in terms of euros had to be the same as the central parity ERM rates in terms of the ECU. The finance ministers and the national central bankers announced the conversion rates in May 1998, about seven months ahead of their effective date.

It was announced, in May 1998, that the central banks had agreed to coordinate monetary policies and intervene in the foreign exchange markets by trading unlimited amounts of currencies until the market rates equalized with the announced conversion rates. The announced bilateral rates became credible, and the foreign exchange speculators sped up the convergence of the market exchange rates to these announced conversion rates. The reason the conversion rates were agreed to and pre-announced instead of set equal to the December 31 central ERM exchange rates was to eliminate any possible manipulation of the

Table 3.1

| Euro Conversion Rates (Number of national currency units per euro) | | |
|---|---|---|
| Belgian francs | BFK | 40.3399 |
| Spanish pesetas | ESP | 166.386 |
| Irish pounds | IRL | 0.78756 |
| Luxembourg francs | LFR | 40.3399 |
| Austria schillings | AS | 13.7603 |
| Finnish markkas | FM | 5.94573 |
| Deutsche marks | DM | 1.95583 |
| French francs | FF | 6.55957 |
| Italian lire | ITL | 1936.27 |
| Dutch guilders | DG | 2.20371 |
| Portuguese escudos | PTE | 200.482 |
| Greek drachmas | GRD | 340.750 |

*Note the conversion rate for the Greek drachma was announced on June 19, 2000.
Source: EU Commission

foreign exchange markets by governments to obtain a favorable competitive exchange rate position. The irrevocable bilateral conversion rates are listed in Table 3.1.

## January 1, 2002–February 28, 2002

During these two months, the euro was introduced for the first time in the form of banknotes and coins. The euro and the national currencies coexisted in this brief sub-period during the withdrawal of national currencies. The replacement of the twelve national currencies with the euro was the largest withdrawal of national currencies recorded in the world's monetary history. It turned out that the introduction of the euro was exceptionally smooth, and the foreign exchange markets were "kind" to the euro during these first critical days.

## March 1, 2002–Present

This was the last sub-period during which the euro replaced the twelve national currencies and became the only legal tender in the EMU countries. The European monetary integration has since been completed.

## A New Currency Is Born—The Euro

Thanks to its geographic position, the French Pacific Ocean island of Reunion was the first European territory to see the euro on January 1, 2002. The first officially recorded cash purchase was that of one kilo of lychees (a white-fleshed, prickly, skinned fruit) in a street market of the capital city, Saint-Denis, for the price of 75 eurocents. The transaction was concluded three seconds after midnight while the event was staged for local television cameras since the buyer, the mayor of the city, Rene-Paul Victoria, made arrangements to televise the historically important and symbolic event. Following Reunion Island, Greece and Finland, the two easternmost Euro Area (Eurozone) countries were the first EMU countries to launch the euro (banknotes and coins) in a jovial atmosphere. Both countries accepted the euro with celebrations and dances under skies lit up from fireworks. The central banks of both countries opened up for the historical event. In Athens, the Prime Minister of Greece, Costas Simitis, drew euro banknotes from an Automated Teller Machine (ATM). In Helsinki, the Bank of Finland opened up for an hour allowing the Finns to be among the first Europeans to receive euros in exchange for their markkas.

There was quite a bit of preparation before the ECB, in cooperation with the 12 Euro Area NCBs, to make the euro (banknotes and coins) available to more than 300 million people. The ECB printed 14.25 billion notes (from 5 euros to 500 euros) in 15 different plants. The NCBs coordinated the minting of 56 billion coins from 1 cent to 2 euros. The total value of banknotes and coins was worth 660 billion euros ($558 billion dollars). The ECB started delivering the euro banknotes to commercial banks in September 2001. If all printed banknotes were placed end to end, they would have covered the distance from the earth to the moon five times. Some 200,000 ATMs had to be converted to handle euro exchanges in the 12 Euro Area countries. It was expected that 90 percent of the euros would be delivered through the ATMs.

The ECB spent 80 million euros to educate the public on the new common currency. In addition, the EU Commission and the NCBs undertook their own campaigns on the arrival of the euro. The introduction and acceptance of the euro was a great success.

See Blitz, J. "Eurozone Gives Thumbs Up to New Currency," *Financial Times Weekend*, January 5–6, 2002.

Also Grant, Jeremy. "Greece, Finland Begins Historic Euro Cash Launch," *World Reuters*, http://dailynews.yahoo.com/h/nm/20011231/wl/euro_dc_5.html

# Performance of the EU Countries in Reference to the Maastricht Convergence Criteria

At the Dublin Summit, in December 1996, the European Council, upon the recommendation of the EU Commission and the EMI, decided that the majority of the EU countries did not meet the Maastricht convergence criteria. This decision meant that the starting date of the EMU would be January 1, 1999. In March 1998, the Commission and the EMI each submitted a new recommendation on the economic performance of the countries in reference to the five Maastricht criteria and the compatibility of national legislations concerning the independence of the central banks. This time, the European Council accepted the recommendations and decided on May 2, 1998, the EMU would begin on January 1, 1999.

The economic performance of all 15 EU countries is examined here for the periods before and after the decision to select the countries that qualified as EMU members. It is useful and informative to observe the past performance of the EU countries in reference to the Maastricht convergence criteria to pinpoint significant changes resulting from new governmental policies motivated by the Maastricht Treaty. It is also interesting to examine the EU countries' performance on all Maastricht convergence criteria for periods after the establishment of the EMU. This is important since the EMU nation states could stop complying with some of the Maastricht convergence criteria in the future. The possibility exists that any of the Euro Area countries may adopt policies that could trigger inflation in the Euro Area. Such behavior may place the EMU at a great risk.

## Inflation and Long-Term Interest Rates

Table 3.2a below shows historical and recent data on the first two Maastricht convergence indicators, which are based on annual statistics for the years 1985, 1990, 1995, 2000, and 2003. The two convergence indicators are the inflation rates and the long-term interest rates.

According to Table 3.2a, all EU15 countries successfully complied with the inflation and long-term interest rates Maastricht convergence criteria. Each country reduced its annual inflation rate to low levels by the year 2000. By 1995, none of the EU15 countries' inflation rates exceeded ten percent. Similarly, in 2000 (with the exception of Ireland), all EU15 countries reduced their inflation rate below five percent.[6] The two countries that succeeded in reducing inflation the most were Portugal and Greece. For this reason, these

Table 3.2a

| Historical Performance of the EU15 Member States According to Two Maastricht Convergence Criteria | | | | | | | | | | |
|---|---|---|---|---|---|---|---|---|---|---|
| | Inflation Rates | | | | | Long-Term Interest Rates | | | | |
| | 1985 | 1990 | 1995 | 2000 | 2003 | 1985 | 1990 | 1995 | 2000 | 2003 |
| Austria | 3.2 | 3.3 | 2.3 | 2.0 | 1.3 | 7.8 | 8.7 | 6.5 | 5.6 | 4.4 |
| Belgium | 4.9 | 3.5 | 1.5 | 2.7 | 1.5 | 10.6 | 10.1 | 7.5 | 5.6 | 4.4 |
| Denmark | 4.6 | 2.7 | 2.1 | 2.7 | 2.0 | 11.3 | 10.7 | 7.6 | 5.5 | 4.5 |
| Finland | 5.9 | 6.1 | 1.0 | 3.0 | 1.3 | 12.7 | 13.2 | 8.8 | 5.5 | 4.3 |
| France | 5.8 | 3.4 | 1.8 | 1.8 | 2.2 | 10.9 | 9.9 | 7.6 | 5.5 | 4.3 |
| Germany | 2.2 | 2.7 | 1.7 | 2.1 | 1.0 | 6.9 | 8.9 | 6.5 | 5.2 | 4.3 |
| Greece | 19.3 | 20.4 | 8.9 | 2.9 | 3.4 | 15.8 | 24.5 | 18.0 | 6.1 | 4.5 |
| Ireland | 5.4 | 3.3 | 2.5 | 5.3 | 4.0 | 12.6 | 10.1 | 8.3 | 5.4 | 4.4 |
| Italy | 9.2 | 6.5 | 5.2 | 2.6 | 2.8 | 13.0 | 11.5 | 12.2 | 5.6 | 4.5 |
| Luxembourg | 4.1 | 3.7 | 1.9 | 3.8 | 2.5 | 9.5 | 8.5 | 6.1 | 5.5 | 3.3 |
| Netherlands | 2.2 | 2.5 | 1.9 | 2.3 | 2.2 | 7.3 | 8.9 | 7.2 | 5.5 | 4.3 |
| Portugal | 19.3 | 13.4 | 4.1 | 2.8 | 3.3 | 20.8 | 18.6 | 10.3 | 5.6 | 4.4 |
| Spain | 8.8 | 6.7 | 4.7 | 3.5 | 3.1 | 13.4 | 14.7 | 11.0 | 5.4 | 4.3 |
| Sweden | 7.4 | 10.5 | 2.5 | 1.3 | 2.3 | 13.1 | 13.1 | 10.2 | 5.4 | 4.9 |
| UK | 6.1 | 7.0 | 2.7 | 0.8 | 1.4 | 10.5 | 11.1 | 8.3 | 4.7 | 4.9 |
| Average | 7.2 | 6.4 | 3.0 | 2.6 | 2.3 | 11.7 | 12.2 | 9.1 | 5.5 | 4.4 |
| Maastricht Reference Value | 4.0 | 4.1 | 2.9 | 2.8 | 2.7 | 7.3 | 9.5 | 7.6 | 5.2 | 6.3 |

*Source: European Economy and International Financial Statistics (IMF)

countries can be considered as the greatest beneficiaries from the formation of the EMU. Italy and Spain were the second group of countries that reduced inflation substantially, followed by Sweden and the UK. These last two countries, along with Denmark, chose not to join the EMU.

Similar success was achieved in the reduction of the long-term interest rates, which in the year 2000 stood in the range of 5–6 percent. In 2003, long-term interest rates for all EU15 countries, with the exception of the UK, were below their 2000 values. This shows that the EMU continues to exert a positive influence on the EU economy since lower long-term interest rates boost investment and growth. Long-term interest rates are closely related to inflation or, more precisely, to expected inflation. This relation, presented below in equation (1), is attributed to the famous American economist Irving Fisher and is known as Fisher's equation:

$$i = r + \pi^e \tag{1}$$

$i$ is the long-term interest rate, $r$ is the real interest rate, and $\pi^e$ is the expected inflation. The real interest rate is considered by many economists to be stable since it depends on personal savings behavior and the productivity of capital, both assumed relatively stable over long periods. Expected inflation rates are related to present and past inflation rates since countries that experienced high inflation rates in the past are likely to experience high inflation rates in the future.

On the micro level, the interaction of borrowers and lenders in the loanable funds market determines the interest rate, i.e., the price of the loanable funds. If lenders, however, expect a high inflation rate in the future, then they will require an inflation risk premium above the real interest rate. Thus, low expected inflation rates imply low long-term nominal interest rates. Inflation rates, prior to the establishment of the EMU, were mainly the result of monetary policies adopted by the NCBs.

Another reason that the Maastricht Treaty required convergence in long-term interest rates was to avoid massive capital movements and disruption of the capital markets between member countries during the transitional period to the EMU. The transitional period here is considered the time from when the exchange rates became irrevocably fixed to the time of the introduction of the euro. Once the exchange rates were irrevocably fixed and one country was maintaining a higher long-term interest rate, this could have caused an incentive for national bond market destabilization. Financial investors will purchase and hold government bonds only from countries with the highest interest rate and sell all other countries' bonds. The above analysis assumes that no other risks were present. Thus, the Maastricht requirement for convergence in long-term interest rates reduced or eliminated such possible disruptive financial behavior.

## Government Deficit and Debt to GDP Ratios in the EU15 Countries

In Table 3.2b, the performance of all the EU15 countries in terms of the two fiscal Maastricht criteria, the government deficit and debt to GDP ratios, are presented for the years 1985, 1990, 1995, 2000, and 2003. A drastic reduction in the government deficit to GDP ratios of all EU15 countries occurred. Most EU countries realized only a small reduction in the government debt to GDP ratios. According

Table 3.2b

| Historical Performance of EU15 Member States According to Two Fiscal Maastricht Criteria | | | | | | | | | |
|---|---|---|---|---|---|---|---|---|---|
| | Government Deficits | | | | | Government Debts | | | | |
| | 1985 | 1990 | 1995 | 2000 | 2003 | 1985 | 1990 | 1995 | 2000 | 2003 |
| Austria | −4.6 | −4.5 | −5.2 | −1.5 | −1.1 | 50 | 58 | 69 | 66 | 65 |
| Belgium | −10.9 | −5.5 | −3.2 | 0.2 | 0.4 | 122 | 129 | 134 | 109 | 100 |
| Denmark | −0.6 | −0.7 | −2.4 | 1.7 | 0.3 | 70 | 58 | 69 | 52 | 46 |
| Finland | −0.8 | 0.2 | −9.5 | 7.1 | 2.3 | 16 | 15 | 57 | 45 | 46 |
| France | −2.7 | −2.1 | −6.5 | −1.4 | −4.1 | 32 | 36 | 54 | 57 | 64 |
| Germany | −1.1 | −1.6 | −1.8 | 1.3 | −3.8 | 42 | 44 | 57 | 60 | 64 |
| Greece | −12.7 | −13.8 | −11.9 | −4.1 | −4.6 | 60 | 89 | 109 | 114 | 110 |
| Ireland | −11.8 | −1.7 | −0.6 | 4.4 | 0.1 | 105 | 98 | 84 | 38 | 32 |
| Italy | −14.6 | −10.5 | −6.9 | −0.6 | −2.4 | 82 | 97 | 123 | 111 | 106 |
| Luxembourg | 9.4 | 4.7 | 2.3 | 6.0 | 0.8 | 10 | 5 | 6 | 5 | 5 |
| Netherlands | −5.2 | −4.1 | −3.5 | 2.2 | −3.2 | 70 | 77 | 77 | 56 | 54 |
| Portugal | −14.8 | −4.6 | −5.0 | −2.8 | −2.8 | 68 | 64 | 64 | 53 | 60 |
| Spain | −6.1 | −2.5 | −5.2 | −0.9 | 0.4 | 43 | 44 | 64 | 61 | 51 |
| Sweden | −7.1 | 1.0 | −8.9 | 5.1 | 0.3 | 62 | 42 | 77 | 53 | 52 |
| UK | −2.9 | 0.6 | −5.4 | 3.8 | −3.3 | 54 | 35 | 52 | 42 | 40 |
| Average | −6.0 | −3.3 | −4.8 | 1.4 | −1.4 | 59 | 59 | 73 | 61 | 60 |
| Maastricht Reference Value | −3% | −3% | −3% | −3% | −3% | 60% | 60% | 60% | 60% | 60% |

to the Maastricht convergence criteria, each country was legally restrained to maintain government deficit and debt to GDP ratios equal to or below 3 and 60 percent, respectively. Table 3.2b shows that, though government deficits were reduced during the first ten years, most countries did not meet the Maastricht reference value of 3 percent in 1995. However, in the year 2000, many countries' deficits gave way to surpluses to the extent that the EU15 average became a surplus of 1.4 percent. The few countries with a deficit in 2000 managed to keep it below the reference Maastricht value of 3 percent. In 2003, however, the situation changed when four countries violated the 3 percent deficit to GDP ratio: Denmark, Greece, Germany, and France. Germany and France violated the deficit to GDP ratio for two years in a row. Greece is likely to be the biggest violator of all as it was accused of falsifying its reported deficit statistics and will be taken to the court by the EU Commission. The new data reported by the Commission for Greece show four years of consecutive deficits, starting in 2000. The new Greek government, elected in 2004, accused the former government of falsifying the deficit data to gain membership to the EMU.

The Maastricht government debt criterion, however, had a relatively small impact on government debt reduction. The EU average debt to GDP ratio in 2000 declined from its 1995 value of 73 percent, but still remained relatively high at 61 percent, slightly above the Maastricht reference value. In 2003, the government debt to GDP ratio declined for most EU countries. As a result, the EU average decreased by one percentage point to 59 percent, only one percent below the Maastricht limit of 60 percent. In light of this evidence, a question arises: "Why were the candidate EMU countries unsuccessful in their effort to reduce their government debt to GDP ratios, thus, risking accession to the EMU?" It turned out heavily indebted countries had trouble reducing their government debt to GDP ratios in a few years. The reason for this failure is that government debt reduction depends on factors independent of the current government policy choice.

Reduction of government debt to GDP ratios depends on several factors: the existing debt levels, the interest rate at which the debt was issued, the economy's growth rate, and the political commitment of the government to run yearly surpluses. The annual government surplus or deficit is the only variable subject to current governmental policy. The government debt reduction problem can be analyzed according to De Grauwe, 2000 by examining the annual government budget constraint shown in equation (2):

$$G - T + iB = \Delta M + \Delta B, \qquad (2)$$

where:

$G$ = Government Expenditures

$T$ = Tax Revenues

$i$ = Interest Rate on the National Debt (Government Bonds)

$B$ = National Debt (Bonds)

$M$ = Currency in Circulation

$\Delta M$ = Change in Currency in Circulation (Seigniorage)

$\Delta B$ = Change in National Debt

On the left-hand side of equation (2), $G - T$ is the primary government deficit or surplus, and the second term ($iB$) is the required amount of interest payments to service the existing outstanding debt ($B$). The amount of the interest payments depends positively on the interest rate and the level of outstanding national debt. For a country to reduce a high government debt to GDP ratio, it needs to generate primary budget surpluses $(G - T)$ continuously in excess of the required interest payments $(iB)$. In addition, a country can reduce its government debt to GDP ratio further if its GDP continues to increase. During recessionary periods when GDP declines, the government debt to GDP ratio will increase since GDP appears in the denominator of the ratio. The right-hand side of equation (2) indicates the sources of financing government expenditures. Financing current deficits can be carried out by printing new money (known as seigniorage) $(\Delta M)$ or by issuing new debt $(\Delta B)$.

Before the Maastricht Treaty, most EU15 countries had abandoned financing their government deficits by printing money. Now, many central banks restrain from monetizing new debt by accommodating their Treasury department when it issues new debt. They do this by refusing to increase the money supply by purchasing government securities. The reason EU countries have adopted this policy is because deficit financing is known to be inflationary and conflicts with the first and most important Maastricht criterion of low inflation.

The inability of the EU countries to reduce the government debt to GDP ratio is demonstrated in Table 3.2b, where even in 2000, three EU countries accumulated a government debt to GDP ratio above 100 percent. Studies conducted by the EU Commission, based on simulations of national debt reductions under optimistic expectations of the performance of high debt EU countries, leave little hope for quick government debt to GDP ratio reductions. It will take several years for the highly indebted countries, according to these studies, to reduce their national debt to GDP ratio to the level of the Maastricht reference value of 60 percent.[7]

Another reason for imposing the government debt to GDP ratio Maastricht criterion was to thwart any possible incentive of countries to engineer unexpected inflation to reduce the real value of their national debt and interest payments. However, the creation of unexpected inflation would have had economic repercussions on the country in the form of higher interest rates, incorporating risk and default premia. Because of higher interest rates, it becomes more expensive for a country to raise funds in the bond market. It is clear that high national debt to GDP ratios are positively related to interest rates and inflation.

One could have expected that these long-term negative effects on the economy would have been obvious to government policymakers and avoided. The problem lies in the attractiveness of short-term benefits to governments from inflationary finance and increases in national debts. These benefits become an irresistible temptation to politicians. For other countries that have successfully stabilized prices for a long period and derive great benefits from price stability, inflationary finance is no longer an option.

These countries will be unwilling to accept other new member countries maintaining high government debt and deficit to GDP ratios in the EMU. Germany supported the inclusion of these two fiscal criteria in the Maastricht Treaty. Germany requested, in addition to the two fiscal Maastricht criteria, the "no bail out clause" be included in the Maastricht Treaty. According to the "no bail out clause," if a high debt country defaults on its government debt, then no other government or the ECB can be forced to bail out that country. Such a provision in the Maastricht Treaty was intended to motivate governments to become more fiscally responsible.

Let us now examine the performance of the EU countries in reference to the two fiscal Maastricht criteria during 1994–2001. This period was chosen to observe whether candidate EMU countries tried to reduce government deficit and debt to GDP ratios, starting from the first year after the Maastricht Treaty was put into effect (Refer to Figure 3.1). On the horizontal axis, the government debt to GDP ratio of all the EU countries is measured, and on the vertical axis, the government surplus (deficit) to GDP ratio is measured. The rectangle formed starting from the origin in the fourth quadrant with coordinates (60, −3) includes all points that correspond to countries that meet both Maastricht criteria. Each country is depicted by an arrow, representing data of the government debts and deficits for the years

Figure 3.1

**Government Deficit and Debt to GDP Ratios All 15 EU Countries**

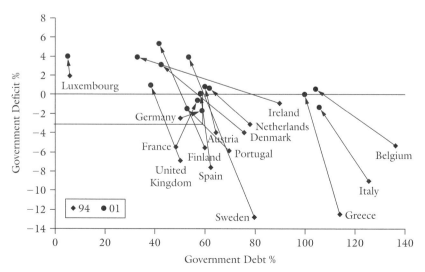

1994 and 2001. The beginning (origin) of the arrows corresponds to data for the year 1994, and the front tip of the arrow (end) corresponds to data for the year 2001. The most important information conveyed by this diagram is that every arrow ended inside the box or it pointed in the expected direction, i.e., northwest, meaning smaller government debt and smaller government deficit, or a larger surplus to GDP ratio. This constitutes strong evidence that the candidate EMU governments seriously considered the incentives of the Maastricht convergence criteria and adopted the appropriate policies. Appropriate fiscal policies were adopted by all countries including Greece, Italy, and Belgium despite their failure to even come close to meeting the 60 percent Maastricht government debt to GDP ratio reference value.

# The Council Decision

Let us now examine the data presented by the EU Commission and the EMI, in March 1998, based upon which the two EU institutions made their recommendations to the European Council. According to the Maastricht Treaty, the Council accepted these reports and, on May 2, 1998, approved the official launching of the EMU beginning January 1, 1999.

The data in Table 3.3 are from the official report of the EU Commission published on March 25, 1998, and submitted to the Council in accordance with Article 109 (J). The performance of all EU15 countries, in reference to the five Maastricht convergence criteria, is summarized and reported in Table 3.3.

## Inflation Rate

The inflation rate was calculated as a percentage change in the arithmetic average of the latest 12-month Harmonized Indices of Consumer Prices (HICPs) in relation to the arithmetic average of the 12 HICPs of the previous period. The HICPs were constructed on the initiative of the EU Commission to make the calculated inflation rates of all EU countries more comparable. The HICPs are based on identical baskets of goods in all candidate EMU countries. All EU countries continue to calculate and report the HICPs. The inflation Maastricht reference value was calculated to be 1.5 percentage points above the average inflation rate of the best three performing countries in terms of price stability. This value was calculated to be 2.7 percent for the year ending January 1998. All EU15 countries made substantial progress toward price stability and achieved convergence in inflation, and, as a result, 14 countries met the Maastricht inflation criterion. The only exception was Greece, which failed to meet all five Maastricht criteria.

Table 3.3

| Performance of EU15 Member States in Relation to the Maastricht Convergence Criteria 1997–1998 | | | | | |
|---|---|---|---|---|---|
| | Inflation HICP January 1998 | Long-Term Interest Rates 1997 | Deficit (% of GDP) 1997 | Debt (% of GDP) 1997 | ERM Participation March 1998 |
| Reference Value | 2.7 | 7.8 | 3 | 60 | |
| Austria | 1.1 | 5.6 | −2.5 | 66.1 | yes |
| Belgium | 1.4 | 5.7 | −2.1 | 122.2 | yes |
| Denmark | 1.9 | 6.2 | 0.7 | 65.1 | yes |
| Finland | 1.3 | 5.9 | −0.9 | 55.8 | yes[1] |
| France | 1.2 | 5.5 | −3.0 | 58.0 | yes |
| Germany | 1.4 | 5.6 | −2.7 | 61.3 | yes |
| Greece | 5.2 | 9.8 | −4.0 | 108.7 | yes[3] |
| Ireland | 1.2 | 6.2 | 0.9 | 66.3 | yes |
| Italy | 1.8 | 6.7 | −2.7 | 121.6 | yes[2] |
| Luxembourg | 1.4 | 5.6 | 1.7 | 6.7 | yes |
| Netherlands | 1.8 | 5.5 | −1.4 | 72.1 | yes |
| Portugal | 1.8 | 6.2 | −2.5 | 62.0 | yes |
| Spain | 1.8 | 6.3 | −2.6 | 68.8 | yes |
| Sweden | 1.9 | 6.5 | −0.8 | 76.6 | no |
| UK | 1.8 | 7.0 | −1.9 | 53.4 | no |
| EU | 1.6 | 6.1 | −2.4 | 72.1 | |

Source: Commission Services, Summary of the 1998 Convergence Report, EURO 1999 Part I: Recommendation   [1]Since October 1996   [2]Since November 1996   [3]Since March 1998

## Long-Term Interest Rate

There was a substantial reduction and convergence in the long-term interest rates of all EU member countries. The Maastricht reference value was 7.8 percent. This was calculated by adding 2 percentage points to the average of the three interest rates of the three best performing EU countries in terms of price stability. The interest rate for each country was measured by the 10-year government bond yield. Fourteen countries met the interest rate Maastricht convergence criterion.[8]

## Government Deficit to GDP Ratio

Drastic reductions of government deficits became a reality for all EU countries. This was a significant change from the large spending trend, which resulted in high deficits by 1993. During that time, most EU countries were applying expansionary fiscal policies to combat the recession. According to Table 3.3, fourteen countries met the government deficit to GDP ratio Maastricht criterion of 3 percent.

## Government Debt to GDP Ratio

Unlike the impressive performance of the EU countries in reducing the government deficits, only four countries met the government debt criterion though almost all EU countries were making substantial progress. The exception was Germany, which was confronted with the extraordinary large cost of the reunification that began in 1989 with the fall of the Berlin Wall. The EU Council decided to ignore the government debt criterion and evaluated the candidate countries according to the other four Maastricht criteria, bending the Maastricht Treaty.

## Exchange Rate

Some bending of the Maastricht rules took place regarding the exchange rate Maastricht criterion. According to this criterion, all candidate EMU countries had to maintain their currencies within the ±2.25 percent ERM normal band for at least two years without devaluing their currencies. The 2-year review period was from March 1996 to February 1998. Two currencies, the Finnish markka and the Italian lira, kept their currencies in the ERM for less than two years. The markka entered in October 1996, and the lira reentered the ERM in November 1996. Thus, both currencies did not complete the two year required period in the ERM. Three currencies, the Greek drachma, the Swedish crown, and the UK pound sterling, did not participate in the ERM during this period.[9] The Council decided that the 12 participating currencies of the ERM were, in general, stable and met the exchange rate Maastricht criterion. The only currency that deviated from the central parity and realigned by 3 percent was the Irish pound. This realignment, however, was a revaluation and, as such, was not considered to be a problem since a currency revaluation indicates strength in terms of price stability and the country's economy.

The Maastricht requirement for each currency to remain in the ERM for two years without devaluation was adopted for two reasons. The first reason was to induce countries to pursue price stability since high-inflation countries' currencies consistently depreciate vis-à-vis currencies of low inflation countries. High inflation countries that participated in the ERM were accustomed to devaluing their currencies periodically. A second reason for the inclusion of the exchange rate Maastricht criterion was to avoid temptations for devaluations intended to gain a competitive advantage during the transitional period of the EMU prior to the withdrawal of the national currencies.

## Other Maastricht Requirements and Problems in Meeting the Maastricht Criteria

Another important requirement of the Maastricht Treaty (Article 107) was compatibility of the national legislations in reference to rendering independence of the NCBs. The Council determined that eight member states adopted legislation compatible with the treaty, whereas four other states were expected to have completed all legislative and legal arrangements to qualify by the beginning of the third stage of the EMU on January 1, 1999. Denmark and the UK, because of their opt-outs from the third stage of the EMU, were not obligated to comply with this requirement of the treaty. Denmark, on its own initiative, had adopted legislation compatible with the Maastricht Treaty, rendering independence to its central bank. Sweden was the most difficult case since its constitution required an amendment to comply with the treaty.[10] All other economic and financial indicators, examined according to the treaty by the Council, were found to be favorable for the launching of the EMU and the new common currency, the euro.

EU countries adopted the appropriate monetary and fiscal policies to meet the Maastricht criteria. Almost all countries were successful in meeting the convergence criteria and complied with the legal requirements of the Maastricht Treaty.[11] Greece was the only laggard country that disqualified for EMU membership on January 1, 1999. Greece subsequently joined the EMU two years later on January 1, 2001.

Meeting the Maastricht criteria required the adoption of austere programs and sacrifices by the citizens of all countries, especially the poorer ones. The poorer countries were required to make major structural adjustments to comply with the Maastricht criteria. Since the EU countries were determined to meet the challenge of the Maastricht Treaty, they imposed on themselves extraordinary fiscal discipline and considered employing various tactics to achieve this objective. Unfortunately, a few of the tactics they considered adopting were only tricks that were referred to by the news media as "creative accounting." A few governments were tempted to consider such questionable tactics. Even Germany, which initiated the Maastricht criteria and demanded strict adherence to price stability and fiscal discipline, risked its own credibility by considering such a tactic.

## Three Challenges to EMU

The voyage to EMU was a "rough sail," as it was popularly referred to by the news media. Three events were considered the most serious challenges to EMU. The first was a political one; this was the rejection of the Maastricht Treaty in the first referendum by the Danes on June 1992 and, to a lesser degree, the marginal passing of the Maastricht Treaty by the French. These election results were strong messages that some EU governments were not in close touch with their own citizens.

The second shock to the EMU was the 1992–1993 exchange rate crisis. This became an embarrassment to the architects of the EMU and the EU governments. Several EMU member countries proved incapable of maintaining the exchange rates against the central parities within the normal band of the ERM at ±2.25 percent prior to irrevocably fixing them. At that time, many people believed that exchange rate stability was a minimum basic precondition prior to the establishment of the EMU. The Council found an interesting way to surpass this unexpected shock by opening up the range of the ERM grid to ±15 percent. This unexpected decision, however, created grave doubts regarding the feasibility of the EMU.

The third challenge to the EMU was the recession that struck the EU countries in the early nineties (1990–1993). During this period, all EU countries needed to apply countercyclical expansionary monetary and fiscal policies to help pull their economies out of the recession. Such policies, however, could not be adopted since the EU countries were legally bound to comply with the Maastricht criteria. The contractionary policies imposed by the Maastricht Treaty during this period, according to De Grauwe (2000) and others, created spillover effects by reducing total spending (decline of the aggregate demands) in all EU countries, which deepened and prolonged the recession.

## Criticism Regarding the Validity of the Maastricht Criteria

Other authors considered the Maastricht criteria to be arbitrary since they had nothing to do with the OCA theory.[12] No explanations were offered why, for example, the Maastricht reference values of 3 percent and 60 percent for the government deficit and debt to GDP ratios were chosen. Similarly, the reference values of the other three Maastricht criteria were arbitrary. Since not all EU economies were similar, it can be argued that the optimal Maastricht reference values for these different EU countries ought to differ. All Maastricht criteria involve nominal variables, and thus, convergence in terms of the Maastricht criteria is a nominal convergence.

The most meaningful convergence, however, is real convergence. This is usually measured with the real per capita GDP, or real per capita income. The Maastricht Treaty did not require real convergence. It is possible that some Euro Area countries may experience real divergence in the future. If real economic divergence occurs and countries experience deterioration in their standards of living, these countries will abandon the EMU.

Another criticism of the government deficit and debt criteria is the absence of distinction in government spending between public consumption and public investment. Many economists agree that reducing public consumption can be beneficial to an economy, but the same cannot be argued for public investment. Public investment yields direct benefits to individuals and enhances productivity in the private sector. A few economists expressed concern that the Maastricht restrictions could create problems for less developed EU countries, which lacked sufficient infrastructure. The main concern was that the Maastricht criteria might deter further economic growth and development of these EU countries.

## The Stability and Growth Pact (SGP)

The Maastricht convergence criteria were designed to assist the European Council in deciding which countries qualified for membership. Once the EMU was established, the ECB, an independent entity from the EU governments, became responsible for the monetary policy in the EMU. The ECB can succeed in pursuing price stability provided the Euro Area countries adhere to their adopted policy of fiscal discipline. However, once countries became members of the EMU, they could have begun generating large annual deficits and accumulated unsustainable government debts.

Large deficits and debts of any EMU country could have had spillover effects to the other EMU member countries. For this reason, upon the initiation and insistence of Germany at the Amsterdam Summit of the European Council in June 1997, the Stability and Growth Pact (SGP) was agreed upon and signed by all the Euro Area countries.

According to the SGP, the EMU countries were responsible for maintaining fiscal discipline after the establishment of the EMU. The SGP aimed to achieve medium-term budget positions of close to balance or in surplus. This means countries were to target their budgets to be in balance or in surplus over the medium-term period. This allowed them to attain a cyclically adjusted position, i.e., incur a balanced budget or surplus during normal economic periods and deficits during recessions. The maximum deficit to GDP ratio, which EMU countries were allowed to reach under the SGP, remained 3 percent. Different countries, depending on their budget positions, could increase spending but were not allowed to incur deficit to GDP ratios in excess of 3 percent.

If countries violated the 3 percent deficit, they were subject to non-interest deposits of 0.2 to 0.5 percent of their GDP, depending on the size of the deficit. If, after two years, countries failed to reduce their deficits, the deposits could become fines. Excluded from such fines were countries that experienced natural disasters or any other special circumstances, which caused an annual GDP reduction of 2 percent or more. If the GDP reduction was within the range of 0.75 and 2 percent, fines would be imposed only when the ECOFIN decided to do so. Lastly, if the GDP declined within the range of 0 to 0.75 percent, the EMU countries agreed not to invoke special circumstances, but must instead pay the fines. Even in this case, however, the Council had to decide whether the fines were appropriate. According to the SGP, the amount of the fines was to be distributed to other EMU member countries as a reward for respecting the SGP.

## Inherent Problems in the SGP

The main objectives of the SGP are economically sound since fiscal stability is a necessary condition for the growth of all economies. However, the SGP has some serious drawbacks. The main concern is that the SGP reduced the flexibility of national fiscal policies. This is particularly important after the creation of the EMU because national governments have lost the independence of their exchange rate and monetary policies. If EU countries experience asymmetric shocks, then the small margin in the government deficit budgets of up to 3 percent of their GDP may be insufficient to help countries fight recession and unemployment.

## The Future of the SGP Is Uncertain

The future of the SGP is not promising since past experience and empirical evidence from the EU recession in the early 1990s indicates that the 3 percent deficits were exceeded by several countries, which exercised counter-cyclical expansionary fiscal policies. A few countries could have been exempted from paying the fines since their GDP had declined by more than 2 percent, but three countries (France, Spain, and Portugal) would have been fined. This indicates that the SGP will be unpopular if similar situations arise in the future as countries that are committed to fighting recession and unemployment will be penalized with fines.

## The SGP, a Restraining Factor for Ireland

A few Euro Area countries may find themselves in a difficult situation when their economies are in desperate need of public investment. A good example of this is Ireland. All political parties in Ireland agreed in 2002, prior to the national elections, that it would be imperative for their next government to invest heavily in infrastructure projects, including roads, hospitals, railroads, waste, and power systems. Ireland attained a phenomenal annual growth rate of 10 percent during the 1992–2002 period. Post-2002 Ireland has found itself, however, in a difficult position since its economy was in desperate need of massive investment in infrastructure to support its booming modern industries. Failure to construct these public projects may translate to a loss of thousands of jobs and substantial loss in revenues from tourism.

The need for such a large public investment was deeply felt and recognized by some big businesses, which began an open campaign in the news media, requesting that the Irish government invest in infrastructure. Prime Minister Bertic Ahern's governing party, Fiana Fail, announced, before the elections, a public investment of 52 billion euros ($46.9 billion) for the period 2000–2006. A large portion of this investment, 27 billion euros, was designated for infrastructure. Yet, the Irish government, despite its excellent performance in public debt reduction, has found its hands tied to invest in infrastructure due to the SGP.

See Champion, M. "In Ireland, Fears that Investment May Stall," *Wall Street Journal,* May 16, 2002.

Some authors are convinced the SGP will become ineffective. These authors predict that when EU member countries experience a recession and are forced to reduce spending, they will resort to "creative accounting."

Perhaps the most serious threat to the SGP is that, during a widespread recession in the EU, it will be difficult for the Council to reach a decision by a qualified majority to impose fines on the majority of the EMU member countries. Such a scenario is plausible since many macroeconomic shocks are highly correlated in the EU countries. As it turned out, most of the possible expected problems of the SGP mentioned above became reality.

## Enforcement of the SGP—An Impossible Task

To strengthen the SGP, the EU finance ministers agreed to balance their government budgets by the end of 2004. They agreed that those countries whose deficits approached close to 3 percent were to receive an official warning from the Commission to reduce their deficits. Germany, France, and Portugal were the first countries considered by the Commission to receive an official warning to reduce their deficits. By the middle of July 2002, such an action was avoided due to the Council's willingness to settle issues by having countries state that they agreed to conform to the SGP. The same issue was expected to reemerge with a possible fine for Portugal, since the ECB estimated that Portugal had violated the 3 percent deficit rule in 2001. Portugal officially admitted that it had violated the 3 percent deficit limit and became the first EU country to report such a violation. The Portuguese finance minister, however, announced that the country adopted fiscal measures to restore fiscal stability in accordance to the SGP.

## French, Italian, and German Defiance of the SGP

Another attack against the SGP surfaced when the German finance minister, Hans Eichel, admitted that Germany would fail to meet the 3 percent deficit limit for the year 2002. This prediction turned out to be correct since, in 2002, the German government deficit was 3.7 percent of GDP. Another attack against the SGP came from the President of the EU Commission, Romano Prodi, who made an unorthodox comment, characterizing the SGP as "stupid, just like all decisions which are rigid."[13]

A new challenge to the SGP came from a victorious Jacques Chirac during the elections of spring 2002 in France when he was reelected as President and his party won an important victory in the parliamentary elections after a major setback of the socialists. President Chirac convinced the other EU leaders at the 2002 Seville Summit that, based on the forecasts of the government deficit and the rate of growth of the French economy, France could not balance the budget by 2004. The EU partner countries were conciliatory with France as they were with Germany and Portugal before.

The French stand encouraged the Italians to voice opposition to the SGP through their finance minister, calling for a revision of the pact. French and Italian leaders promised tax reductions they found difficult to deliver to their constituency because of the SGP. Though the Commission remained steadfast and adjusted Italy's reported deficit upward for 2001, the Prime Minister of Italy, Silvio Berlusconi, announced the biggest tax cut in Italian history. Such large tax cuts, if implemented, would place the SGP at risk. This initiative constitutes further evidence that Italy was determined to weaken the SGP and challenge the EU Commission.[14]

On November 14, 2002, after pressure from the EU Commission, France and Germany agreed to reduce their deficits. However, toward the end of January 2003, France received another warning from the ECOFIN to stop challenging "the rules underpinning the euro." This warning was a response to the French defiance at the ECOFIN meeting in the previous week. At that time, the French finance minister, Francis Mer, refused the request by the other 11 ministers to bring the French government deficit "close to balance by 2006."[15] From that time on, the French remained defiant of the SGP. Together with the Germans, they forced their view on the Commission and on a few smaller countries to relax financial fines against them for violating the SGP.

On November 26, 2003, France and Germany convinced their colleagues at the ECOFIN meeting to "freeze the mechanics" of the SGP. Such a decision angered some Euro Area partners due to fear of high interest rates and a sharp euro depreciation.

In early January 2004, the EU Commission decided to take the ECOFIN to court over its November 20, 2003, decision to allow France and Germany to exceed the Maastricht limit of 3 percent government deficits. On July 24, 2004, the European Court of Justice decided that France and Germany violated the SGP but were not obligated to take corrective action recommended by the Commission. After a two-year dispute between the Commission and EU countries regarding the SGP, Romano Prodi, the president of the Commission, announced a plan that would loosen the SGP. The main points of the Prodi Plan are summarized below.

1. Countries should be allowed a deficit of more than three percent of their GDPs for longer periods of time to combat recession.

2. Countries with low debt to GDP ratios should be allowed to run bigger deficits.

3. Peer pressure should be applied to encourage countries to run balanced budgets or surpluses during normal economic times.

4. Broad guidelines, agreed upon by the EU leaders, should be used to coordinate reforms.

The Prodi Plan provides a starting point for discussion to the EU leaders when they meet in March 2005 to revise the SGP.

## SUMMARY

Since March 1, 2002, 12 EU countries formed the EMU and now share a common currency, the euro. The ECB was established in Frankfurt, Germany. The Eurosystem that consists of the ECB and the 12 NCBs is solely responsible for the monetary policy of the twelve EU countries, which are often referred to as Euro Area, Eurozone, or Euroland. The formation of the EMU was a successful event of unparalleled and historic significance for the international financial system. Never before had such a large number of independent nations surrendered their monetary and exchange rate policies, replacing their national currencies for a new, untested common currency. The EMU is the most recent and important development toward European integration which, after the end of World War II, was cemented with the Treaty of Paris (1951), the Treaty of Rome (1957), and the Single European Act (SEA) (1986). The EMU is the ultimate accomplishment of the European monetary integration that began with the Werner Plan, the Delors Report, and finalized with the Maastricht Treaty in 1991.

Under the Maastricht Treaty, countries agreed to a gradual approach to establish the EMU in three stages. This time period was considered essential for the EU countries to prepare their economies for the EMU. Candidate EMU countries were required to demonstrate price stability and fiscal discipline. This requirement for EMU membership preoccupied the economies and politics of the EU during the entire decade. Candidate EMU countries could join the EMU after they met the five Maastricht convergence criteria. Once countries became members of the EMU, they could have become fiscally imprudent and begun large spending or tax reduction policies, leading to unsustainable debts. Upon the insistence of Germany, the EMU countries signed the SGP. According to the SGP, EMU countries are legally responsible to be fiscally prudent and maintain deficit spending below 3 percent. EMU countries have agreed to attain medium-term budget positions of close to balance or in surplus. The SGP was first violated by a few EU countries during the 2002–2004 period. The ECOFIN ministers decided to freeze the mechanics of the SGP rather than face fines from the Commission. The SGP is expected to be revised in March 2005.

## Essay Questions

1. Identify and discuss the five Maastricht convergence criteria. Be sure to explain the importance of each of the five Maastricht criteria. Do you think that the five Maastricht convergence criteria

were the most appropriate indicators to determine the candidate countries' qualifications for membership to the EMU? Explain.

2. According to the Maastricht Treaty, the formation of the EMU was going to be timely and gradual. Discuss in chronological order each of the three stages of the formation of the EMU. Explain the most important events that took place during each of the three stages.

3. In addition to the five convergence criteria, the Maastricht Treaty required that candidate EMU countries render independence to their central bank. Explain why independence of the central bank was imposed as an additional requirement.

4. The voyage to the EMU according to the popular news media was a "rough sail." Discuss three important challenges to the EMU that almost shook its foundation.

5. The SGP was agreed upon in June 1997. What are the objectives of the SGP? What challenges does the SGP currently face? Evaluate the SGP.

6. Discuss the Delors Report—explain the significance of the Delors Report for the formation of the EMU.

# chapter 4

# Monetary Policy in the Euro Area

## Introduction

On January 1, 1999, with the formation of the Economic and Monetary Union (EMU), 11 Euro Area (Eurozone) countries surrendered their independent national monetary policies in exchange for a common monetary policy. Two years later, Greece joined the EMU as the twelfth member. On March 1, 2002, the Euro Area countries became a complete monetary union after adopting a common currency, the euro, as the only legal tender in all 12 countries that presently constitute the EMU.

The establishment of the EMU was an unprecedented and historic event in international economic and monetary history. Many people considered the creation of the EMU a brave step toward the completion of the Single European Market (SEM) and, possibly, the most important building block in advancing European economic integration. Despite the long-term preparation and planning of the EMU by its architects and the enthusiastic commitment of all Euro Area governments to launch the euro, the future of the EMU is still not free of risk. The media's skepticism toward the success of the euro is well demonstrated by its description of the launching of the euro as a "jump in the dark." This characterization was suggested because the future of such a daring and unprecedented project could not be predicted with certainty. The survival of the EMU, however, depends on the success of the common Euro Area monetary policy.

## The Eurosystem

Monetary policy in the Euro Area was entrusted to the Eurosystem. This consists of the European Central Bank (ECB) and the 12 National Central Banks (NCBs) of the countries that have adopted the euro. The ECB is the central bank of the Euro Area. Its organizational structure resembles the Federal Reserve System (the Fed), the central bank of the United States (US). It is only a coincidence that the Eurosystem is presently comprised of twelve NCBs, a number equal with the Fed's regional US banks. The number of the NCBs in the Euro Area will change whenever new member countries join the EMU.

Two main administrative bodies formulate and implement monetary policy in the Euro Area: the Governing Council and the Executive Board. A third entity, the General Council, serves as an advisory body to the ECB. The ECB, located in Frankfurt, Germany, together with the NCBs that are located in major cities of the EU25 member states, constitute the European System of Central Banks (ESCB). The ESCB does not have governing bodies of its own. The distinction between the Eurosystem and the ESCB will continue to exist as long as some EU countries have not adopted the euro. When all EU member countries join the EMU and adopt the euro, the Eurosystem and the ESCB will become one entity, the ESCB.

In Figure 4.1, the Eurosystem and the ESCB are portrayed in a diagram that depicts the most important features and functions of the

Figure 4.1　European System of Central Banks (ESCB)

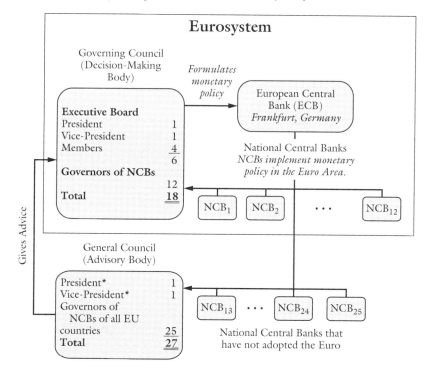

*The President and the Vice-President of Executive Board are also members of the General Council.

two related European monetary institutions. The Eurosystem, which is responsible for the monetary policy of the Euro Area countries, is placed in the center of the diagram. The ESCB and the thirteen NCBs of the countries that have not adopted the euro and the General Council are shown outside the Eurosystem rectangle. If all EU countries join the EMU, the General Council will be dissolved and the Eurosystem will become the same as the ESCB. The ESCB will then consist of the ECB and all the NCBs, which will be responsible for monetary policy in the entire EU.

# The Governing Council

The Governing Council, which formulates the monetary policy of the Euro Area, consists of eighteen members. The European Council and the twelve Euro Area governments appoint the first six members. This takes place after a common accord is reached among the Euro Area government representatives in consultation with the European Parliament. From these six members, two hold the offices of the president and the vice president. The other twelve members of the Governing Council are the governors of the NCBs of the Euro Area member countries.

The central bank governors are appointed by the Euro Area member state governments to serve a minimum of five-year renewable terms according to the Maastricht Treaty. The Governing Council is the supreme decision-making body in the Eurosystem. It formulates monetary policy and is responsible for all decisions pertinent to its implementation in the Euro Area. The Maastricht Treaty requires the Governing Council to convene at least ten times a year, but it usually meets twice each month in the Eurotower in Frankfurt, Germany. A major function of the Governing Council is to provide liquidity to the entire Euro Area banking and financial system. Another responsibility of the Governing Council is the establishment of an efficient payments mechanism in the EU, while pursuing its most important objective, the promotion of price stability.

To achieve its goals, the Governing Council exercises its authority by controlling bank reserves and setting certain key short-term interest rates that permit it to influence credit and, ultimately, the money supply in the Euro Area. Each member of the Governing Council is allocated one vote. All members of the Governing Council are established professionals with reputations and experience in monetary policymaking or in commercial banking.

The first president of the Governing Council, Willem Duisenberg, was the governor of the Dutch Central Bank for several years. Similarly, the second president of the ECB, Jean-Claude Trichet, was the president of the French Central Bank prior to his appointment as the ECB president. Both ECB executives have had successful careers and significant real-world experience in applied monetary policy. Willem Duisenberg was responsible for establishing price stability in the Netherlands that led to the continuous appreciation of the Dutch currency, the guilder, which became one of the strongest currencies in the EMS along with the Deutsche mark.

Jean-Claude Trichet is credited with the price stabilization policy in France established during the years of the EMS. Trichet is responsible for the adamant "franc fort" policy by resisting devaluation of the franc against the Deutsche mark. Likewise, the current vice president of the Governing Council, Lucas Papademos, served as the governor of the Central Bank of Greece. Lucas Papademos is credited with a successful price stabilization campaign in Greece that opened the doors to EMU membership on January 1, 2001.

# The Executive Board

The Executive Board is comprised of the first six members of the Governing Council. To provide continuity of experienced members on the Executive Board, its members are selected to serve eight-year, nonrenewable, staggered appointments. There are different arrangements for the members of the inaugural executive board. For example, the vice president of the Executive Board was elected for four years.

The Executive Board is responsible for implementing the Euro Area monetary policy on a daily basis. To implement the decisions made by the Governing Council, the Board instructs the NCBs to undertake the appropriate transactions within their respective national financial markets. This approach to the implementation of monetary policy was adopted because the NCBs are better suited than the ECB to carry out such responsibilities in their own money and financial markets. It would have been difficult, if not impossible, for the ECB to oversee the implementation of monetary policy on a daily basis from Frankfurt. This arrangement was decided because of the distance between the ECB and the twelve national financial and money markets and the lack of familiarity of the ECB with the functioning of these national financial markets.

Below is a list of the Executive Board members with their responsibilities:

1. The ECB President, Jean-Claude Trichet, External Relations, Secretariat, Protocol and Conferences, and Internal Audit.

2. The ECB Vice President, Lucas Papademos, Administration and Personnel, Legal Services and the Middle Office. He is one of the ECB's two members of the Economic and Financial Committee.

3. José Manuel González-Páramo, Information Systems, Statistics, and Banknotes. Previously a member of the Executive Board of the Bank of Spain.

4. Gertrude Tumpel-Gugerell, Operations and Controlling and Organization. The only woman in the Executive Board and previously the vice-governor of the Austrian Central Bank (Oesterreichische Nationalbank).

5. Otmar Issing, Economics and Research. He is also one of the ECB's two members of the Economic and Financial Committee. Previously chief economist of the Bundesbank.

6. Tommaso Padoa–Schioppa, International and European Relations, Payments Systems and Prudential Supervision. Previously deputy director general of the Central Bank of Italy.

### A Scandal Regarding the Succession of the ECB Presidency

In early 1998, before the announcement of the EU to appoint Willem Duisenberg as the first ECB president, a problem developed concerning his tenure in office and replacement. This happened when the French chose to support their own candidate to the key position of the ECB presidency. President Jacques Chirac campaigned for the appointment of Jean-Claude Trichet, the governor of the Central Bank of France, an intelligent and well-respected central banker. The French had hoped that Trichet's appointment would counterbalance the German influence in formulating monetary policy after the EU's decision to locate the ECB in Frankfurt, Germany.

According to rumors, the final appointment of Duisenberg was a "backroom deal" and the presidency position would be equally divided between Duisenberg and Trichet. Once on the job, the ECB president Duisenberg later denied that he had secretly agreed to serve only half of the eight-year term. He admitted later that because of his age he might not be able to serve the entire eight-year term. Duisenberg announced that he would step down in July 2003.

This arrangement would have been ideal if it was certain that Trichet could succeed Duisenberg as the next ECB president. Trichet was confronted with a lengthy legal investigation for his role in a scandal involving the French Bank Credit Lyonnais. He was accused of manipulating the accounts of the Credit Lyonnais when he was the director general of the treasury in the finance ministry in the late 1980s. At the end of a month-long trial, prosecutors demanded a ten-month suspended sentence for Trichet.

The outcome of this trial would determine the succession of the ECB presidency, an important decision for the future of the EMU and the euro. On February 12, 2003, a Parisian court announced that it would pronounce a verdict on Jean-Claude Trichet on June 18, 2003, only 21 days before he was expected to take over the presidency from Willem Duisenberg. Duisenberg, however, agreed to remain on the job another six months until Trichet's name was cleared or until the EU agreed to appoint another candidate. Trichet's name has been cleared from any accusations and, on November 1, 2003, Jean-Claude Trichet became the second president of the ECB.

Source: Mallet, V. "Trial order jeopardizes Trichet bid to leave" (2002). *Financial Times.* July 17.

# The General Council

To coordinate those activities pertinent to the exchange rate and other monetary arrangements between the "ins" (i.e., the EU members that adopted the euro) and the "outs" (i.e., the EU members that did not adopt the euro), the General Council was created. The General Council is comprised of the president and the vice president of the Governing Council along with the governors of the NCBs of all EU countries. The General Council has only an advisory role in formulating monetary policy in the Euro Area.[1]

The General Council inherited all the responsibilities of the European Monetary Institute (EMI), which was dissolved in October 1998 with the establishment of the ECB. Because not all EU countries have adopted the euro, a number of organizational and financial issues had to be resolved during the third stage of the EMU. The General

Council became responsible for issues pertinent to the exchange rates between the ins and outs. The General Council assists the ECB with the collection of statistical data and the writing of the annual ECB reports. Finally, the General Council is responsible for the standardization of all the accounting reports prepared by the NCBs.

Since three EU15 countries chose not to adopt the euro, the creation of the General Council proved to be the most appropriate institution in dealing with the exchange rate arrangements between the members and non-members of the Euro Area countries. As long as some EU countries have not adopted the euro, the General Council will remain the official institution of the ESCB. The decision of the EU to include ten more countries on May 1, 2004, increased the members of the General Council to 27. As a result of the EU enlargement, the tasks of the General Council in advising the ESCB on monetary and exchange rate issues are more important and difficult. The main role of the General Council is the coordination of the exchange rate and monetary policies between the Euro Area and EU countries, which did not adopt the euro, and to prepare the ground for the full EMU membership of all EU countries.

## The ECOFIN and the Eurogroup

The Council of Ministers of Economics and Finance (ECOFIN) is comprised of the economics or finance ministers of all EU member countries and is responsible for economic and exchange rate policies in the EU. The exchange rate policy, however, is implemented by the ECB, which is consulted before any decisions regarding exchange rate policy are adopted by the ECOFIN. The NCBs of the 13 countries that have not adopted the euro are members of the ESCB, but are excluded from the decision-making process regarding the common monetary policy and its implementation. The finance ministers of the *euro 12* or *euro X* (X denoting the current number of the Euro Area countries) are known as the Eurogroup. The Eurogroup economics and finance ministers meet prior to the ECOFIN meetings to discuss euro-related issues.

The Eurosystem is a unique central bank in regards to its organization and function.[2] It combines unity in decision making with decentralized implementation. Individual NCBs are delegated the authority to implement monetary and exchange rate policies in their own national money and financial markets, according to decisions adopted by the Governing Council. The NCBs contribute to the design of the Euro Area monetary policy because their governors are members of the Governing Council. In this sense, they are not totally subordinated by the Governing Council though they appear at the bottom of the Eurosystem's organizational chart.

Such an arrangement, under which the ECB has delegated the implementation of the monetary policy to the NCBs, is consistent with the principle of "subsidiarity" that is customarily practiced by the EU in other areas. According to the subsidiarity principle, EU institutions should have authority over those activities that cannot be carried out more efficiently by the nation-states or the local authorities. Supervision of banks and other financial institutions in the Euro Area resides within the jurisdiction of the Euro Area member states. Nevertheless, this arrangement could cause future problems, especially if nation-states do not act to adopt the appropriate policies necessary for the smooth functioning of the EMU.[3]

## Objectives, Independence, Accountability, and Transparency of the ECB

The primary objective of the ECB is the pursuance of price stability for the entire Euro Area, stated in Article 105 of the Treaty, which established the European Community (EC). Though other objectives are stated in Article 2 of the Treaty, these are of secondary importance.[4]

To pursue price stability, the ECB was granted political independence from all other EU institutions and national governments. As of today, the ECB is considered the most independent central bank in the world. It was designed to become more independent than the German Central Bank, the Bundesbank, after which the ECB was modeled.[5]

The ECB is prohibited from financing government deficits. Deficit spending is considered a major source of high inflation. Many developed countries have resolved the high inflation problem by rendering a high degree of political independence to their central banks. These independent central banks are not obligated to "monetize government debt." They do this by refusing to purchase newly issued government securities.

To further solidify the ECB's independence, the Treaty provided that the ECB would become institutionally and financially independent from the EU institutions by having its own budget. It was, therefore, decided that the ECB's capital would be provided by the NCBs' subscriptions, instead of the EU budget. This allocation of the ECB capital was based on the population and GDP of each country in relation to the total EU population and GDP. In addition, to enhance the ECB's independence, the members of the Governing Council are appointed for relatively long terms to minimize external political influences.

An interesting question arises as to whether the ECB's independence is equally matched with accountability and transparency. The first president of the Governing Council, Willem Duisenberg, advocated in one of his early speeches that ECB transparency is necessary to create the appropriate expectations among economic agents, which enhances the effectiveness of monetary policy.[6] In the same speech, he stated, ". . . in a democratic society, a central bank ought to be accountable for its policies and transparent." As a reflection of this concern, the Treaty establishing the European Community imposed stringent reporting obligations on the ECB. Specifically, the ECB is required to publish a weekly consolidated financial statement of the Eurosystem and at least one report on the ESCB activities every quarter. Such publications and many others are available on the ECB web site in at least 11 languages of the EU. The ECB's Monthly Bulletin web site contains detailed information on the Governing Council's assessments of the economic outlook and price developments in the Euro Area.

Beyond these publications, the ECB is legally obligated to deliver an annual report of its activities to the three main EU governing institutions: the European Parliament, the EU Commission, and the EU Council. The European Parliament frequently organizes debates regarding the ECB Annual Reports. The president of the ECB and other members of the Executive Board may participate in these debates and present their views to the various committees.

The Eurosystem goes beyond the minimum requirements in providing information regarding its activities and assessing the financial situation and price developments in the Euro Area. The president of the ECB holds a press conference after the first meeting of the Governing Council every month, explaining the decisions of the Governing Council on monetary policy and the status of price developments and expectations. Unlike the Federal Reserve of the US, the ECB does not publish the voting record of the members of the Governing Council. The official position of the ECB is that secrecy is necessary to protect the independence of the members of the Governing Council from external pressure in exercising their duties.

## Price Stability Strategy

The principles under which the Eurosystem directs its monetary policy are based upon the ECB's stability-oriented monetary policy strategy, which was announced on October 13, 1998. The ECB's stability-oriented monetary policy consists of two "pillars" and a quantitative definition of price stability. The first pillar is based on the conviction that inflation is mainly a monetary phenomenon. Such a strong perception of the cause of inflation forced the ECB to set a reference value for the growth rate of the money supply. The ECB chose the broader measure of the money supply growth (M3) as an intermediate monetary indicator to guide monetary policy. This choice of money supply growth as a reference value requires the existence of a stable relationship between this monetary aggregate and the aggregate price level.

Figure 4.2   Annual Growth Rate of the Euro Area M3 Money Supply

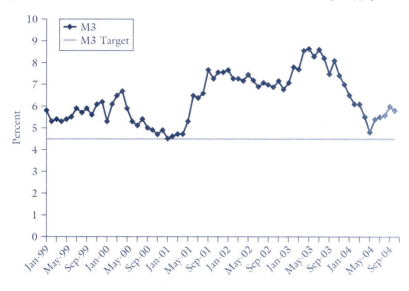

Source: ECB

Such a relationship is usually depicted with the equation of exchange $M.V. = P.Q.$[7] The actual annual growth rate of the money supply, M3, is shown in Figure 4.2 together with the target rate of M3. From January 1, 1999, to May 2001, the rate of growth of M3 converged toward its target rate. Starting in May 2001, the growth rate of M3 rose above its target value of 4.5 percent. The target growth rate of M3, however, was set at only 4.5 percent in January 1999 when the EMU was launched, and it has not changed since. Many analysts consider the growth rates of M3 relatively high. Some Governing Council members expressed their dissatisfaction with the ECB's repeated failures to control M3 growth. Previous poor performance of the Bundesbank in targeting M3 directed the architects of the EMU to seek a second pillar in guiding its monetary policy.

The second pillar is a broad assessment of the outlook for future price developments in the Euro Area. For this purpose, a comprehensive group of real economic and financial indicators is constantly surveyed in the entire Euro Area. ECB officials consider these indicators crucial in conveying useful information for future price changes. Such indicators include wages, exchange rates, long-term interest rates, various measures of economic activity, fiscal policy indicators, and cost indices.

Prior to the establishment of the EMU, the EMI introduced an improved measure of inflation while preparing the groundwork for the common currency. The EU Commission now publishes this new measure of inflation regularly, which is based on the construction of new price data sets more consistent and comparable among all EU countries. Based on this new approach, inflation rates of the EU countries are calculated according to the year-on-year percent change of the Harmonized Indices of Consumer Prices (HICP).

The ECB, along with other central banks of some developed countries (UK, Sweden, New Zealand, and Canada), has adopted a quantitative definition of price stability by targeting the inflation rate over the medium term. The Governing Council targeted the annual inflation rate in the range of 1 to 2 percent. However, no economic theory provides convincing evidence that this target rate is the optimum inflation rate for the Euro Area. A few authors have suggested that some industries or companies experiencing negative shocks can only remain competitive and survive if they manage to reduce real wages. Such a reduction in real wages may not be institutionally feasible unless it is introduced indirectly via an increase in the price level (See Akerlof, et al., 1996). The actual annualized inflation rate for most of 2004 was above the maximum target of 2 percent, set by the ECB.

## Monetary Policy Instruments

The ECB utilizes three different monetary instruments to implement monetary policy. These monetary instruments are Required Reserves, Permanent Standing Facilities, and Open Market Operations.

**1. Required Reserves:** Reserve deposits are held in the vaults of the NCBs and earn an interest rate equal to the repurchase transactions (repo) rate.[8] In 2004, the legal required reserve ratio in the Euro Area was between 1.5 and 2.5 percent of the bank's liabilities. Though required reserves constitute the most basic monetary tool, it is rarely employed for the implementation of monetary policy. The Fed follows this practice and rarely changes the legal reserve requirement ratio. Commercial banks and financial institutions cannot lend out the required reserves, which constitute a constraint on the banks' ability to make loans.

An increase in the reserve requirement ratio set by the ECB implies a contractionary monetary policy since it reduces excess reserves, i.e., bank deposits available for new loans. This action by the ECB will decrease the money supply. Similarly, a reduction in the reserve requirement ratio will tend to increase loans and ultimately the money supply. Money supply changes affect interest rates that influence real economic variables such as consumption, investment, and eventually national income.

**2. Permanent Standing Facilities:** The ECB provides overnight emergency loans through the NCBs to those banks requesting such loans when they find themselves short of liquidity.[9] Some overnight loans are obtained in the form of overnight repurchase agreements, and others are based on a collateral agreement under which the counterparty provides government securities to the NCB as collateral.[10,11] This arrangement of the ECB is known as marginal lending facility. The Governing Council sets the interest rates on these loans higher than any other ECB interest rate.

If banks accumulate excessive overnight liquidity, then they have the option to deposit their extra liquidity with their respective NCBs. Counterparties, i.e., banks and other credit institutions, can carry out such transactions by utilizing the ECB's short-term standing deposit facility. Financial institutions depositing short-term liquidity with the NCBs earn interest payments based on the marginal deposit rate, which is lower than any other ECB interest rate. Thus, the two interest rates of the standing facility form a corridor of movement for overnight market interest rates. The Governing Council is vested with the authority to change the operating terms of the facility and even to discontinue its operations if necessary.

During its November 7, 2002, meeting, the Governing Council decided not to change the two short-term interest rates of the marginal lending and deposit facilities. These two interest rates, the overnight lending rate and the overnight deposit rate, were left at their previous values of 4.25 and 2.25 percent, respectively. The Governing Council had set these same values on November 9, 2001. On December 6, 2002, after tremendous political pressure, the ECB reduced the marginal lending rate and the marginal deposit rate by a half of one percent to 3.75 and 1.75 percent, respectively. This reduction in the two interest rates took place only after France and Germany indicated they were committed to fiscal discipline. Similarly, on March 6, 2003, the ECB reduced its two key interest rates by 25 basis points and the deposit rate was set at 1.5 percent; the marginal lending rate was set at 3.5 percent. Lastly, on June 6, 2003, the ECB reduced both interest rates by 50 basis points and did not change them again in 2003 or 2004.

**3. Open Market Operations:** Permanent standing, lending, and borrowing facilities are not the most important monetary tools available to the ECB in implementing the monetary policy of the Eurosystem. Instead, the Eurosystem relies mainly on open market operations to implement monetary policy. Through open market operations, the Eurosystem steers the interest rates and manages liquidity in the Euro Area market.

There are four distinct categories regarding the "aim, regularity and procedures" of open market operations. These categories are a) main refinancing operations, b) longer-term refinancing operations,

c) fine-tuning operations, and d) structural operations. Reverse repurchase transactions are utilized in all four categories.

a) **Main refinancing operations:** When financial institutions find themselves short of liquidity, they have the option to borrow on a competitive basis from the NCBs. The NCBs offer such loans on the condition that they buy high-quality bonds from the borrowing financial institutions, which they hold as collateral for these loans. The financial institutions promise to repurchase the same bonds in two weeks when their loans are repaid.

The Governing Council sets the interest rate charged on these loans. Such transactions occur every week according to a pre-specified schedule, and they are known as short-term refinancing. Commercial banks and other financial institutions offer bids to NCBs for liquidity. As a result, these loans are granted to the highest bidders. Such transactions undertaken by the NCBs are known as reverse purchase agreements or repurchase agreements (repos). For this reason, the interest rate charged on these loans is known as the main refinancing rate (repo rate). Main refinancing operations are the most important monetary tool and are frequently used by the Eurosystem. They provide the greatest volume of refinancing to the entire financial sector of the Euro Area. On December 6, 2002, the ECB reduced the repo rate by 50 basis points and on March 6, 2003, by another 25 basis points. On June 6, 2003, the repo rate was reduced by another 50 basis points to 2 percent, a record low value since its introduction on January 1, 1999 and was not changed again in 2003 or 2004.

b) **Longer-term refinancing operations:** The Eurosystem, through its longer-term refinancing operations, provides additional liquidity to the financial institutions. Long-term refinancing is implemented through regular refinancing once a month. These loans have a maturity of three months and are issued on a competitive basis. All eligible counterparties are allowed to submit bids for the longer-term refinancing operations to their respective NCBs. Because the longer-term refinancing operations constitute only a limited part of the ECB's refinancing volume, the Eurosystem does not rely on these operations to transmit signals to the money markets. Thus, the Eurosystem is a rate taker rather than a rate setter in the longer-term refinancing operations.

c) **Fine-tuning operations:** To smooth out the fluctuations of interest rates that may result from unexpected volatility in the liquidity market, the Eurosystem undertakes fine-tuning operations. These are conducted with reverse open market transactions. The Eurosystem employs three additional types of operations to provide

or absorb liquidity. Specifically, fine-tuning operations can be executed with outright transactions, foreign exchange swaps, and the
collection of fixed-term deposits.[12] The availability of these additional transactions enhances the flexibility and effectiveness of the
Eurosystem in affecting the liquidity situation in the Euro Area.

**d) Structural operations:** Whenever the Eurosystem considers it
necessary to adjust its structural financial position in relation to the
Euro Area financial sector, the Eurosystem conducts structural operations. These are carried out when the NCBs issue debt certificates
using reverse and outright transactions. Such operations alter the
composition of the balance sheet of both the Eurosystem and the
financial institutions.

# A Tabular Presentation of Monetary Operations

A concise summary of all the Eurosystem's monetary policy operations
is presented in Table 4.1 below. In this table, monetary instruments are
arranged according to their importance in carrying out monetary operations. Thus, open market operations are listed first since this is the
Eurosystem's preferred monetary tool. The Eurosystem utilizes four
distinct methods to conduct monetary policy using open market operations. These methods are listed in Column 1. The most important of
these four methods for the conduct of open market operations and the
exercise of monetary policy is the main refinancing operations. The
other three methods, longer-term refinancing, fine-tuning, and structural operations, are useful since they complement the main refinancing
operations. These three methods strengthen the Euro Area monetary
policy because they enhance the ECB's flexibility.

The next monetary operation is the standing facility. Lending and
borrowing under this facility are initiated by the financial institutions
and not by the ECB. Lastly, the minimum required reserves are
listed on the bottom of Table 4.1 even though the required reserve
ratio is not generally used to conduct monetary policy. The required
reserve ratio, however, is available to the ECB and can be utilized
whenever a drastic intervention may be necessary to affect money
supply.

In the second column of Table 4.1, the various types of transactions
utilized by the Eurosystem are listed next to the corresponding
monetary policy operations. Such transactions are available to provide
or absorb liquidity. The next two columns indicate the maturity and
the frequency of each transaction, respectively. The last column indicates the exact procedure employed for the implementation of each
transaction.

Table 4.1

## Eurosystem Monetary Policy Operations

| Monetary Policy Operations | Types of Transactions | | Maturity | Frequency | Procedure |
|---|---|---|---|---|---|
| | Provisions of Liquidity | Absorption of Liquidity | | | |
| **1. Open Market Operations** | | | | | |
| a. Main Refinancing Operations | Reverse Transactions | | Two weeks | Weekly | Standard Tenders |
| b. Longer-term Refinancing Operations | Reverse Transactions | | Two months | Monthly | Standard Tenders |
| c. Fine-tuning Operations | Reverse Transactions Foreign Exchange Swaps | | | | |
| | Outright Purchases | Outright Sales | | Non-Regular | Bilateral Procedures |
| d. Structural Operations | Reverse Transactions | Issuance of Debt Certificates | Standardized/ Non-Standardized | Regular and Non-Regular | Standard Tenders |
| | Outright Purchases | Outright Sales | | Non-Regular | Bilateral Procedures |
| **2. Standing Facilities** | | | | | |
| a. Marginal Lending Facility | Reverse Transactions | | Overnight | Access at the discretion of counterparties | |
| b. Deposit Facility | | Deposits | Overnight | Access at the discretion of counterparties | |
| **3. Minimum Required Reserves** | | | | | |

*Source:"The Single Monetary Policy in the Euro Area: General documentation on Eurosystem Monetary Policy Instruments and Procedures." *European Central Bank,* April 2002. Definitions of some of the terms used in this table are found also in the Glossary at the end of this chapter.

Though commercial banks and other credit institutions in the Eurozone can borrow liquidity from the NCBs, most of the borrowing for the purpose of meeting the reserve requirement is conducted in the interbank market. Only when the entire banking system is short of liquidity will the ECB inject the necessary liquidity to the Euro Area financial institutions. The ECB, however, is not legally bound to serve as a lender of last resort, unlike its counterpart in the US, the Fed. In the US, commercial bank members of the Fed borrow from each other when they are short in reserves. The interest rate on these overnight loans is the federal funds rate and is set by the Fed.

Implementation of monetary policy in the Euro Area is much more complicated than it is in the US. One of the reasons for this difference is that the Eurosystem inherited different monetary instruments and procedures from the various NCBs, most notably from the Bundesbank. These NCBs conducted monetary policies in their respective countries prior to 1999. In particular, the main refinancing operations, the most important Eurosystem monetary tool, were used by most NCBs prior to the establishment of the Eurosystem in 1999.

## Three Key ECB Interest Rates

Monetary policy in the Euro Area is mainly exercised through changes in interest rates. The Governing Council sets the minimum bid rate that affects excess reserves, i.e., available credit for loans in the entire Euro Area banking system. A reduction in the minimum bid rate (the repo) indicates an expansionary monetary policy since a lower repo rate makes borrowing from the ECB more attractive and profitable. At its November 7, 2002 meeting, the Governing Council chose to leave the minimum bid repo rate unchanged at 3.25 percent. This rate was left unchanged despite expectations and pressure from Euro Area governments for an interest rate reduction to promote economic growth. The ECB first set the repo at 3.25 percent on November 9, 2001. On December 6, 2002, the ECB reduced the repo rate by half a percentage point to 2.75 percent. On March 7, 2003, the ECB reduced the repo rate by another 25 basis points to 2.50 percent. This long awaited reduction of the repo was expected to have beneficial effects to the Euro Area economy, which at this time was experiencing a slow rate of growth related to geopolitical tensions caused by the fear of war in the Middle East. On June 6, 2003, the ECB reduced the repo rate another 50 basis points to 2 percent, which was a record low.

In Table 4.2 below, historic data for the three key ECB interest rates are shown since January 1, 1999. The three key ECB interest rates are the repo rate and the two rates of the marginal standing facility, the deposit and the lending rates.

Table 4.2

| The Three Key ECB Interest Rates | | | | |
|---|---|---|---|---|
| Date | Deposit Facility | Main Refinancing Operation (Repo Interest Rate) | | |
| With Effect From: | Marginal Deposit Rate | Fixed Rate Tenders | Variable Rate Tenders | Marginal Lending Rate |
| | | Fixed Rate | Minimum Bid Rate | |
| 6-Jun-03 | 1.00 | | 2.00 | 3.00 |
| 7-Mar-03 | 1.50 | | 2.50 | 3.50 |
| 6-Dec-02 | 1.75 | | 2.75 | 3.75 |
| 9-Nov-01 | 2.25 | | 3.25 | 4.25 |
| 18-Sep-01 | 2.75 | | 3.75 | 4.75 |
| 31-Aug-01 | 3.25 | | 4.25 | 5.25 |
| 11-May-01 | 3.50 | | 4.50 | 5.50 |
| 6-Oct-00 | 3.75 | | 4.75 | 5.75 |
| 1-Sep-00 | 3.50 | | 4.50 | 5.50 |
| 28-Jun-00 | 3.25 | | 4.25 | 5.25 |
| 9-Jun-00 | 3.25 | 4.25 | | 5.25 |
| 28-Apr-00 | 2.75 | 3.75 | | 4.75 |
| 17-Mar-00 | 2.50 | 3.50 | | 4.50 |
| 4-Feb-00 | 2.25 | 3.25 | | 4.25 |
| 5-Nov-99 | 2.00 | 3.00 | | 4.00 |
| 9-Apr-99 | 1.50 | 2.50 | | 3.50 |
| 22-Jan-99 | 2.00 | 3.00 | | 4.50 |
| 4-Jan-99 | 2.75 | 3.00 | | 3.25 |
| 1-Jan-99 | 2.00 | 3.00 | | 4.50 |

Source: ECB. http://www.ecb.int

From January 1, 1999, to June 27, 2000, the repo interest rate of the main refinancing operations was set as a "fixed rate tender." This means that the counterparties were competing only on the amounts of liquidity they wanted to borrow from the ECB (see Table 4.2). Starting on June 28, 2000, the main refinancing operations were conducted at "variable rate tenders." This implies that the counterparties were competing on the amount of liquidity and the interest rate they offered for the transaction. The interest rate at which

Figure 4.3   Key ECB Interest Rates

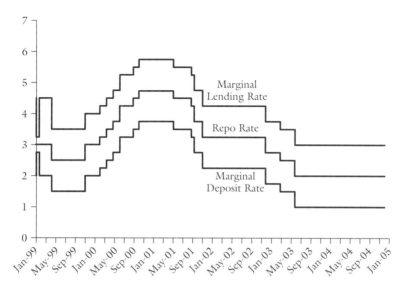

Source of data: ECB, http://www.ecb.int

counterparties place their bids is known as "minimum bid rate," or repo rate.

In Figure 4.3, the three key ECB interest rates shown in Table 4.2 are presented as time plots. The marginal deposit rate constitutes a floor rate; the marginal lending rate constitutes a ceiling interest rate. The repo interest rate is set by the ECB in between the two rates of the standing facility. In Figure 4.2, we observe the existence of a pattern in all three interest rates. Since April 9, 1999, all three interest rates moved in the same direction, changing by equal increments of 25 or 50 basis points at a time while maintaining equal spreads between each other. For example, the spread between the marginal lending and deposit rate was permanently set at 2 percent (200 basis points). The ECB has kept the repo rate equal to the average of the two interest rates of the standing facility. This is depicted in Figure 4.3 with the center time plot in equal distance from the two other time plots after April 9, 1999.

From November 5, 1999 to October 6, 2000, the ECB applied contractionary monetary policy that resulted in a cumulative increase of 225 basis points (2.25 percent) for every one of the three target interest rates. From October 6, 2000, until June 6, 2003, the ECB applied expansionary monetary policy that resulted in a reduction of all interest rates by 275 basis points (2.75 percent). On December 6, 2002, the ECB reduced the three key interest rates by half of a percentage point (50 basis points). Similarly, on March 7, 2003, the ECB

Figure 4.4    Main Refinancing Operation (Repo) and EONIA Interest Rates

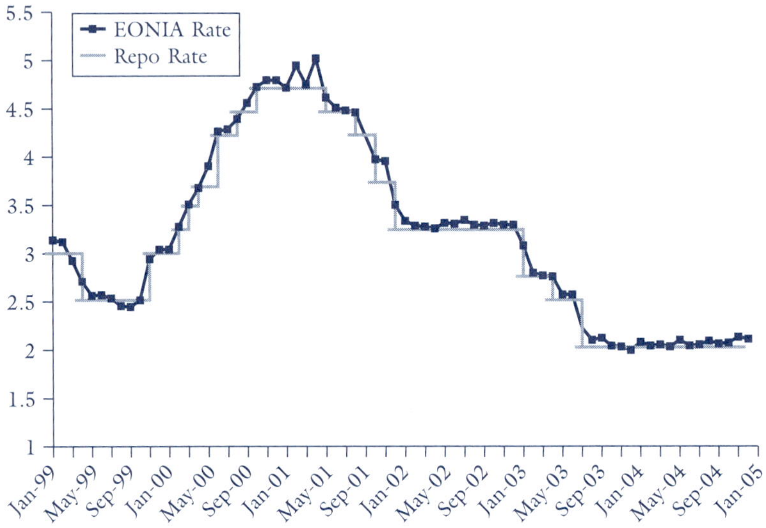

Source: ECB, http://www.ecb.int

reduced all three interest rates by another 25 basis points and on June 6, 2003, the ECB reduced the repo and the two marginal rates by another 50 basis points. Thus, the repo rates was set at 2 percent, and the marginal deposit and lending rates were at 1 and 3 percent, respectively. The ECB announced that an all-time low repo rate would help the recovery of the Euro Area economy. The repo rate, however, was still double the federal funds rate of the US in 2003. This implied that the monetary policy in the Euro Area was more contractionary than the US monetary policy.

As the ECB sets the repo rate, the interbank overnight borrowing rate, known as the Euro Overnight Index Average (EONIA), which is the equivalent of the US federal funds market rate, is affected. In the US, the Fed sets the target federal funds rate to influence the market federal funds rate. The latter is the rate that banks charge when borrowing overnight reserves from each other to meet their minimum reserve requirements. In the Euro Area, the EONIA and the repo rates move closely as indicated in Figure 4.4.

## An Evaluation of the EMU

A relatively short time has passed since the establishment of the EMU on January 1, 1999. However, such a short period can provide sufficient time to form a reasonably accurate opinion regarding the survival of the EMU and the common currency, the euro.

The EMU passed the first test in early 1999 when the euro was successfully introduced in the form of bank deposits for firms, individuals, and interbank transactions. The most critical test of the EMU took place, in early January 2002, when euro coins and banknotes were introduced and enthusiastically accepted by the public of the 12 Euro Area countries. The French governor of the Banque de France at that time and now the second president of the ECB, Jean-Claude Trichet, described the early success of the euro as ". . . an indisputable success from the technical and operational point of view."[13]

This favorable evaluation of the EMU based on the quick and wide acceptance of the euro does not imply that the EMU will be free of risks in the future. The EMU could suffer major setbacks for various reasons. The most serious threat to the EMU is the possibility that asymmetric shocks may occur in the Euro Area. In this case, EMU countries may require different monetary and fiscal policies. A common monetary policy that results in the same interest rate for the entire Euro Area will not be the most appropriate monetary policy for all countries if one or a few countries experience a recession and others do not. A worse scenario is if the economies of one or more countries experience a recession, and other economies expand rapidly. A "one size fits all" monetary policy may not work well for the Euro Area. An example of this occurred when a few countries, such as Germany, experienced a recession after January 1, 1999, yet others, such as Ireland and Greece, experienced a boom.

## Fiscal Problems in the Euro Area

Compliance with the Stability and Growth Pact (SGP) and the loss of the exchange rate policy has pushed some countries into a difficult and strenuous situation. In the fall of 2002, for example, a low projected annual growth rate for the Euro Area led many to predict that the EU countries would temporarily relax compliance with the SGP or, alternatively, abrogate it altogether. In either situation and particularly in the latter, interest rates and foreign exchange markets were expected to react adversely toward the euro. Depending on the magnitude of the reaction of the foreign exchange and capital markets, many predicted that the outcome of such a scenario could be destructive for the euro and the future of the EMU.

In the fall of 2002, four Euro Area countries (France, Germany, Italy and Portugal) experienced difficulties in balancing their government budgets. This was widely publicized, raising public concern questioning the survival of the SGP. To avoid further embarrassment, the EU Commission decided, on September 16, 2002, to extend the deadline of balancing the budgets of the four countries by two more years, i.e., December 2006, instead of December 2004, which was required by all other Euro Area countries. On October 8, 2002, the French finance minister, Francis Mer, was outvoted in the Eurogroup meeting by the 11 other finance ministers on his government's adamant position not to reduce the 2002 government deficit. The French government adopted an extreme position in total defiance of the SGP after the reelection of President Chirac. At the time of the meeting, an official reprimand was expected to be issued against France. The French government was determined to keep the pre-election promises by President Chirac to cut taxes and increase government expenditures to boost growth in the French economy.

In his quarterly testimony in the fall of 2002 to the European Parliament, Willem Duisenberg criticized the three large EU countries (France, Germany, and Italy) for failing to put their public finances in order at a time when the Euro Area was not in a recession. In the same testimony, Willem Duisenberg vehemently refused an interest rate reduction even though inflationary pressures were weak in the Euro Area.

Monetary policy in the Euro Area in 2002 was considered tight. At a time when the global economy was overshadowed by uncertainty caused by the fear of war in the Middle East, the ECB took an adamant position against an interest rate reduction. The tight monetary policy of the ECB had, consequently, frustrated many politicians and economists. They publicly raised doubts whether the target inflation rate of two percent was an appropriate one when the Euro Area countries were heading for a recession.

The ECB had one good reason to resist political pressure in conducting what many considered a tight monetary policy. This reason was the negative political friction in the Euro Area regarding the SGP's future. A revision or abrogation of the SGP seemed likely in the near future. If this was going to happen and no other common agreement would be reached to safeguard fiscal discipline, Euro Area countries might begin experiencing large deficits and debts. In this situation, it would be impossible for the ECB to pursue price stability. This was the main reason why the ECB refused to reduce interest rates.

To many economists, however, interest rate reduction in the Euro Area economy was necessary. The decision taken by the ECB on November 7, 2002, not to reduce interest rates was the opposite from the one taken by the Fed which one day earlier, reduced the federal funds and the discount rates by a half of a percentage point to boost the US economy. During 2001, the Fed applied expansionary monetary policy and reduced the federal funds rate 11 times.

Finally, some good news for the SGP came on November 14, 2002, when the EU Commission ordered France and Germany to reduce their deficits.[14] As a result, both countries, through their finance ministers, Francis Mer and Hans Eichel, agreed that noncompliance with the SGP would weaken the euro. This was a significant change in the fiscal policy of both countries.[15] Such an important attitude change toward the SGP by the two largest EU countries made it possible for the ECB to reduce the three key interest rates on December 5, 2002, by one half of one percent. This improved climate regarding the SGP did not last long.

France and Germany violated the 3 percent deficit two years in a row and were heading for a third and fourth. To avoid sanctions from the Commission, the French and German finance ministers convinced the other finance ministers of the ECOFIN to "freeze the mechanics of the SGP" and, thus, avoid sanctions. In March 2005, the SGP is going to be revised and likely will become more flexible. Despite the problems with the SGP and the rising deficits, the euro kept appreciating during 2004 against the dollar and other currencies, breaking record highs.

# The Moral Hazard Problem

The possibility of moral hazard is a problem that can be associated with the creation of the EMU. This could occur when an NCB, by abusing its financing facilities of the ECB, creates a favorable climate for its own banks at the expense of other Euro Area countries' banks. Such a situation is likely to be corrected if it is brought to the attention of the ECB governing bodies. Nonetheless, since the ECB does not directly regulate or supervise the banks and other financial institutions in the individual countries, moral hazard will remain a potential problem in the EMU.

If economic conditions deteriorate in one or more countries, the governments of these countries could decide to break apart from the EMU based on purely short-term, cost-benefit considerations. This decision could be influenced by public opinion voiced in a national referendum. Under a worst-case scenario, one country's decision could trigger the EMU's total collapse. An EMU disaster could be avoided if the governing bodies of the EMU and the national governments demonstrate a commitment to confront adverse economic trends aggressively. Therefore, a firm commitment to unity by the Euro Area governments can safeguard confidence in the euro. This firm commitment should encourage the adoption of more flexible rules by the EU institutions and governments. The promotion of further economic integration and the adoption of structural reforms can transform the EU into a dynamic and internationally competitive economy.

Such a favorable scenario for the EMU and the euro is likely to prevail. This optimistic outlook is based on the previous experiences of the EU countries in overcoming obstacles to economic integration. This decision by the vast majority of the EU countries to pursue further integration was based on the belief that the benefits of further integration would outweigh the costs. Economic integration, however, was disrupted during the most recent experience with the EMU by Sweden, the UK, and Denmark, which chose not to adopt the euro. It is expected that these countries may seek full EMU membership as they reconsider their benefits and costs.

## Monetary Financial Integration in the Euro Area

Because economic and monetary integration is a dynamic process, most of the benefits from integration will be realized over a long time. Once economic and financial integration is complete, many of the benefits of integration will become permanent. An initial beneficial effect of monetary integration began with the introduction and adoption of the new electronic interbank payments system for all the EU countries. The new payments system is called the Trans-European Automated Real-time Gross settlement Express Transfer (TARGET). Payments within this efficient electronic system are received within a few seconds. For example, each day during the second quarter of 2002, an average of 251,340 total payments for domestic and cross-border transactions, representing a value of 1,062 billion euros, took place.[16]

Financial integration can help Euro Area countries cope with asymmetric shocks. The replacement of national currencies with the euro eliminated the exchange rate risk from holding assets in different EU countries' national currencies. Firms and citizens of every Euro Area country diversify their investment portfolios by holding various securities issued in other Euro Area countries. As a result of financial integration, negative effects caused by a recession in a particular country are mitigated as residents of this country receive income earned from their investments in other Euro Area countries. Thus, financial integration works as a shock absorber that provides some assurance for the citizens of a Euro Area country experiencing an asymmetric shock. In the absence of large fiscal stimuli from the EU, which is lacking a substantial budget, financial integration can play a critical role in the success of the euro.

Monetary policy can only be implemented successfully in an integrated monetary and financial market. Since the objective of the ECB is to direct interest rates to affect real economic variables, control of a stable monetary aggregate is crucial. The introduction of the euro created an integrated money market for the first time in the Euro Area. Similarly, since most credit (liquidity) obtained from the ECB is based on collateral, an efficient securities market in the Euro Area is essential. Much progress has been achieved in integrating the securities market. A few legal and technical barriers still remain. Therefore, additional progress is necessary to integrate financial markets fully in the Euro Area.

# Long-Term Interest Rates

Since January 1, 1999, the Eurosystem has successfully pursued its primary objective of stabilizing prices in the Euro Area. In the early winter of 2005, the inflation rate in the Euro Area was slightly above two percent, which was close to the ECB's target value. In Figure 4.5, the long-term interest rate time plots of the Euro Area, the US, and Japan are presented. These interest rates are measured by the 10-year bond yield for the period 1997–2004. It is clear from Figure 4.5 that Euro Area long-term interest rates have declined since the beginning of 2000. A similar pattern was followed by the US long-term interest rate. During 2004, however, all three long-term interest rates increased slightly. Long-term interest rates include an expected inflation premium above the short-term interest rates if the price level is expected to increase in the long run. A declining long-term interest rate is an indication the ECB is gaining credibility in stabilizing prices. The

Figure 4.5   Ten-Year Government Bond Yields

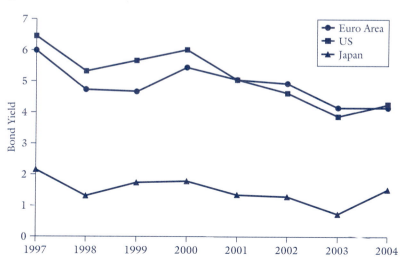

Source: ECB Monthly Bulletin, http://www.ecb.int

ECB's price credibility is the main reason for the reduction of the long-term interest rate.

In Figure 4.5, the Japanese long-term interest rate (10-year bond yield) is presented along with the comparable US and Euro Area long-term interest rates. The Japanese long-term interest rate is lower than the US and Euro Area interest rates. This large difference in the long-term interest rates is explained primarily by the deflation of the Japanese economy in the last few years.

Another reason for the decline of the Euro Area and US long-term interest rates is prevailing uncertainty in the global economy, especially after the September 11, 2001, tragedy. This uncertainty led many investors to shift their portfolios to more liquid and safer government bonds and away from stocks (equities). Demand for government bonds increased the prices of bonds and reduced the yield (long-term interest rate) since the two are inversely related.

## SUMMARY

The Eurosystem, which consists of the ECB and the 12 NCBs of each country, conducts monetary policy in the Euro Area. The ECB and the 25 NCBs constitute the ESCB. When all EU countries adopt the euro, no distinction will be made between the Eurosystem and the ESCB.

The Eurosystem is administered by three governing bodies: The Governing Council is the supreme governing body, which consists of 18 members and is entrusted with the formulation of the monetary policy. The Executive Board is comprised of six members and is responsible for the implementation of the monetary policy on a daily basis. The General Council consists of the president and the vice president of the executive board and the EU25 central bank governors. The General Council is responsible for issues pertinent to the exchange rates between Euro Area and EU non-Euro Area countries. The Treaty, establishing the EC and the statutes of the ECB, requires that the ECB be independent from all other EU institutions as well as the national governments. Additionally, the ECB must be accountable and transparent.

The monetary policy of the Euro Area is guided by the ECB's stability-oriented monetary policy strategy, which consists of two pillars and a quantitative definition of price stability. The first pillar recognizes inflation purely as a monetary phenomenon; therefore, price stability requires control of a monetary aggregate. The second pillar broadly assesses the outlook of future price developments in the Euro Area. In addition, the Eurosystem targets inflation in the Euro Area, which reflects the ECB's aim for a quantitative definition of price stability.

The ECB utilizes three monetary instruments to implement monetary policy: Required Reserves, Permanent Standing Facilities, and Open Market Operations. The most important of the three is open market operations, which are conducted with four distinct methods that aim to steer interest rates and manage liquidity: main refinancing operations, longer-term refinancing operations, fine-tuning operations, and structural operations. The ECB relies primarily on its main refinancing operations to conduct monetary policy in the Euro Area. It sets the interest rate for the main refinancing operation, which is known as the repo interest rate. The ECB sets two other short-term interest rates of the standing facility: the deposit rate and the lending rate. Changes in these two interest rates affect all other interest rates in the Euro Area.

Many considered monetary policy in the Euro Area, since 2002, to be contractionary. The ECB refused to reduce its key interest rates because the three largest Euro Area countries chose not to reduce their government deficits. A temporary shift in attitude of the large Euro Area countries toward fiscal stability and compliance with SGP allowed the ECB on December 5, 2002, and March 7, 2003, to reduce its three key interest rates. Such a decision was expected to have a favorable effect on the Euro Area economy.

In the early hours of Tuesday, November 25, 2003, the ECOFIN ministers of the Euro Area countries agreed to suspend sanctions against Germany and France, which refused to conform to the SGP. Though the foreign exchange markets did not respond negatively against the euro, the fear remains that the long-term interest rates will rise in the Euro Area. This will happen unless the SGP is revised by a new pact that will guarantee price stability and growth in the Euro Area and restore trust among Euro Area countries. Furthermore, the EC Commission announced the SGP will be revised in March 2005 and become more flexible.

## Essay Questions

1. The Eurosystem was entrusted with the monetary policy of the Euro Area. Describe the two institutions of the Eurosystem: the ECB and the NCBs of the Euro Area member countries. What are the functions of each of the two institutions in the conduct of monetary policy in the Euro Area? Explain.

2. Describe the functions of the Governing Council in exercising monetary policy in the Euro Area. How many members does the Governing Council consist of?

3. Discuss the role, functions, and responsibilities of the ECB's Executive Board. How many members does the ECB Board consist

of? Name the two most important positions on the Executive Board. What are the names of the officers that are serving in these two top positions of the Board?

4. The ECB is responsible for the monetary policy of the Euro Area. To pursue its objective, the ECB was granted independence from all other EU institutions and national governments. Explain why ECB independence is such an important factor for the successful exercise of monetary policy.

5. On October 13, 1998, the Euro Area countries adopted the Single Monetary Policy. Discuss the two pillars and the quantitative definition of the ECB's stability-oriented monetary policy.

6. The ECB utilizes various monetary instruments to carry out the Single Monetary Policy in the Euro Area. Discuss each of the ECB's monetary instruments. Which is the most important monetary instrument that the ECB utilizes most frequently to implement monetary policy?

7. Write a definition for each of the following terms:

   a. repo rate

   b. permanent standing facilities

   c. main refinancing operations

   d. fine-tuning operations

   e. structural operations

# chapter 5

# Performance of the Euro: The First Six Years

## Introduction

The purchasing power of a currency, measured by the amount of goods and services a national currency unit can buy within a domestic economy, will vary from period to period. Various factors can affect the purchasing power of a national currency. Such factors include changes in expectations regarding the strength of the economy and movements in real and/or nominal economic variables in the country. Two major economic variables that affect the purchasing power of national currencies are the rates of growth of real output (GDP) and the country's inflation or deflation rate.

The same factors responsible for changes in the purchasing power of a currency within the domestic economy will affect the value of a country's currency in relation to its trading partners' currencies. Assume, for example, that a currency's purchasing power decreases within the national market while the purchasing power of a trading partner's currency increases or remains unchanged. In this situation, it is plausible and almost certain the domestic currency will be worth fewer units of the trading partner's currency. The number of domestic currency units that one foreign currency unit is traded for is called the foreign exchange rate. For example, on December 21, 2004, the $/1€ exchange rate was 1.336, i.e., 1.336 US dollars per 1 euro.[1]

The international rules and arrangements under which foreign currencies are regulated, controlled, and traded for each other are known as exchange rate regimes or exchange rate systems. Two distinct and diametrically opposite exchange rate regimes exist. A few variations exist between these two polar cases. The first of these two extreme cases is the fixed exchange rate regime while the second is the flexible, or floating, exchange rate system. Under the fixed exchange rate system, all participating countries fix the price of their official exchange rates multilaterally. These systems were adopted during one of the few historical and well-publicized international monetary and exchange rate conferences and agreements. The Gold Standard (1870–1914) and the Bretton Woods International Monetary System (1946–1971) were fixed exchange rate regimes. All member countries under these exchange rate systems had agreed to fix their foreign exchange rates with respect to gold and the US dollar accordingly and, therefore, indirectly with respect to all other currencies. Gold and the US dollar were the international reserves under these two exchange rate systems, respectively.

The exchange rates under the fixed exchange rate regimes were known as official parity rates and rarely changed. Official exchange rate changes occurred only when it was certain that the existing rates were misaligned, which meant that they substantially deviated from what was perceived to be their long-run equilibrium values. In such situations, currencies were overvalued or undervalued.

Since 1973, many developed economies have adopted the flexible exchange rate regime. Foreign exchange prices under this regime are mainly determined in the foreign exchange markets where currencies are traded daily. Demand and supply of foreign currencies simultaneously determine the foreign exchange prices. The US dollar, the euro, the Japanese yen, the UK pound sterling, the Canadian dollar, and the Australian dollar are a few such currencies traded in the foreign exchange markets.

Under the present foreign exchange system, many developing countries peg (fix) their exchange rates to a currency of one of their major trading partners that has joined the flexible exchange rate regime. This currency is usually an important world currency such as the US dollar, the euro, or the UK pound. Because foreign exchange markets are scattered around the globe, one or more foreign exchange markets are guaranteed to be open 24 hours a day. According to Jennifer Hughes of the *Financial Times,* the foreign exchange market is "the largest and most dynamic market in the world that literally does not sleep."

Foreign exchange markets are over-the-counter markets, i.e., they are not located in any specific geographic area where currency traders meet to exchange currencies. Foreign exchange transactions are mainly conducted by specialized foreign exchange rate departments of large banks via telephone lines and fax but mostly through the Internet. Most of these banks are centered in Tokyo, London, and New York. Foreign exchange dealers in these banks advertise on the Internet, sharing information of their bids and offers of all major currencies. What currency dealers are offering to buy and sell in this highly competitive market are bank demand deposits (i.e., checking account deposits) of various currencies in amounts worth over $1 million and often in multiples of $1 billion. Paper notes and coins of foreign currencies are purchased in smaller amounts by tourists and others from bank branches usually located in international airports or in big cities. Such small transactions of foreign currencies are not carried out at the most favorable exchange rates for the customer due to high transaction costs.

Under the present flexible exchange rate regime, exchange rates are not determined exclusively by market forces. Governments sometimes interfere in the foreign exchange markets by buying and/or selling currencies to influence certain exchange rates. This happens when governments are convinced that a particular exchange rate has deviated from what was perceived to be its long-run equilibrium value. Because of the presence of such governmental interferences in the foreign exchange markets, the flexible exchange rate regime is often called a "managed float" or "dirty float."

There have been a few times in the past when a group of large developed countries has agreed to influence the foreign exchange rate of certain currencies. To achieve this objective, these countries jointly intervened by buying and/or selling massive amounts of these currencies. The end result of this decision was to affect the foreign exchange rate of the targeted currency, which was considered overvalued or undervalued. A massive interference in the foreign exchange market was decided by the Plaza Agreement in 1985 that aimed to reduce the rising value of the dollar, which was perceived to be overvalued and was feared to become detrimental to the US export sector. The opposite was agreed upon two years later with the Louvre Accord in 1987, when the US dollar was thought to be undervalued. A joint effort was also undertaken in September 2000 to prevent a further slide of the euro, which had bottomed out at about $0.83.

Since the establishment of the Economic and Monetary Union (EMU) and the adoption of the euro on January 1, 1999, the Euro Area (Eurozone) countries have agreed to let their currency float against all currencies that had joined the flexible exchange rate regime.

This chapter aims to present the euro's historical performance in relation to other major world currencies. Nominal and real exchange rates of the euro versus several major world currencies will be presented as time plots and will be discussed and analyzed thoroughly. Nominal and real trade-weighted exchange rates of the euro and other major world currencies are presented graphically to evaluate the overall performance of the euro and the other currencies. In the following two chapters, all key factors that may have played an important role in the determination of the euro exchange rates, will be studied. Similarly, all existing exchange rate theories will be introduced and tested to examine whether they explain the empirical performance of the euro since its introduction as a new currency in January 1999.

# The US Dollars per Euro Nominal Exchange Rate ($NE_{\$/€}$)

Figure 5.1 below portrays the nominal US dollar per euro exchange rate ($NE_{\$/€}$) from January 4, 1999, the day the new Euro Area currency was introduced and traded in the foreign exchange market against other currencies. The euro was introduced at $1.168, a rate equal to the US dollars/ECU official exchange rate on December 31, 1998. After this date, the European Currency Unit (ECU) ceased to exist since it was replaced by the euro. The first recorded trading transaction of the euro took place in Australia on January 4, 1999, at a rate of $1.175. In Europe, the euro began trading at a rate of $1.1855.

## The Decline of the Euro: A Downward Trend

Immediately after its introduction in January 1999, the euro embarked on a rough sail as it started depreciating against the US dollar as shown by the downward trend in Figure 5.1. This depreciation persisted until the end of 2000. The euro's path, however, is a series of random, short-run fluctuations during the entire period starting January 1999. Two noticeable breaks in the euro's downward trend occurred in July 1999 and in May 2000. Toward the end of the first two years, the euro hit its all-time low value against the dollar when it sank to $0.8252 on October 26, 2000. During the next year (2001) and the first two months of 2002, the dollar/euro exchange rate remained relatively stable, dancing around the $0.90 mark.

## The Appreciation of the Euro: An Upward Trend

Starting in February 2002, the euro began appreciating, following an upward trend against the US dollar. The continuous appreciation of the euro caused uneasiness among many European businesses, government officials, the EU Commission, and the ECB. The reason for their concern was the fear that the appreciation of the euro against the US dollar and other currencies would damage the Euro Area export sector and disrupt the perceived anemic and fragile Euro Area recovery, which was believed to have begun during the last quarter of 2003. On December 24, 2004, Christmas Eve, the euro reached a record value

Figure 5.1   US Dollars per Euro Nominal Exchange Rate

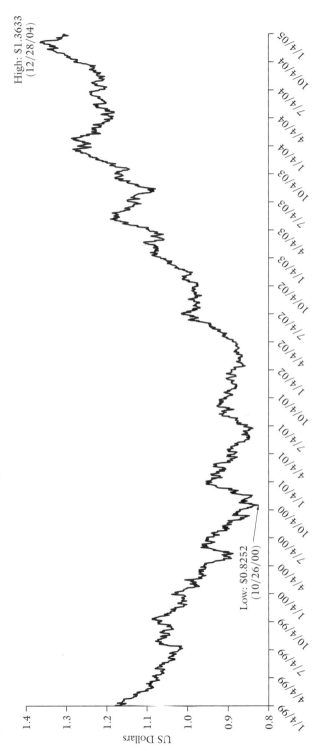

High: $1.3633
(12/28/04)

Low: $0.8252
(10/26/00)

US Dollars

1.4
1.3
1.2
1.1
1.0
0.9
0.8

1/4/99
4/4/99
7/4/99
10/4/99
1/4/00
4/4/00
7/4/00
10/4/00
1/4/01
4/4/01
7/4/01
10/4/01
1/4/02
4/4/02
7/4/02
10/4/02
1/4/03
4/4/03
7/4/03
10/4/03
1/4/04
4/4/04
7/4/04
10/4/04
1/4/05

Source: Data are based on daily rates collected by the ECB at 2:15 p.m. ECB time.

against the US dollar at $1.3542. On December 28, the euro again reached an all-time record high value of $1.3633.

Figure 5.1 reveals evidence of tremendous volatility in the $/1€ nominal exchange rate during the first six years of the euro's life. For example, from January 1999 to October 26, 2000, the euro had depreciated by 30 percent to its lowest recorded value of $0.8252. Similarly, the euro appreciated by 65.2 percent from October 26, 2000, to December 28, 2004, the day the euro rose to its all-time high value of $1.3633. The percentage appreciation of the euro versus the US dollar from its introductory value on January 4, 1999 to December 28, 2004 was 15.64 percent.

These statistics indicate that the euro has fluctuated substantially against the US dollar since 1999 and, in the end of 2004, it surpassed its initial value of $1.168.

## The Nominal Euro Exchange Rates Versus Other Currencies

In Figure 5.2, the nominal euro exchange rates versus the currencies of eight economically important countries are presented in time plots similar to that of the $NE_{\$/€}$. By observing these graphs, it can be seen that the exchange rates of the Japanese yen, the UK pound sterling, the Swiss franc, the Canadian dollar, the South Korean won, and the Chinese yuan (renminbi) resemble the graphs of the $NE_{\$/€}$. The first five out of the above six mentioned currencies' exchange rates are market-driven, floating exchange rates, influenced occasionally by governmental interference. The Chinese renminbi is pegged to the US dollar at 8.27 renminbis per US dollar. As a result, the renminbi/euro nominal exchange rate is similar to the $NE_{\$/€}$. Therefore, it is not surprising that these currencies pegged to the US dollar first-appreciated, stabilized, and then depreciated against the euro.

The time plots of these six exchange rates follow U-shaped paths. Similarly, U-shaped time plots were observed for the euro exchange rates with several other currencies. The parabolic U-shaped paths of the euro exchange rates in relation to so many currencies were not coincidental but were caused by economic factors inherent in the global business cycle and the Euro Area economy.

One of the euro exchange rates that did not follow a U-shaped path was the Australian dollar. The exchange rate of the Australian dollar (aussie) and a few other currencies with respect to the euro, which are known as commodity exchange rates, are mostly influenced by the movements in the prices of certain commodities that are found in

Figure 5.2   Nominal Euro Exchange Rates of Eight Currencies

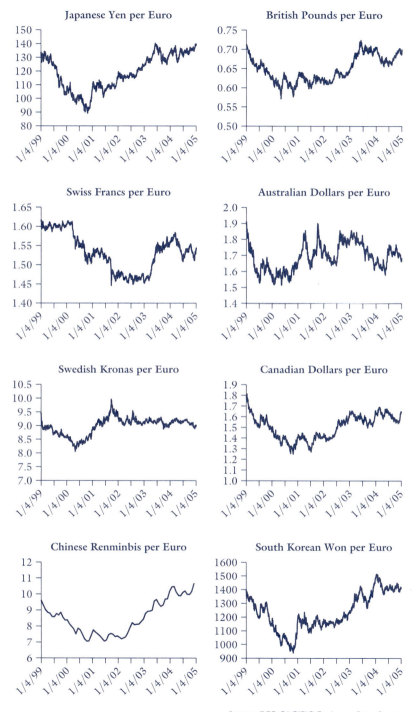

Source: ECB, PACIFIC Exchange Rate Service

abundance in these countries and are exported. The aussie/euro exchange rate followed a path independent from any other countries' exchange rates with respect to the euro. The aussie appreciated the first year and then depreciated following a turbulent upward trend for about a year; it has since been appreciating until June 2004, exhibiting overall relative stability.

Similar to the Australian dollar, the Swedish krona/euro exchange rate has been stable because the Swedish government was considering joining the EMU and has been preparing to adopt the euro. According to the Maastricht Treaty, Sweden, as a candidate EMU country, was obligated to maintain a stable currency versus the euro prior to joining the EMU.[2] In a national referendum, however, in September 2003, the Swedes decided against joining the EMU and rejected the euro.

Figure 5.3 portrays the performance of the euro in relation to 11 world currencies as measured by the respective nominal exchange rates. The 11 currencies are the Chinese renminbi, the South Korean won, the Canadian dollar, the Australian dollar, the Norwegian krone, the Swiss franc, the Swedish krona, the UK pound sterling, the Danish krone, the Japanese yen, and the US dollar. Eight of these currencies are presented in terms of time plots in Figure 5.2.

Figure 5.3 consists of three different bar charts that demonstrate the performance of the euro during two sub-periods and during the period from the introduction of the euro until it reached its all-time high value against the US dollar.

The first sub-period covers the time from January 4, 1999, to October 26, 2000, the date the euro reached its minimum value against the dollar. This sub-period, which lasted a little less than two years, can be referred to as the euro depreciation period since the euro depreciated against all eleven currencies. The euro depreciated the most against the Japanese yen and the Korean won by approximately 33.22 and 32.88 percent, respectively. Similarly, the euro depreciated against the Chinese renminbi, and the US and Canadian dollars at 29.93, 30, and 30.62 percent, respectively.

The second period spans from October 26, 2000, to December 28, 2004. During this interval, the euro appreciated the most against the US dollar and reached its maximum value at the end of this period (see the middle bar chart in Figure 5.3). This time can be referred to as the euro appreciation period since the euro appreciated against 10 of the 11 currencies. The euro, nonetheless, appreciated the most against the US dollar (65.21 percent), the Chinese renminbi (62.38 percent), the Japanese yen (57.32 percent), and the South Korean won (51.40 percent).

Figure 5.3   Nominal Euro Exchange Rate Percent Change Against Eleven
Currencies During the Period (1/4/99–12/28/04)

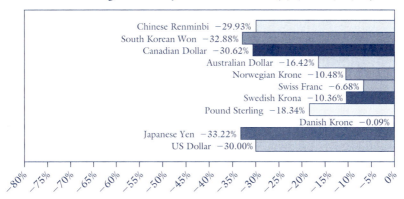

Euro % Change Versus Major World Currencies (1/4/99–10/26/00)

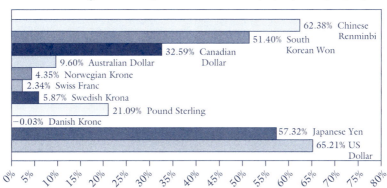

Euro % Change Versus Major World Currencies (10/26/00–12/28/04)

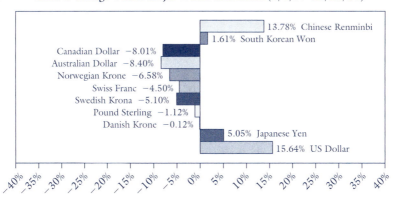

Euro % Change Versus Major World Currencies (1/4/99–12/28/04)

Source of data: ECB, OANDA

Lastly, the third period spans from January 4, 1999, to December 28, 2004. This period covers the time from the introduction of the euro to the day it reached its maximum value against the US dollar. The bar chart at the bottom of Figure 5.3 shows that a more balanced position was attained by the euro since it appreciated against four currencies and depreciated against seven others. All the percentage changes of the euro exchange rates, whether they indicated an appreciation or depreciation, were relatively small at less than 16 percent. The Australian dollar (Aussie) appreciated 8.40 percent against the euro. Similarly, the Canadian dollar (looney) appreciated 8.01 percent against the euro. Currency dealers often refer to the Canadian dollar as a "looney" for the name of the exotic bird's picture that appears on one side of this currency. This bar chart provides evidence that the nominal exchange rate of the euro, after a two-year dive, gradually recovered. On July 14, 2004, after about five and a half years, the euro was trading against the dollar a little above its initial introductory value of January 4, 1999, but toward the end of 2004, the euro gained strength against the US dollar.

## Nominal Versus Real Exchange Rates

Knowledge of the nominal exchange rate provides information regarding the exact number of foreign currency units that can be exchanged for one domestic currency unit. More useful information than this would be knowing the amount of goods and services that a domestic currency unit could buy in a foreign country after it is converted into a foreign currency.

To demonstrate this point, let us hypothesize that you are a college student who has decided to take a trip to Europe and intend to visit some Euro Area countries. You know you must exchange a certain number of dollars for euros, but you do not know how many dollars will be sufficient to cover all of your trip's expenses. These expenditures may include restaurant meals, admission tickets to museums, operas, concerts, soccer games, and bus and train tickets. You will need money for lodging (for inexpensive youth hostels) or maybe more expensive motels along with all other possible expenditures.

Before you depart for your European trip, you must ensure you have enough money to cover all your trip's expenses. To resolve this issue, you must decide how many dollars you will exchange into euros. You must, therefore, be concerned about changing a sufficient number of dollars into euros so you can afford to accomplish all the things you have planned for your transatlantic trip. Talking to a few of your friends who went on a European trip last summer can help you decide how much your European adventure will cost. Their advice will be valuable provided that no substantial cost of living changes have developed since last summer.

What would happen to the cost of the trip if prices in the Euro Area countries increased by more than prices in the US? You may be accustomed to following the news and keeping up with international macroeconomics and financial statistics. In such a case, you will be well aware of these price differences and of the current value of the $NE_{\$/\matheuro}$. If you are a rational person, then you will consider all new relevant information prior to exchanging your dollars to euros. Knowledge of the nominal exchange rates alone, however, will provide insufficient information to help you decide how many dollars you need to exchange into euros.

People who do not closely follow the news or bother to ask questions pertinent to the cost of living in foreign countries may be surprised when they travel abroad. When price differences develop between two countries, the exchange rate that reflects and provides the most correct and relevant information is the real exchange rate. The real exchange rate captures the relative price of a particular basket of goods purchased in the two countries. In your case, the relative price of the two baskets of goods refers to the cost of all those goods you will consume in the Euro Area countries versus the cost of a similar basket of goods in the US.

An alternative vacation elsewhere, though not a perfect substitute for you and others, may become an option. If, for example, the real dollar/euro exchange rate ($RE_{\$/\matheuro}$) increases and, thus, the US dollar depreciates with respect to the euro in real terms, a US vacation may become more attractive. Many Americans, because of the real depreciation of the dollar after the end of 2001, switched their vacation destinations to home instead of Europe. Similarly, many Europeans began arriving on the eastern shores of the US to visit Walt Disney World and other US tourist attractions.

The real US dollar/euro real exchange rate ($RE_{\$/\matheuro}$) is given by formula (1):

$$RE_{\$/\matheuro} = NE_{\$/\matheuro}\left(\frac{P_{EA}}{P_{US}}\right) \tag{1}$$

$NE_{\$/\matheuro}$ and $RE_{\$/\matheuro}$ are the nominal and real $\$/1\matheuro$ exchange rates, respectively. $P_{EA}$ and $P_{US}$ are the market basket prices of the Euro Area and the US as they are measured by their respective EU and US consumer price indices (CPIs). The CPIs were chosen because we are interested in the consumer prices of the entire economies and not in any particular market basket.

Figure 5.4 depicts the nominal and real US dollar/euro exchange rates. These time plots demonstrate that the two exchange rates move closely to each other. Such a finding should not be surprising since the real exchange rate is defined as the product of the nominal exchange rate with the Euro Area to the US CPI ratio.

Figure 5.4   Nominal and Real Exchange rates (Dollars per Euro)

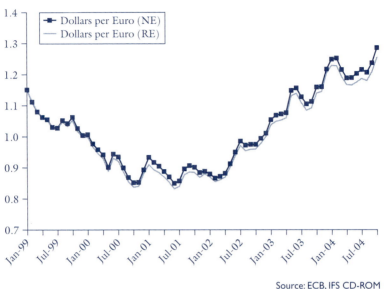

Source: ECB, IFS CD-ROM

Figure 5.4 shows that the real exchange rate is almost always below the nominal exchange rate. A main reason for this is that the nominal exchange rates react faster than prices do to any signals regarding the actual or expected growth and stability of the two economies.

If changes in nominal exchange rates are completely offset by changes in the relative price ratio, then the real exchange rate will remain constant. However, this is not correct as shown in Figure 5.4. Real exchange rates change and are, therefore, crucial in determining the international competitiveness of countries and the directions of international trade and foreign investment.

## Nominal Trade-Weighted or Nominal Effective Exchange Rates (NEERs)

The overall performance of a currency with respect to all other currencies jointly can be evaluated by examining the trade-weighted exchange rate or nominal effective exchange rate (NEER).[3] This exchange rate differs from the nominal bilateral exchange rate discussed in the previous section since it is a weighted average, theoretically, of all nominal bilateral exchange rates of the country's trading partners. The weights of the various exchange rates on a country's trade-weighted exchange rate are determined by the importance of each trading partner in terms of trade share in the total trade of the country. The NEERs are constructed as price indices.

Figure 5.5   Nominal Effective Exchange Rates (NEERs)

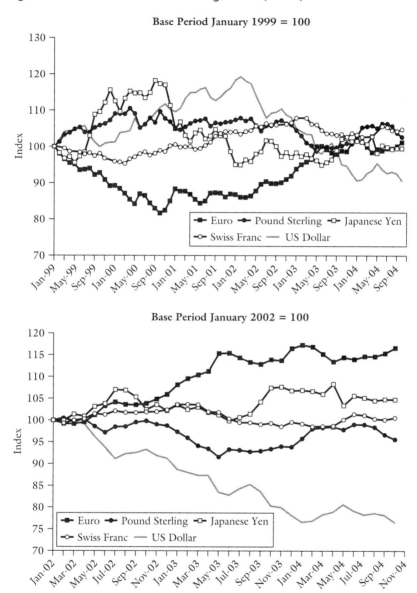

Source: IFS CD-ROM

In Figure 5.5, the NEERs or the trade-weighted exchange rates of five economically important currencies are presented as monthly indices. These currencies are the euro, the UK pound sterling, the Japanese yen, the Swiss franc, and the US dollar. The International Monetary Fund (IMF) constructs such NEERs. The Bank of England, which constructs NEERs, follows the IMF's method.

In the upper part of Figure 5.5, all of the NEERs were constructed with the month of January 1999 as the base period. Since the data utilized to construct the NEERs are monthly, the exchange rate indices of all currencies are set equal to 100 during the base period. This graph shows that the NEER of the euro resembles the U-shape of the $NE_{\$/\euro}$ bilateral exchange rate (see Figure 5.1) and the other exchange rates versus the euro, presented in Figure 5.2.

In contrast to the euro time plot, the NEER of the US dollar followed a path resembling a mirror image of the $NE_{\$/\euro}$, an upside-down U-shape. Similar trends to the US dollar NEER were followed by the NEER time plots of the UK pound sterling and the Japanese yen. According to these graphs, these two currencies appreciated, reaching their peaks at different dates, and then depreciated. The UK pound sterling, according to the NEER time plots, fluctuated less than the dollar or yen. The NEER of the Swiss franc has followed an independent path from the other currencies' NEERs. This is probably due to the idiosyncrasy and uniqueness of the Swiss economy.

The lower part of Figure 5.5 portrays the trade-weighted exchange rates of the same five currencies for the period starting January 2002, the time the euro was launched and circulated for the first time as a paper and coin currency in the 12 Euro Area countries. The trade-weighted exchange rates or NEERs in this graph are constructed as indices with January 2002 as the base period, equal to 100 for all five currencies. (The IMF originally published data using 1995 as the base year and treated the euro as an extension of its predecessor, the ECU.)

This graph covers a sub-period of the upper graph of Figure 5.5. It is evident from this graph that the euro's NEER appreciated continuously during the period 2002–2004, and the US dollar depreciated during the same period. The British magazine *The Economist* and a few daily newspapers that provide coverage on exchange rate developments publicized similar graphs to emphasize the euro's appreciation after January 2002. The remaining three currencies were stable during the same period as seen in the lower half of Figure 5.5, which indicates the NEERs of these three currencies converging toward the base period value of 100 or remaining close to 100.

## Real Trade-Weighted or Real Effective Exchange Rate (REER)

As described in a previous section, real exchange rates can be constructed from bilateral nominal exchange rates and the two countries' price indices. By deflating the NEER by a selected price index, REERs are constructed. The procedure of constructing the REERs is identical

Figure 5.6    Real Trade-Weighted or Real Effective Exchange Rates (REERs)

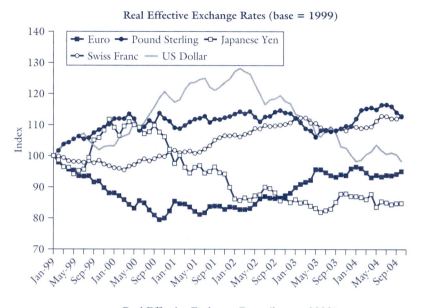

Real Effective Exchange Rates (base = 1999)

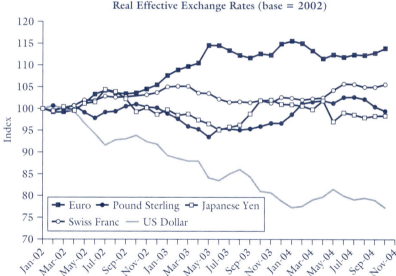

Real Effective Exchange Rates (base = 2002)

Source of data: IFS CD-ROM

to NEER construction. An important issue that must be resolved in REER construction is the selection of the appropriate price index. Figure 5.6 portrays the real trade-weighted or REERs of the same five currencies for which the NEERs were presented in Figure 5.5.

The REER time plots of the euro, the UK pound sterling, the dollar, and the Swiss franc portray similar paths with those of the NEERs

Figure 5.7

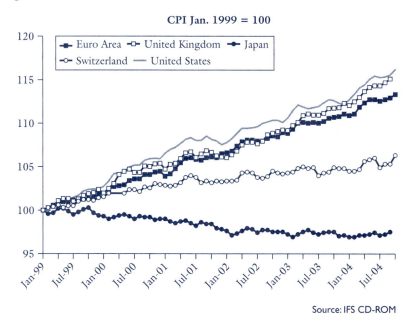

CPI Jan. 1999 = 100

Source: IFS CD-ROM

presented in Figure 5.5. The NEER and the REER time plots of these four currencies do not differ much because they all reflect similar price developments and inflation rates in these countries. The only exception is the REER of the Japanese yen, which declined. A major factor causing the real trade-weighted yen exchange rate to decline (depreciate) is that Japan, unlike any of the four other countries, has been experiencing prolonged deflation.

This can be seen in Figure 5.7, where the CPIs of the Euro Area, UK, Japan, Switzerland, and the US are depicted as time plots starting in January 1999. Only the Japanese CPI follows a negative trend during the entire period starting in January 1999. Japanese deflation was considered a major cause of Japan's long recession, which lasted more than ten years. Japanese deflation, coupled with interferences by the Central Bank of Japan to hold the value of the yen against the US dollar, caused a depreciation of the yen's REER. A depreciating REER benefits a country since it strengthens its international competitiveness position, thus promoting exports while discouraging imports.[4] The overall international competitiveness of a country, however, cannot be evaluated only by examining the country's REER. Additional information, such as the quality of its products and related non-price competition factors at the firm level, must be considered.

In the lower part of Figure 5.6, the same five REERs are presented. These have been constructed with January 2002 as the base period. This graph covers a sub-period of the upper graph of Figure 5.6, starting January 2002. It shows that the euro's REER has been appreciating during this period and the dollar has been depreciating. As for the other three currencies' REERs, each converged to its initial January 2002 value of 100. A substantial real appreciation of the euro and a greater depreciation of the US dollar occurred beginning March 2002. This situation caused great concern for possible loss in the international competitiveness of the Euro Area. One can, therefore, understand the eagerness of the Europeans to suppress the rising value of the euro and the lack of any interest by American officials to reverse the depreciation of the greenback. The US government has unofficially welcomed the dollar's depreciation as a means to deal with an increasing US current account deficit. Such an approach of the US government, however, has been unsuccessful in 2004.

## Three Euro Trade-Weighted Exchange Rates

The ECB constructs three different euro trade-weighted exchange rates, or NEERs. The first one is a weighted average of the exchange rates of a narrow (core) group of 12 countries. The second is a weighted average of the exchange rates of a group of 23 trading partner countries of the Euro Area. Finally, the third is a weighted average of the exchange rates of a broader group of 42 countries.[5] The US dollar and the UK pound have been assigned the largest weights in the calculation of the three ECB trade-weighted exchange rates in the same order, respectively.

The ECB constructs the euro's REERs for the NEER-23 and the NEER-42. To construct the REERs, the NEERs are deflated (divided) by two different price indices, the CPI and the producer price index (PPI). In total, three REERs are constructed by the ECB. The CPI and the PPI were utilized in the construction of the two REERs corresponding to the group of 23 countries. None of the price indices above is the perfect, flawless index. Each has its own advantages and shortcomings. Two of the three REERs are based on the group of 23 countries, and the third one is based on the broader group of 42 countries. What is encouraging, however, is that all three REERs in Figure 5.8, constructed with these two deflators, move closely with each other along with the NEER of the broader group of countries, which remains higher than all three. This implies that any one of these three REERs can perform well as a proxy index of the international competitiveness of the Euro Area.

In Figure 5.8, the time plots of three different REERs of the euro, along with two euro NEERs, are presented.

Figure 5.8

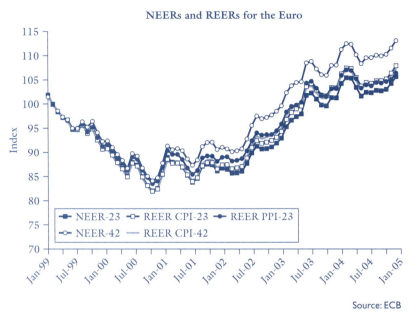

Source: ECB

The time plots of the three REERs and the two NEERs of the euro are consistent with previous graphs of the NEER and REER of the euro that were presented in Figures 5 and 6, based on the IMF NEER and REER data. This finding can be reassuring in that the path of the dollar-euro exchange rate indicates a depreciation of the euro during the first two years, a leveling off during the third year, and an appreciation during the last two years.

## SUMMARY

In this chapter, the nominal US dollar-euro exchange rate ($NE_{\$/\text{€}}$) was examined beginning with its introduction in the Euro Area countries on January 4, 1999. The euro's performance, in relation to other economically important countries' currencies, was studied by observing and analyzing the time plots of the nominal bilateral exchange rates with respect to other countries' currencies. Nominal bilateral exchange rates, however, do not explicitly reflect all the changes in the relative prices between two countries.

For a non-Euro Area firm such as an American importing company, or an American tourist visiting the Euro Area countries, the true cost of buying Euro Area goods or visiting the Euro Area countries can be determined only by knowing the real exchange rate. The real exchange rate captures changes in the relative prices of the two countries. For this purpose, the $RE_{\$/€}$ was constructed and graphed as a time plot.

The overall performance of a currency vis-à-vis the currencies of its trading partners is evaluated by examining the nominal trade-weighted exchange rate or NEERs. The IMF, the Bank of England, the European Central Bank (ECB), and other central banks construct NEERs for a number of important currencies. The NEER time plots of the euro, the US dollar, the UK pound sterling, the Japanese yen, and the Swiss franc were presented and analyzed in the chapter.

To determine the international competitiveness of a country, one must study the REER or real trade-weighted exchange rate. This takes into consideration not only the NEERs of the trading partner countries but also the changes in its prices in relation to partner countries. The REERs of the euro and four major world currencies were constructed and presented graphically in this chapter.

## Essay Questions

1. Describe the performance of the nominal euro exchange rate with respect to some major world currencies, such as the US dollar, the UK pound, and the Japanese yen. Can one observe any common pattern among the euro exchange rates of these currencies or any other currencies? If yes, explain any such pattern(s).

2. Economists are often interested in assessing the performance of a country's currency in relation to a group of trading partner currencies. For this purpose, they construct the nominal trade-weighted or NEERs. Five such NEERs are discussed and presented graphically in this chapter for the euro, the pound sterling, the Japanese yen, the Swiss franc, and the US dollar. Discuss the NEERs of these five currencies, particularly of the US dollar and the euro. How are the NEERs constructed? Do you think the NEERs can be useful?

3. What is the difference between the nominal and the real exchange rate? Which of the two exchange rates is more useful and why? Write out the formula for the dollars per euro real exchange rate. Under what economic conditions will the real exchange rate be particularly useful?

4. Explain how the real trade-weighted exchange rates or REERs are constructed. How are the REERs different from the NEERs? What is the most important information that one can derive from the REERs? In Figure 5.6, the REERs of five currencies

were depicted. What is the meaning of the REER graphs? What can you say about the euro, US dollar, and Japanese yen REERs by observing their corresponding time plots?

5. The ECB constructs three different nominal trade-weighted euro exchange rates or NEERs. The ECB constructs REERs based on the three NEERs. Explain how the NEERs and REERs are constructed. Explain the purpose and usefulness of the NEERs and REERs. What do the graphs of the euro NEERs and REERs (see Figure 5.8) reveal about the euro?

chapter 6

# The Exchange Rate Determination of the Euro

## Introduction

What determines a currency's foreign exchange rate? Several economic theories have been developed to address this issue. A few of these theories pertain to the short-run; others focus on the long-run. Nothing is more difficult in economics than explaining and accurately forecasting exchange rates. Currency speculators often expose the financial capital of their firms to great risk when they invest heavily in the foreign exchange market.

It is difficult, if not impossible, for someone to forecast and profit in the foreign exchange market by purchasing only "winners," in other words, those currencies that end up appreciating.[1] However, one can easily gain knowledge and insight into the foreign exchange market. This can be accomplished by studying all the exchange rate theories and identifying the crucial factors responsible for the movement and determination of exchange rates. Since exchange rate determination is an important topic in economics, many researchers have studied this area, developed theories, and tested the validity of these theories. The findings of the main empirical results of these theories will be reported in this and the next chapter. These two chapters will investigate if the historical performance of the euro exchange rates in relation to the dollar and other currencies can be explained by any existing exchange rate theories.

Exchange rates are difficult to understand because they are affected by many variables. Exchange rates, for example, are influenced by numerous microeconomic decisions. These decisions can involve individuals who may have chosen to visit a foreign country or a business firm that has decided to invest, buy, or sell commodities and services to or from another country. Similarly, financial investors who decide to invest in a foreign country by purchasing financial assets affect exchange rates.

A country's macroeconomic policies influence exchange rates. When governments formulate and exercise monetary and fiscal policies, they affect price levels, national deficits, national debts, interest rates, and the countries' growth rates. Changes in these variables almost always have an impact on a country's foreign exchange rate. A few countries deliberately pursue active foreign exchange rate policies for the purpose of promoting exports and discouraging imports. These countries intervene through their treasury departments, their central banks, or both to alter and direct the foreign exchange rate by selling their own currency and buying other foreign currencies. Occasionally, a number of countries join forces to affect the foreign exchange rate of a certain currency. They achieve this by massively intervening in the foreign exchange markets by buying or selling large amounts of foreign currencies.

In this analysis, the initial two year depreciation of the euro against the US dollar will first be addressed. This will be followed by a discussion of the appreciation of the euro that occurred after approximately one year of relative stability. A few economists have suggested that the introductory dollar-euro nominal exchange rate ($NE_{\$/€}$), agreed upon by the Euro Area (Eurozone) countries, was much higher than what they perceived to be its long-run equilibrium value. It was inevitable, therefore, that the euro would eventually depreciate. This interpretation is no longer supported since, after six years, the euro has appreciated beyond its initial introductory value.

Another explanation for the continuous depreciation of the euro versus the US dollar and other currencies was an extreme view that the euro had no chance for survival as a currency (Feldstein, 1997). The reason behind this pessimistic view was that the euro became the legal currency of 12 independent states that did not form an Optimum Currency Area (OCA). Other authors also believed that the unprecedented project of the euro had an uncertain future and was doomed for failure. Such a view of the euro is no longer convincing after the euro's appreciation, beginning in 2002, and its success as a major world currency with the US dollar.

Not all candidate EU member countries constituted an OCA prior to joining the EMU; however, all present EMU members adhered to strict monetary and fiscal discipline to meet the Maastricht convergence criteria. As a result, all Euro Area countries attained price stability and adopted the appropriate policies to become a more integrated region.

## Economic and Political Developments

What are the primary economic variables affecting foreign exchange rates? Since a currency is a claim on the goods and services produced by a country, it becomes plausible that the output (GDP) of this country is one of the most important variables. Table 6.1 presents data of

Table 6.1

| Basic Statistics on the Euro Area, US, and Japan (2003) | | | |
|---|---|---|---|
| | **Euro Area** | **US** | **Japan** |
| **Population (in millions)** | 307.8 | 291.1 | 127.4 |
| **GDP per capita in € (thousands, PPP)** | €23.5 | €34.1 | €25.1 |
| **GDP (share of world GDP)** | 15% | 21.1% | 7.1% |
| | | | Source: ECB |

some basic economic statistics for the Euro Area, the US, and Japan, the three largest world market economies. The relative economic performance of a country in comparison to its trading partners is more important than the absolute economic performance in affecting the foreign exchange rate. Therefore, one should compare the economic performance of the Euro Area economy with the trading partner economies to study the euro exchange rate in relation to the currencies of these countries.

According to Table 6.1, the Euro Area's population is larger than the populations of Japan and the US. The Euro Area's per capita GDP is almost the same as that of Japan but is lower than that of the US. The Euro Area produces 15 percent of the world's output (GDP). This percentage is more than double Japan's share of the world GDP but smaller than the US's share, which produces more than one fifth of the world's output. The above statistics strongly support the position that the euro is a currency of an economically vital and relatively wealthy group of countries.

With the enlargement of the EU, which took place on May 1, 2004, some new EU member countries will seek EMU membership and will adopt the euro. In this case, the Euro Area's population and GDP share of the world output will increase. The per capita GDP will decrease since these countries are poorer than the present members.

The wealth and national income composition of the world economy will change for many reasons. One such reason is that at least a few emerging economies on the global economic scene will become more important. For example, China and India attained high growth rates after 1999 and have affected the international economy in many ways. The increased importance of these countries and other emerging economies such as Brazil and Russia, to mention a few, will probably continue. Such political and economic developments will change the world economy and will affect the euro.

Figure 6.1

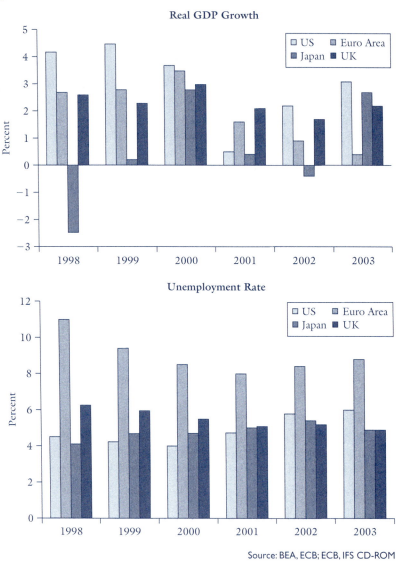

Source: BEA, ECB; ECB, IFS CD-ROM

Exchange rates are influenced by the relative economic performance of countries. In Figure 6.1, two crucial macroeconomic indicators, the real GDP growth and the unemployment rates of the US, the Euro Area, Japan, and the UK, are presented as bar charts. In a comparison of the real GDP growth and the unemployment rates, the US outperformed the Euro Area, Japan, and the UK during 1999 and 2000 (the first two years of the EMU). In these first two years, the euro depreciated against the US dollar and the other currencies.

During 1990–2000, the US economy attained high real GDP and labor productivity growth rates due to unparalleled innovation in information technology that made in-roads in all sectors of the US and the world economy. The GDP growth rate in the UK was lower than the Euro Area GDP growth rate during the first two years of the euro (1999 and 2000) but exceeded the Euro Area real GDP growth every year after 2001. The rate of Japan's real GDP growth was the lowest during 1998–2002, but in 2003, it exceeded the rate of growth of the Euro Area and the UK but not the US.

US economic expansion in 1998–2000 resulted in low unemployment rates. In 2000, for example, the US unemployment rate reached 4 percent, a rate less than half the unemployment rate of the Euro Area. Most Euro Area countries, in contrast to the US, had experienced high unemployment rates for many years prior to the formation of the EMU, but these rates steadily declined after 1999. Starting in 2001, the US and the Euro Area unemployment rates began increasing. The UK reduced its unemployment rate by two percentage points during 1999–2003. During the first six years, the euro depreciated and then appreciated against the UK pound sterling. Based on this information, one cannot make a clear association between indicators of economic performance of countries and the exchange rates.

US real GDP growth, during 1990–2000, a time period that overlaps with the first two years of the euro, induced increases in US imports and caused large US current account (CA) deficits. This relation should have caused depreciation of the dollar and appreciation of the euro. The US expansion should have contributed to the appreciation of the euro against the dollar. However, the relatively higher US growth rates attracted foreign capital inflows to the US to take advantage of the higher rates of return. Foreigners were eager to invest in a growing US economy, assuming the US currency would remain stable. In 1999 and 2000, the capital inflows into the US affected the determination of the value of the euro by more than the increased US import demand. In 2001, the US grew at a lower rate than the GDP growth rate of the UK and the Euro Area. After 2001, the US experienced a higher growth rate than the Euro Area, the UK, and Japan, but unprecedented events affected the US and the world economy and, subsequently, the dollar-euro exchange rate.

The supply and demand model of euros helps explain the determination of the foreign exchange ($NE_{\$/€}$). This is demonstrated in a hypothetical example in Figures 6.2a, 6.2b, and 6.2c for the daily dollar-euro market.

# The Foreign Exchange Market Model of Supply and Demand

## The Demand for Euros

The supply and demand model of exchange rate determination is presented here with a hypothetical example regarding the euro-dollar market.[2]

On the horizontal axis, the quantity demanded of euros is measured; on the vertical axis, the foreign exchange price expressed in dollars per euro is measured. The line labeled $D_\epsilon$ is the demand for euros by Americans or by anyone else who demands euros and is willing to pay with dollars. American residents and US firms, for example, demand euros since they are interested in buying Euro Area goods and services. Some Americans demand euros to visit Euro Area countries, and others demand euros to invest in financial and real assets in the Euro Area. The higher the price of the euro in terms of dollars, the more expensive any purchase from the Euro Area becomes for Americans, and, therefore, they will demand fewer euros.

Assume that the dollar-euro exchange rate is equal to $1, corresponding to Point E of the demand curve. According to Figure 6.2a, at this point €500 billion are demanded. If the price of the euro rises to $1.15, then only €300 billion will be demanded, as there will be a movement from Point E to Point A along the demand curve for euros. Similarly, if the price of the euro declines from $1.00 to $0.85, then US residents and firms will demand €700 billion, as there will be a

Figure 6.2a    Demand for Foreign Exchange (euros)

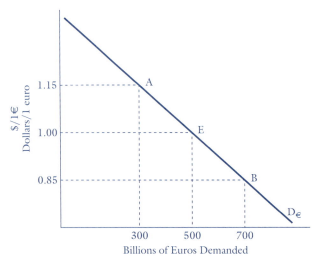

movement from Point E to Point B along the demand curve for euros. According to the hypothetical example of Figure 6.2a, a negative relationship exists between the price of the foreign exchange (the price of the euro) and the quantity demanded of the foreign exchange (the quantity demanded of euros). Such a negative relationship is not a unique and special case for this particular example but is one application of a well-established economic relation that economists refer to as the law of demand.[3]

The law of demand applies to the demand for the foreign exchange. Demand curves for commodities shift for certain reasons known as shift factors.[4] Similarly, the demand curve for foreign exchange can shift. If, for some reason other than the change in the price of the exchange rate, US firms and residents decide to demand more euros, then the demand curve for euros will shift to the right (increase) but will shift to the left (decrease) if US firms and residents choose to demand fewer euros. The US demand for foreign exchange (euros) is affected by different factors. Some of the most common shift factors of the demand for foreign exchange are changes in the domestic income, changes in the relative price levels of the two countries, and more importantly, changes in the domestic and foreign interest rates.

A change in US real GDP or real national income will induce changes in import demand for goods and services from the Euro Area countries and, as a result, will affect the demand for euros. Similarly, a change in the Euro Area interest rates is another shift factor of the demand for euros by US firms and residents. Higher Euro Area interest rates will induce US capital outflow to the Euro Area countries and an increase in the US demand curve for euros. Reduction of Euro Area interest rates will cause a reduction in the demand curve for euros since Americans will not be interested in investing in the Euro Area countries.

In Figure 6.2b, the supply of euros is drawn on a graph with the price of the euro on the vertical axis and the quantity supplied of euros on the horizontal axis. Euro Area residents and firms supply euros in exchange for dollars to be able to carry out their purchase from the US. Thus, the supply of euros arises because of the demand for dollars by the Euro Area residents and firms.

## The Supply of Euros

When the price of the euro is equal to $1, corresponding to Point E of the supply curve for euros, €500 billion are supplied by Euro Area residents and firms. An increase in the price of the euro to $1.15 induces Euro Area residents and firms to supply €800 billion, which is a movement from Point E to Point A' along the supply curve for euros. Why did the quantity supplied of euros increase? An increase in the price of

Figure 6.2b   Supply for Foreign Exchange (euros)

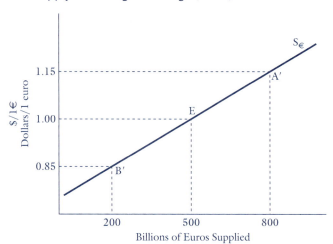

the euro versus the dollar makes all purchases of goods, services, and assets priced in dollars a better deal for Euro Area firms and residents. A rise in the price of the euro amounts to the same thing as a reduction in the dollar prices of the US goods, services, and assets. Euro Area firms and businesses will demand more dollar-priced goods and services. Thus, they will supply more euros for dollars. Similarly, if the price of the euro declines from $1.00 to $0.85, only €200 billion will be supplied, denoting a movement along the supply curve from Point E to Point B'. This will happen because a reduction in the price of a euro makes all US goods, services, and assets more expensive. Therefore, fewer amounts of each will be demanded. Consequently, Euro Area firms and residents will supply a smaller amount of euros.

The discussion above shows that the supply of euros will slope upward, implying a positive relation between the price of the euro and the amount of the euros supplied. This is a familiar economic relation, similar to the supply curve for any commodity. The supply of euros will shift to the right (increase) or shift to the left (decrease) if certain variables change, these variables are known as shift factors.[5] The supply of euros arises because Euro Area businesses and individuals demand US goods, services, and financial assets. To complete these transactions, the Euro Area firms and residents supply euros to purchase dollars. The greater the amount of imports, services, and assets purchased from the US by the Euro Area countries, the larger the increase in the supply of euros.

## Demand and Supply Together

In Figure 6.2c, the demand and supply curves for euros are presented in the same graph with the euro exchange rate on the vertical axis and the quantity demanded and quantity supplied of euros on the

Figure 6.2c   Supply and Demand for Foreign Exchange (euros)

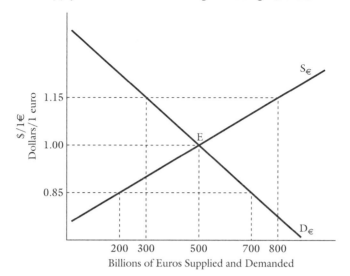

Billions of Euros Supplied and Demanded

horizontal axis. The graph indicates the quantities demanded and supplied of euros at different euro prices. For example, at the highest price
of the euro ($1.15) as shown in the graph, the quantity supplied is
€800 billion, but the quantity demanded is only €300 billion. At this
high euro price in terms of US dollars, there is an excess supply or surplus of euros in the market equal to the amount of €500 billion
(€800 − €300). This excess supply of euros in the market will put pressure on the price of the euro and the euro will start depreciating against
the dollar. As long as a surplus exists in the euro market, the euro will
continue depreciating.

The depreciation of the euro versus the dollar will stop when the
price of the euro equals one dollar. At this price of the euro, the quantity demanded of euros equals the quantity supplied. Point E is the
intersection of the supply and demand and is called the market equilibrium point. The price of one dollar per euro is referred to as the equilibrium price. This is the price of the euro that clears the market. At equilibrium, the quantity demanded of euros equals the quantity supplied,
as can be seen in Figure 6.2c where both are equal to €500 billion.
Lastly, at the price of $0.85 per euro, the quantity demanded of euros
exceeds quantity supplied by €500 billion (€700 − €200). At this relatively low euro price, an excess demand or shortage of euros exists.
Therefore, market forces will bid up the price of the euro versus the
dollar and the euro will keep appreciating as long as a shortage remains.
The market will reach equilibrium at point E where the price will be
one dollar per euro and the amount of the euros and dollars traded will
be both equal to 500.

## An Application of the Supply and Demand Model for Euros: The US Experience (1999–2004)

The supply and demand model of the euro exchange rate determination will be utilized to understand and explain the foreign exchange price of the euro in relation to the dollar. The initial supply and demand curves intersecting at equilibrium point $E_0$ are $S_€$ and $D_€$, respectively, and the equilibrium price and quantity of the foreign exchange are $€_0$ and $q_0^€$. The US has attained phenomenal growth rates during 1990–2000. Higher real US incomes and growth rates than the rest of the world induced increases of US imports. US imports from the newly established Euro Area countries have increased. To pay for its imports, the US needed to acquire euros. Therefore, the US firms and residents needed to exchange their dollars for euros. In terms of the supply and demand model, this meant that during the first two years of the euro in 1999 and 2000, the US demand for euros increased substantially. This is denoted in Figure 6.3, with an increase or a shift out in demand for euros to the right from $D_€$ to $D_€^I$.

If nothing else had occurred, then the increased demand for the euros would have resulted in a new equilibrium, $E_1$, with a higher equilibrium price of the euro, $€_1$, versus the dollar, and larger equilibrium amount of euros traded equal to $q_1^€$. However, this was not the only thing that had happened, thus, $E_1$ was not the final equilibrium point toward the end of 2000.

Figure 6.3   Supply and Demand for Foreign Exchange (euros)

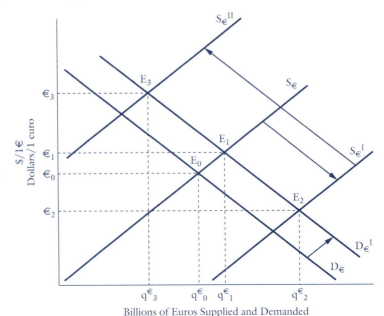

Billions of Euros Supplied and Demanded

During the 1990–2000 information technology revolution, the growing US economy had attracted vast amounts of foreign capital because the rates of return in the US were much higher than elsewhere in the world. The Euro Area businesses and residents, attracted by higher US rates of return, invested in the US. To carry out their US investment transactions, Euro Area firms and individuals needed to exchange their euros for dollars in the foreign exchange market. In terms of Figure 6.3, this is interpreted as an increase in the supply of euros or a shift to the right to $S_\epsilon^1$. The increase of the supply of euros was large and induced a euro depreciation below the euro's initial value €$_0$, corresponding to equilibrium point $E_0$. The lower value of the euro was equal to €$_2$ and the amount of euros traded at this new equilibrium is equal to $q_2^\epsilon$. This is an explanation for the euro's depreciation in 1999 and 2000.

In 2001, the US experienced a recession caused by three unprecedented events that generated lasting negative effects and had an impact on the US dollar. First, came a abrupt drop in stock market prices. The stock market crash begun in July of 2000 with the collapse of the NASDAQ stock exchange that lists shares of the new information technology (IT) companies. Some economic analysts had predicted this contraction since, by that time, most US companies had overinvested in IT and had no other option but to cut additional investments.

The second event that affected the US economy was a terrorist attack on September 11, 2001, when the two World Trade Towers in New York City and the US Pentagon were hit by three hijacked commercial jetplanes. These attacks destroyed both World Trade Towers. This US national tragedy claimed the lives of about 3,000 people, and caused substantial property damage. The horrific terrorist attacks on civilians and the loss of so many lives irrevocably changed the US, its economy, and the world. After the September 11 national tragedy, US security measures increased to unprecedented levels. Such security measures raised the costs of production and slowed down air travel and product delivery. The economic and political environment of the country also changed significantly. Businesses reduced investment and consumers reduced consumption. As a bold reaction to September 11, the US went to war in Afghanistan and Iraq. These two wars cost the US billions of dollars while keeping the US Army, the Congress, and the president preoccupied.

The third factor that negatively affected the US economy was a number of corporate embezzlements and financial scandals involving once reputable corporations, such as Enron, WorldCom, and Arthur Anderson. Such scandals left many workers and shareholders financially destroyed as their lifetime savings dissipated. The corporate scandals caused more damage by undermining the people's trust in the American economic system. These three factors negatively affected the dollar since all three factors influenced the perception of Americans and foreigners regarding the strength of the US economy.

Foreign investors, as a result, lost some confidence in the US dollar. Euro Area businesses and individuals revealed a hesitancy to invest in the US, a long-time favorite destination for their investment. In the meantime, to fight the recession, the US Federal Reserve (the Fed) reduced the federal funds rate to a 41-year low, equal to 1 percent and, thus, succeeded in driving down all other US interest rates. A reduction in the rate of return in the US reversed the direction of some capital flows from the US to the Euro Area. In terms of Figure 6.3, this means the supply of euros was reduced (shifted left) to $S_\epsilon^{II}$. This drastic reduction of the euro supply triggered a rapid appreciation of the euro as was discussed in Chapter 5. In Figure 6.3, the new equilibrium $E_3$ is shown as the price of the euro increased to $\epsilon_3$, indicating an appreciation of the euro versus the dollar above its introductory value $\epsilon_0$ of January 4, 1999. The new equilibrium amount of euros traded is equal to $q_3^\epsilon$.

Since the US real national income had declined, US imports from the Euro Area countries should have also declined. This implies that the demand for euros must have declined (shifted to the left) and, thus, should have triggered some appreciation of the dollar. This depreciation of the euro, however, was not large enough to drive its value below its January 4, 1999, introductory value. In terms of the graph, the new euro exchange rate, after the US income decline, should have settled below $\epsilon_3$ but above $\epsilon_0$. For the purpose of not crowding the graph, this new equilibrium is not shown in Figure 6.3.

The disproportional effects of income and interest rate changes on the euro exchange rate discussed in this section can be supported by the fact that only about 20 percent of the volume of all transactions of the foreign exchange market is associated with the financing of international trade. The rest of it is related to capital flows for financial investments between countries. Capital outflows (inflows) between countries are mainly responding to real rates of return in investments and real interest rate differentials. It is concluded that real interest rates play the most important role in the determination of exchange rates. At least this was the dollar-euro experience since January 4, 1999.

# Current Account (CA)

## Introduction

A country's currency is demanded and held for various reasons by foreign individuals, firms, and governments. One reason that a foreign currency is demanded by foreign entities is to facilitate international trade. For example, if a US company decides to import goods from a

Euro Area firm, then the American firm must first secure the necessary amount of euros to pay for the imports from the Euro Area. One reason that economic relations among nations differ from domestic economic relations in trade and finance is the existence of different national currencies. The price of the foreign exchange affects each country's balance of payments accounts. The price of the foreign exchange is, however, affected by developments in a country's national and international accounts. For this reason, one must have a clear understanding of the national accounts and the balance of payments accounts that may play a crucial role in affecting the determination of the price of the foreign exchange.

## A Graphical Presentation of the Balance of Payment Accounts

Figure 6.4 below shows graphically the two most broad accounts of the balance of payments for the Euro Area and for three of the world's most economically important countries: the US, Japan, and China. The two broad accounts of the balance of payments depicted in Figure 6.4 are the CA and the financial account (FA). Since the Euro Area, along with the other three countries, constitute a large part of the world economy, many international economic issues can be analyzed and discussed by observing the balance of payments accounts presented in Figure 6.4.[6] Not surprisingly, these international statistics provide explanations for the determination of the euro exchange rates.

Before analyzing the information presented in Figure 6.4, let us first define the two economic variables depicted in the graphs. The CA includes the balance of goods and services of a country with the rest of the world. Specifically, when a country sells goods and services to the rest of the world, it generates an income flow equal to the value of goods and services sold. Similarly, the value of goods and services that a country buys from foreign countries results in payments by the country to the rest of the world. The difference between the payments received minus the payments made to the rest of the world is known as the balance on goods and services or the trade balance. If the net income received from abroad, i.e., income received by US factors of production abroad minus income paid to foreign factors of production employed in the US, is added to the balance of goods and services, this results in the balance of goods, services, and income.[7] By adding net unilateral transfers to this sum, we get the balance of the CA.

When a country's trade balance is positive, a country receives net income flows from the rest of the world. For this reason, surpluses in the trade balance were looked upon favorably in the distant past. In the 17th and 18th century, a school of economic thought known as

Figure 6.4   Balance of Payments Accounts

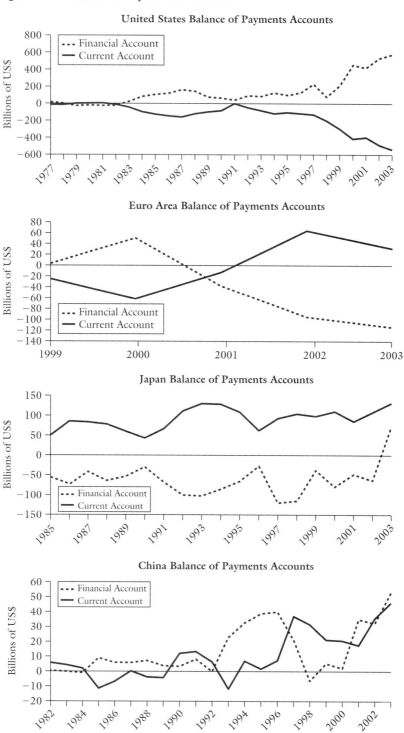

"mercantilism" advocated international trade only to the extent that it resulted in trade surpluses. According to mercantilists, trade surpluses enable a country to earn gold and silver and, consequently, enhance the country's wealth. This perception of international trade is self-defeating since all countries cannot simultaneously attain trade surpluses.

Presently, trade deficits are not necessarily considered undesirable provided they do not become too large and persistent, causing unsustainable foreign indebtedness to a country. The CA includes other sub-accounts in addition to the trade balance of goods and services, as was pointed out previously. Therefore, it is important when addressing issues regarding the CA that one considers all the components of the CA and not only the trade balance.

A large and increasing CA deficit has been experienced by the US since 1999, as can be seen in Figure 6.4 and in the appendix of this chapter. The CA, the FA, and other international sub-accounts are presented graphically for the US, the Euro Area, Japan, and China in the appendix of this chapter. Starting in the late 1990s, the CA deficit of the US began rising, reaching high levels in terms of absolute dollars and as a percent of US GDP. In 2003, the US CA deficit reached the amount of $542 billion, or approximately 5 percent of GDP (see Figure 6.4). In 2004, the CA increased to a record of $617 billion, or 5.3 percent of GDP. Both Japan and China experienced CA surpluses almost every year since the 1980s.

The Euro Area began with a negative CA balance in 1999, which turned positive after 2001 and kept increasing until 2002 when it began declining, but remained positive.

The persistent and growing deficit of the US CA has become a problem for the US economy, especially when combined with a large and growing government budget deficit.[8] As a result, the US CA deficit has affected the dollar-euro exchange rate, a concern that the Euro Area representatives have often raised especially since 2003. Japan and China experienced persistent CA surpluses that they do not perceive as problems, but rather as beneficial to their economies since CA surpluses induce economic growth in these countries. Japan and China earned large amounts of dollars from their exports to the US and to other countries. During the first ten months of 2004, the Euro Area, according to Eurostat, recorded a €41 billion trade deficit with China. The Euro Area, however, incurred trade surpluses with the US and UK of €50.3 billion and €53.2 billion, respectively. Despite the euro appreciation, the Euro Area recorded overall trade balance and CA surpluses of $94.7 billion and $47.3 billion from October 2003 to October 2004. Germany maintained its position as the leading exporter country of the world in 2004.

# Financial Account (FA)

The FA includes changes in a country's net assets abroad and changes in foreign assets in the country. The financial account is mainly divided into two principal sub-accounts: foreign direct investment (FDI) and portfolio investment (PI).[9]

For many countries, the FA is almost the mirror image of the CA. The FA indicates the sources of financing the CA. For example, in the US, the CA is negative while its FA is positive. This means that foreigners bought more financial and real assets in the US with their earned dollars than the financial and real assets purchased by US citizens, businesses, and the US government abroad. In the US, the two accounts move in opposite directions, creating a difficult situation since further growth of the US CA requires an increase in the FA. An increase in the FA implies that foreigners are willing to invest their earned dollars back in the US.

Japan's position is opposite to the US position (up to 2002). Japan has persistently generated large CA surpluses and negative but smaller FA deficits; therefore, it has been buying assets in the US with the earned dollars from the CA surpluses. An exception was the year 2003 when the Japanese FA turned positive. The Euro Area differs from Japan and the US because the CA and FA are a mirror image of one another and because they alternate from positive to negative, and vice versa, while remaining symmetric. China's situation is unique since its CA and FA are increasing and remaining positive after 1999. It makes sense for China's CA to be positive and rising, but it is not obvious why China's FA is positive and rising. Such a phenomenon is rare, but it has been observed in the past in other countries. In the case of China, this phenomenon can be explained by examining the two major components of its FA in Figure 6.5.

In Figure 6.5, the FA accounts of the US, the Euro Area, Japan, and China are broken up into their two main components: the FDI and the PI. FDI refers to purchases of foreign production facilities, such as factories, warehouses, and real estate. PI refers to purchases and acquisitions of foreign financial assets, such as bonds, stocks, and loans. In Figure 6.5, it can be seen that the US, starting in 1993, has been receiving increasing amounts of net PI. The US, however, has recorded smaller amounts of fluctuating net FDI that were positive and negative during the last two decades but started declining after 2000 and turned negative in 2002.

In the Euro Area, FDI is negative. This means that the Euro Area countries were purchasing production facilities abroad. Though PI started negative in the Euro Area, it turned positive in 2001. FDI and PI were each less than $50 billion in 2003.

For Japan, net FDI and PI were mostly negative. This means that Japan was investing in physical assets such as factories and other

Figure 6.5

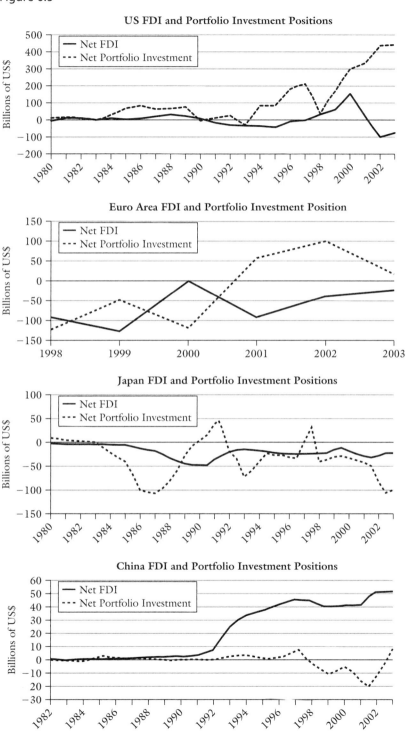

Source: IFS CD-ROM

production facilities abroad. The Japanese FDI was low but stable. On the contrary, the PI was volatile and mostly negative, meaning the Japanese were significant buyers of foreign financial assets.

China's FDI is positive and growing. This can be explained by the many foreign companies that have found China to be an attractive country to locate their production facilities. The main reason for this is that many foreign companies perceive new investment opportunities in China, a vast new market of 1.3 billion people with an emerging economy. Foreign businesses have perceived profitable opportunities to produce in China with a low labor cost and export to the world market. Net PI, however, was low and negative, which means the Chinese were not eager to invest much abroad. The sum of the Chinese FDI and PI is positive, thus causing a puzzle of an overall positive balance of payments. This puzzle is resolved if we consider the accumulation of China's official reserves that have risen $116.8 billion in 2003 and by $206.7 billion in 2004 to reach a total of $609 billion at the end of 2004.[10]

Figure 6.6 portrays the CA and the net international investment as a percent of GDP for the US and the Euro Area. The US CA deficit as a percentage of GDP (right axis) has reached close to 5 percent in 2003 and, in 2004, increased to 5.3 percent. This is an uncomfortable percentage that the US economy is unlikely to sustain for a long period. Studies have pointed out that lower CA to GDP deficits, even as low as 4.2 percent, were empirically found to be too large and a reason for concern (Mann 1999). Persistent US CA deficits have resulted in large long-term indebtedness of the US to foreign countries as is measured by the net US international investment (left axis), which is negative and has reached over 25 percent of the US GDP. In contrast to the US, the Euro Area countries have a small CA surplus, approximately 1 percent of the GDP and a small but negative net international investment of −10 percent of the GDP in 2003.

The growing CA deficit led the US to be dependent on the willingness of foreign countries to provide the US with "loans" to finance the CA deficits. During 2003 and 2004, foreign investors chose, for the first time, to reduce investments by cutting down purchases of US stocks and bonds. Such a decline in the capital inflow to the US was the result of perceived weaknesses in the US economy. Furthermore, the persistent US trade deficits, which had to be financed and required continuous capital inflows to the US, were perceived as an additional weakness.

For a long time, the Japanese government stood steadfast and determined not to let the yen appreciate versus the US dollar. This was a policy that Japan followed to promote its export sector. The Bank of Japan pursued this aggressive policy by intervening in the foreign exchange market and buying dollars. In the year 2003 alone, the Bank of Japan bought $278 billion and continued to intervene in the foreign

Figure 6.6

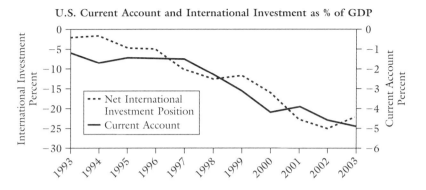

U.S. Current Account and International Investment as % of GDP

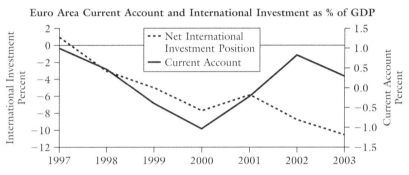

Euro Area Current Account and International Investment as % of GDP

Source: BEA, ECB, IFS CD-ROM

exchange market. It purchased $150 billion in the first quarter of 2004. However, in April 2004, Japanese officials announced their decision to let the yen appreciate, and since then, the Bank of Japan has not interfered in the foreign exchange market by buying dollars. Such a shift in policy led to an appreciation of the yen, but nobody knows Japan's future exchange rate policy position.

The Chinese peg their currency to the US dollar. As a result, the US cannot reduce the CA deficit with China, particularly when the yuan is kept undervalued. Trade imbalances of the US with Japan and China have not been corrected. The only source of adjustment has come from the depreciation of the dollar versus the euro. Economists believe the euro absorbed most of the shock while the Asian currencies, with the exception of the yen, maintained their rigidity. This situation led to the appreciation of the euro above its long-run equilibrium value. To resolve the US trade imbalance with Japan and China, these two countries, along with other Asian countries, will have to adopt and maintain permanent flexible exchange rate policies. If this happens, it will contribute to the stabilization of the dollar-euro exchange rate. A different way that the CA imbalance may be corrected is when Asian countries decide that they cannot tolerate further losses on their accumulated dollars. This will force them to sell a massive amount of dollars, inducing a sharp dollar depreciation. As a result of the sharp dollar depreciation, the US CA will improve but the US economy will experience a prolonged recession. A more desirable alternative will be for a gradual correction (soft landing) without abrupt changes in foreign US dollar holdings. This might have already begun as the Financial Times reported in a front page article, that many central banks have started shifting some of their reserves from dollar denominated US assets to assets held in euros (see Financial Times, January 25, 2005).

## Sources of Current Account Imbalances

A popular belief exists that CA imbalances are caused mainly by differences in the international competitiveness of countries. Current account imbalances, however, can be caused by other factors. For example, CA imbalances can be caused by certain developments in the national income accounts of countries. This can be demonstrated by analyzing the national income accounts of a country starting from the macroeconomic identity of a closed economy:

$$Y = C + I + G$$

$Y$ = national output or national income

$C$ = private consumption

$I$ = gross private investment

$G$ = government expenditures

$T$ = taxes

$C + I + G$ is the domestic national demand, indicating the amount of national output demanded by consumers, businesses, and the government, which is referred to by economists as absorption. If national output ($Y$) is greater than domestic demand, $Y > C + I + G$, then the country generates a surplus. The surplus can be lent abroad. Such an imbalance can arise under two different situations. The first situation occurs when a country's private saving ($S$) exceeds domestic investment ($I$), $S > I$, and the country's government budget is in balance ($G = T$). The second situation arises when the government's budget is in surplus ($T > G$) and private saving is equal to private investment ($I = S$). In this situation, the country generates a surplus that it can lend to other countries. A country can generate a surplus in both accounts and, thus, generate private and public saving.

If total domestic demand exceeds national output, $Y < C + I + G$, then the entire country spends more than it produces. The only way this can happen is for the country to develop a CA deficit. This implies that the country is dissaving by borrowing from abroad. In other words, the accumulation of CA surpluses allows a country to become a creditor nation to other countries while CA deficits transform a country to a debtor nation.

Every year, each country can generate a certain amount of gross saving that consists of two components: the private saving and public saving. Private saving is transformed into private investment with the aid of financial intermediary institutions such as banks. Entrepreneurs who undertake private investment projects transform households' private saving into equipment, machinery, and factories, therefore, enhancing the ability of a country to produce goods and services and, thus, increasing the country's wealth.

Government surpluses can be allocated to the private sector to finance a situation in which private investment demand exceeds private saving. In general, if total saving, private and public, exceeds private investment and government expenditures, $S + T > I + G$, then the country generates excess saving that can be lent out to foreign countries resulting in a CA surplus. A sequence of annual CA surpluses will lead the country to a net creditor position and allow it to build up its ownership of assets abroad and, thus, increase its future income receipts from abroad.

The opposite will occur if a country's private investment and government expenditures exceed the sum of private saving and taxes, $I + G > S + T$. In this situation, the country must borrow from abroad by running a CA deficit to finance its total expenditures. A country's sustained CA deficits will increase the indebtedness to other countries. As a result, the country will be obligated to remit annual income payments to other countries that have purchased some of its real and financial assets.

Identity (1) below states that CA imbalances are the result of internal imbalances in the domestic economy. If a country experiences CA deficits as the US has, this is a result of low saving in relation to investment and/or government budget deficits. Similarly, CA surpluses in a country are the result of surpluses in the government budget and/or excess of private saving over private investment.

Each country must satisfy the following identity:

$$(S - I) \quad + \quad (T - G) \quad = \quad CA \quad\quad (1)$$

| Private Saving (dissaving) | Public Saving (dissaving) | Current Account Surplus (deficit) | |
|---|---|---|---|

As was mentioned, the common belief that surpluses are beneficial and deficits are detrimental to an economy generally is incorrect. Persistent CA deficits, however, are criticized because they can lead a country into heavy indebtedness, requiring continuous income payments to foreign countries. Economists assess the effects of CA deficits according to how a CA deficit country allocates the borrowed funds. If borrowed funds are invested in capital plant and equipment or public infrastructure, then such deficits are expected to benefit the country. However, if borrowed funds are used for private or public consumption, such deficits will burden future generations and reduce the country's future standard of living.

## Saving and Investment Comparisons

Comparison of private saving investment balances of the US, the European Union (EU), and Japan, as a percentage of GDP in Figure 6.7, reveals substantial differences.[11] For example, investment in the US was higher than saving for the years 1999–2002. In 2003, saving and investment were almost equal.

The EU and Japan generated higher saving rates than the US. Unlike the situation in the US, saving in the EU and Japan exceeded investment. It is evident from Figure 6.7 that though the EU and Japan are net savers in the private economy, the US was dissaving most of the years. During the last three years, the US has been closing the gap between saving and investment. This can be a welcome structural change for the US economy. An increase in the US saving rate could rectify international imbalances, but it is difficult for government policy to influence private saving.

Raising taxes for the purpose of generating public saving will have the same positive effect of reducing CA deficits. Raising taxes is, however, an unpopular policy many politicians avoid. Equally unpopular are reductions in government expenditures (G) and the adoption of policies that reduce investment. Government expenditures and investment reductions will depress national income. It is, therefore, concluded that the reduction of CA deficits through the adoption of recession promoting policies is unpopular. For a long time, the IMF and the World Bank have pursued such policies in many countries experiencing balance of payments problems. Not surprisingly, many riots and demonstrations against the IMF and the World Bank were organized in many third world countries.

Though the US closed the private saving-investment gap in 2003, its government deficit balance decreased slightly from its 2003 value of 4.6 percent to 4.4 percent. This, however, was below Japan's government deficit, which reached an exceptionally high level of approximately 6.5 percent. The Euro Area average government deficit for 2004 was the lowest of the three, at 2.9 percent. This analysis suggests that a correction of national income imbalances in the US of public and private saving will be helpful in improving the US CA problem and stabilizing the dollar-euro exchange rate. An increased US savings rate will be beneficial to the US economy and will contribute to solving the problem of the chronic US bloated CA deficit.

Figure 6.7

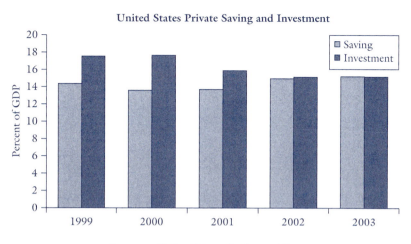

United States Private Saving and Investment

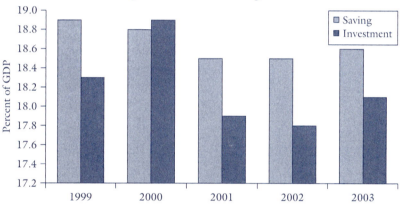

European Union Private Saving and Investment

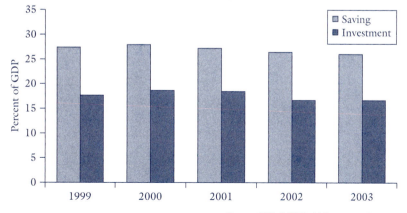

Japan Private Saving and Investment

Source: BEA, IMF World Economic Outlook

## SUMMARY

In this chapter, factors were examined that played a crucial role in determining the euro exchange rate. It was found that the relative performance of countries' economies is an important factor affecting exchange rates. Several variables can be employed to assess a country's economic performance. Such variables include real GDP, real GDP growth rates, unemployment rates, and a few others. What determines the value of an exchange rate is a complicated phenomenon since many variables simultaneously affect exchange rates in the short-run and long-run. The economist's task in explaining exchange rate determination is to focus on the most important variables and to construct a logical and convincing scenario (an economic model) of how exchange rates are determined.

The supply and demand model of the foreign exchange market was employed to explain the dollar-euro exchange rate. Changes in relative economic performance of countries, such as change in real GDP, play an important role in the determination of exchange rates. A higher national income increases a country's imports and the demand of foreign exchange. In addition, real GDP growth increases a country's rate of return and interest rates. The latter causes movements in capital inflows and outflows that play a important role in the determination of foreign exchange rates. This was found to be the case for the US dollar-euro exchange rates. During 1999 and 2000, Euro Area businesses and financial investors, attracted by high rates of return in an expanding US economy, chose to invest in the US. As a result, capital inflows in the US increased, contributing to the appreciation of the dollar versus the euro. After 2000, the situation reversed as Euro Area firms and investors, for various reasons, became hesitant to invest in the US. Such reductions in capital flows in the US played a determining role in the depreciation of the dollar and the appreciation of the euro after 2001.

Structural imbalances in the US CA deficits accompanied with low US private saving rates and high US government deficits have caused a depreciation of the dollar-euro exchange rate.

## Essay Questions

1. Compare the Euro Area with the US and Japan (the world's two largest market economies). Base your comparison, on factors such as population, GDP per capita, GDP, and share of world GDP. Do you believe that the Euro Area is an economically

strong and vital world economy that will sustain one of the most important world currencies (the euro)?

2. Use the supply and demand of the foreign exchange model for euros to show what has affected the dollars-euro exchange rate. Discuss all major events that took place in the US economy starting in the early 1990s that had an impact on the dollar-euro exchange rate. Be sure to include factors that affected the US CA balance as well as the US FA. Does your model explain the path of the dollar-euro exchange during the period 1999–2004?

3. The continuous appreciation of the euro versus the dollar was caused, according to many economists and the news media, by the large US CA deficit. Is this a valid argument? How does the large CA deficit affect the dollar-euro exchange rate? Explain.

4. CA deficits are usually accompanied by FA surpluses, at least that is the case for the US and most other countries. However, not all countries seem to follow the same pattern. China and Japan, since 2003, experienced simultaneously CA and FA surpluses. Comment on the CA and FA balances of these two countries and describe how they are related to the US CA deficits. Do you believe the decision of the central banks of these countries on how to invest their earned US dollars can affect the dollar-euro exchange rate? Explain.

5. With the growing US CA deficits, in terms of absolute dollar amounts and as a percentage of US GDP, many economists are troubled since a country's CA deficit is directly related to its net international investment position. In your opinion, do you think a large economy, such as the US, needs to take these concerns into consideration? Discuss the current US situation regarding its international investment position.

6. Many economists believe the continuous depreciation of the dollar versus the euro is the result of insufficient private US saving and continuous government budget deficits $(G > T)$. Do you agree with this explanation regarding the prolonged depreciation of the dollar versus the euro? If yes, explain how.

# APPENDIX

In Table 6.2, the CA and FA are shown for the years 1999–2003 for the US, Euro Area, Japan, and China. The data in this table are the same with those used to construct Figure 6.4.

Table 6.2

| | United States (billions of US dollars) | | Japan (billions of US dollars) | | Euro Area (billions of US dollars) | | China (billions of US dollars) | |
|---|---|---|---|---|---|---|---|---|
| | Current Account | Financial Account | Current Account | Financial Account | Current Account | Financial Account | Current Account | Financial Account |
| 1999 | −290.87 | 227.82 | 114.6 | −38.85 | −25.17 | 3.34 | 21.12 | 5.2 |
| 2000 | −411.46 | 456.63 | 119.66 | −78.31 | −61.96 | 49.87 | 20.52 | 1.96 |
| 2001 | −393.74 | 420.5 | 87.8 | −48.16 | −12.93 | −37.12 | 17.4 | 34.83 |
| 2002 | −480.86 | 531.68 | 112.45 | −63.38 | 64.39 | −94.56 | 35.42 | 32.34 |
| 2003 | −541.8 | 579 | 136.22 | 71.92 | 32.21 | −113.11 | 45.87 | 52.77 |

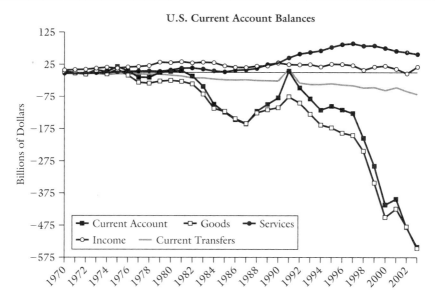

U.S. Current Account Balances

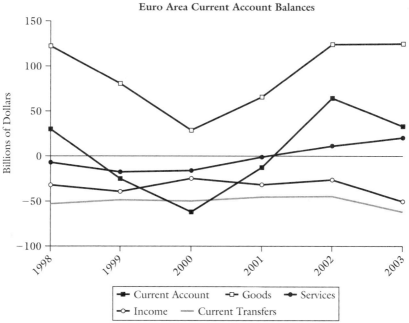

Euro Area Current Account Balances

Source: IFS CD-ROM

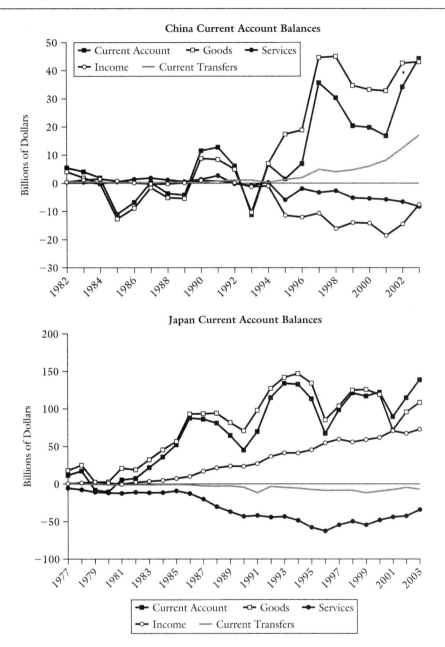

China Current Account Balances

Japan Current Account Balances

Source: IMF

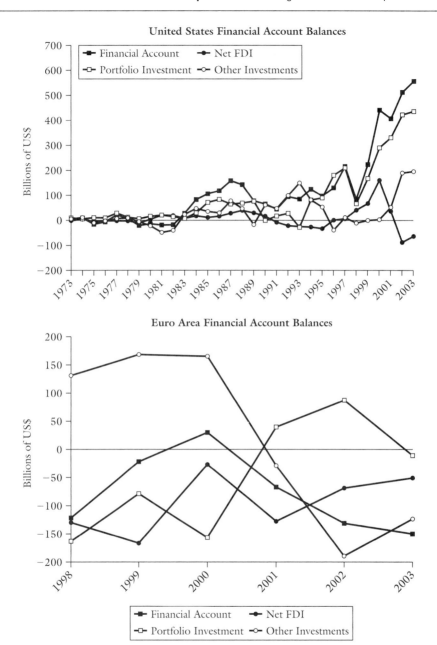

United States Financial Account Balances

Euro Area Financial Account Balances

Source: IFS CD-ROM

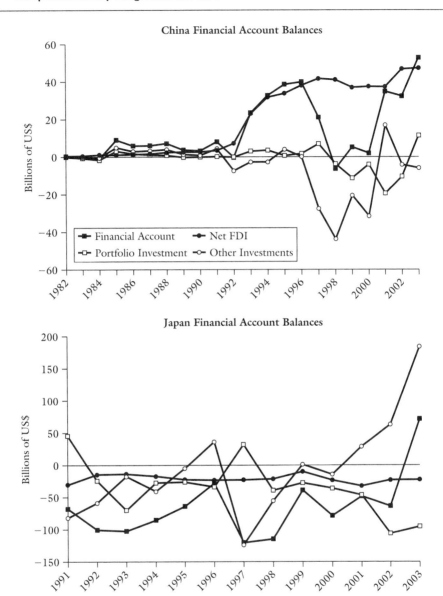

Source: IFS CD-ROM

# chapter 7

# Exchange Rate Theories and the Euro

Chapter Five provided some empirical evidence regarding the historical performance of the euro in reference to selected major world currencies. This was accomplished by studying the bilateral nominal and real exchange rates of the euro in relation to other currencies and analyzing the nominal and real trade-weighted exchange rates of the euro and other currencies. In Chapter Six, variables that were considered to be influential in affecting the euro exchange rate were examined along with some statistics pertinent to the Euro Area (Eurozone), the US, Japan, and the UK. The supply and demand model of the foreign exchange that was presented in the same chapter was utilized to capture all possible movements in the exchange rate caused by factors affecting the supply and demand of the foreign exchange. These factors consist of market fundamentals and market expectations.

Three market fundamentals were previously introduced in Chapter Six. These variables were the real Gross Domestic Product (GDP) growth, the unemployment rate, and the current account (CA). Other market fundamentals included inflation rates, nominal and real interest rates, fiscal, monetary and trade policies, as well as changes in productivity and consumer preferences.[1] Market expectations reflect news on market fundamentals and views or opinions about future exchange rates. It was suggested that the supply and demand of the foreign exchange model captures all movements of exchange rates, but it does not sufficiently explain any of them. This observation leads to the introduction and discussion of alternative exchange rate theories that more explicitly relate the exchange rate to pertinent variables. In Chapter Six, a low US saving rate and a high government deficit were shown to cause imbalances in the CA between countries. This triggers capital flows, generating persistent and one-way movements of exchange rates.

Two variables have historically played a crucial and central role in the development of exchange rate determination theories. These two variables are the interest rate (both nominal and real) and the price level of a country or the annual percent change of the price level (the inflation rate).

## Nominal Target Interest Rates and the Euro

Figure 7.1 illustrates the nominal short-term interest rates targeted by the central banks and the nominal long-term interest rates for the Euro Area and the US. Most central banks of the developed countries exercise monetary policy by setting a target interest rate. Once a central bank sets its target rate, all other interest rates generally follow, moving together with the target rate, which enables the central bank to influence the economy.

When a country's economy begins to slow down and inflation does not seem to be a threat to the economy, the central bank reduces its target interest rate to fight recession and unemployment. Low interest rates encourage borrowing by consumers and businesses. Once an economy approaches full employment and prices begin rising, then this is the time for the central bank to press the brakes on the growth of money supply and slow down the economy to restrain inflation. To achieve this objective, central banks raise target interest rates, discouraging borrowing by consumers and businesses. The US Federal Reserve (the Fed) controls the federal funds rate, while the European Central Bank (ECB) controls the repo rate. Both of these target rates are short-term overnight lending rates that affect the total reserves in the banking system, the money supply, and ultimately, employment, and the growth of the economy.

In the upper part of Figure 7.1, the short-term overnight interest rates (monetary instruments) targeted by the Fed and the ECB are shown starting in January 1999. According to this graph, the US federal funds rate exceeded the Euro Area repo rate during the first two and a half years. At the end of 2000, the Fed began reducing the federal funds rate to fight the emerging US recession. Since then, the federal funds rate was gradually reduced from 6.5 percent to a historic 41-year record low rate of 1 percent. After four years of easy monetary policy, the Fed began raising the federal funds rate by a quarter of 1 percent (25 basis points) to 1.25 percent on June 30, 2004 to curtail anticipated inflation in the US. Since then, the Fed increased the federal funds rate four more times in 2004. The last increase was on December 14, 2004, when the Fed increased the federal funds rate by another one quarter of one percent to 2.25 percent. This rate was above the ECB's repo rate for the first time since the US recession in 2001. The ECB has not changed the repo rate since June 7, 2003. On February 2, 2005, the Fed increased the federal funds rate by another 25 basis points to 2.5 percent.

A pattern similar to short-term target interest rates exists between the corresponding long-term interest rates of the US and the Euro

Figure 7.1    Nominal Interest Rates for the US and the Euro Area

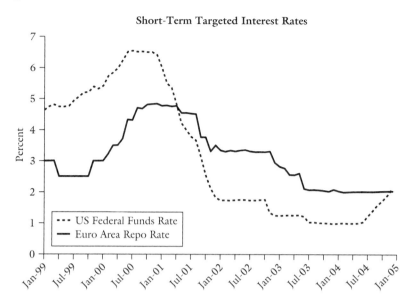

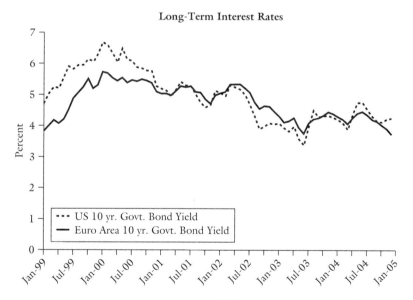

Source: ECB, Federal Reserve of St. Louis; IFS CD-ROM

Area as these are measured by their respective 10-year bond yields. Starting in January 1999, the US long-term interest rate was above the Euro Area long-term interest rate until June 2001. Since June 2001, the US long-term interest rate declined below the Euro Area long-term interest rate. However, the two long-term interest rates have tended to move together since the beginning of 2003.

This particular pattern of the US and Euro Area interest rates has probably affected the dollar-euro ($NE_{\$/\epsilon}$) exchange rate. In the early years when US interest rates were above the Euro Area interest rates, the dollar was appreciating against the euro. Contrary to this, when the US interest rates were driven below the Euro Area interest rates, the dollar started depreciating against the euro. Such a relationship was both expected and plausible because high interest rates attract capital inflows to a country, causing an appreciation of the country's currency. Lower and decreasing interest rates trigger capital outflows from the country causing depreciation of the country's currency. Empirical evidence shows this was the case for capital flows between the US and the Euro Area.

## Real Short-Term Interest Rates and the Nominal Euro Exchange Rate ($NE_{\$/\epsilon}$)

As explained, high short-term and long-term interest in the US and the Euro Area played a crucial role in the determination of the nominal dollar-euro ($NE_{\$/\epsilon}$) exchange rate. Economists, however, pointed out long ago that the most important variable to affect capital flows is the real interest rate. The real interest rate is defined as the nominal interest rate minus the expected rate of inflation, $r = i - \pi^e$, where $r$ is the real interest rate, $i$ is the nominal interest rate, and $\pi^e$ is the expected rate of inflation spanning from the beginning to the end of the period that a security is held by the investor.[2] In effect, investors base their decisions on the after-tax expected real rate of return.

In Figure 7.2, the 3-month real US Treasury bill rate is shown in a bar chart along with the 3-month real interbank rate of the Euro Area, both measured along the left-hand side of the vertical axis. In the same graph, the $NE_{\$/\epsilon}$ exchange rate is presented as a time plot measured along the right-hand side of the vertical axis.

According to this graph, during 1999 and 2000, when the US real interest rate was higher than the Euro Area real interest rate, the euro was depreciating. However, the euro depreciation continued until 2001, a year during which the Euro Area short-term interest rate was higher than the corresponding US interest rate. During 2002–2004, the Euro Area real interest rate was higher than the US real interest rate and consequently the euro was appreciating. The results regarding the relationship of real interest rates in the US and the Euro Area and the $NE_{\$/\epsilon}$ exchange rate are identical to the results involving the $NE_{\$/\epsilon}$ exchange rate and the nominal US and Euro Area interest rates shown in Figure 7.1.

Economists are convinced that exchange rates are simultaneously determined by many factors operating under three different time

Figure 7.2

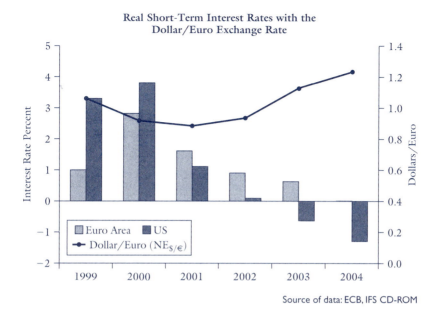

Real Short-Term Interest Rates with the
Dollar/Euro Exchange Rate

Source of data: ECB, IFS CD-ROM

horizons: the short-run, the medium-run, and the long-run. Different factors affect exchange rates under each of the three time horizons. The same factors, however, are cited by many economists as operating under more than one time horizon. As a result, the distinction and classification of these factors under the three time horizons is unclear.

The short-run is often defined to be a period of time that lasts less than one year. The most important variable affecting exchange rates during this time period is financial capital flows. Financial capital flows depend primarily on interest rates. Presently, financial markets in developed countries are becoming increasingly liberalized and integrated, causing countries with the highest real interest rates to attract the most financial capital. In this modern electronic era, international capital flows are facilitated and encouraged by transaction costs that are close to zero. Currency traders routinely transfer foreign currencies worth billions of dollars with a single mouse click to the other side of the globe in less than a second's time. Total world foreign exchange transactions amount to approximately $1.2 trillion per day with most of this triggered by changes in interest rates. Higher real interest rates attract foreign capital inflows provided that risk from holding assets denominated in foreign currencies is absent. If such risk exists, foreign investors require a risk premium to invest in foreign currency-denominated assets. As a result, real interest rates will have to be higher by a certain percentage to compensate investors for holding such risky assets.

Assuming everything else is the same between the two countries, a country with higher interest rates generally can expect to attract capital inflows, and a country with lower interest rates should expect to experience capital outflows. This result is based on the behavior of a typical profit maximizing investor who diversifies the portfolio by purchasing an increasing amount of foreign currency-denominated assets. Exchange rate volatility makes investing abroad different from investing in the home country. A question arises, however, for typical international investors. Is there a criterion upon which typical investors can determine the optimal composition of their portfolios in terms of domestic and foreign currency-denominated assets?

Indeed, there exists such an optimum, profit-maximizing rule that typical investors could follow. According to this optimization rule, profit maximizing investors will keep increasing purchases of foreign currency denominated securities as long as the foreign real after-tax rate of return exceeds the domestic after-tax real rate of return. Capital outflows to a foreign country, however, will tend to cause a reduction of foreign interest rates and an appreciation of the foreign currency. Financial capital movements and changes in other market fundamentals affect the spot (present) exchange rate and affect the expected or future exchange rate. Expectations regarding future exchange rates in the short-run play the most crucial role in affecting spot exchange rates.

## Uncovered Interest Rate Parity

In a financially integrated market, a typical investor will stop transferring funds from a low interest rate country to a high interest rate country only when the rates of return in the two countries are equalized. This situation can be demonstrated with a hypothetical example involving a potential US financial investor. Assume the hypothetical American investor has the option to invest in the US and receive an interest rate equal to $i_{US}$ or invest in the Euro Area to receive an interest rate equal to $i_{EA}$. The American investor will keep moving financial capital between the US and the Euro Area by pursuing a higher rate of return until there is no longer a motive to continue doing so. This will happen when the two rates of return in the US and the Euro Area are approximately equal to one another. Such investor behavior leads to the equalization of the rates of return and is known as arbitrage. Arbitrage occurs not only in financial markets but also in the commodity markets. In the commodity markets, arbitrageurs are responsible for the convergence, or the tendency for convergence, in commodity prices between regions and countries. This is accomplished when an arbitrageur buys a commodity from a location at a low price and sells the same commodity in another market at a higher price in pursuit of profit.

In the financial markets, arbitrage is responsible for the equalization of the rates of return of financial investments between two countries. The rate of return on the US investment is the short-term interest rate, $i_{US}$, which the American investor receives by buying an interest-bearing security, such as a US Treasury bill or bond. A similar investment in the Euro Area yields a rate of return that consists of two components: the short-term interest rate paid for holding the Euro Area asset, $i_{EA}$, and the expected percentage appreciation (depreciation) of the euro during the period the asset is held. If the two rates of return are approximately equal, as shown in Equation (1), then the American investor will be indifferent as to investing in the US or in the Euro Area.[3]

$$i_{US} \approx i_{EA} + E[\%\Delta(NE)] \quad \text{Uncovered Interest Rate Parity} \quad (1)$$

Equation (1) is called the uncovered interest rate parity condition, where $E[\%\Delta(NE)]$ denotes the expected percent change of the nominal exchange rate ($NE_{\$/€}$) during the period that the two bonds are held and pay $i_{US}$ and $i_{EA}$ interest rates in the US and in the Euro Area, respectively.[4]

The uncovered interest parity condition can be rewritten if Equation (1) is rearranged. The interest rate parity condition of Equation (1) can be written as:

$$i_{US} - i_{EA} \approx E[\%\Delta(NE)]. \quad (1a)$$

Equation (1a) denotes that the interest rate differential or spread among the US and the Euro Area will be approximately equal to the expected exchange rate depreciation of the currency with the high interest rate.

For example, if the US interest rate is much higher than the Euro Area interest rate, an American investor will be indifferent to investing in the US and the Euro Area if the US interest rate is equal to the sum of the Euro Area interest rate and the percent appreciation of the euro in relation to the dollar. The sum of the two terms is the expected rate of return from investing in a Euro Area bond.

A numerical example will clarify the uncovered interest rate parity condition. Assume that a short-term security in the US pays a 7 percent annual interest rate, and a similar security in the Euro Area pays only 4 percent. Assume equal inflation rates and all types of risks to be equal or nonexistent. A US financial investor will invest in the US if the euro is expected to remain unchanged or depreciate. The same investor will prefer to invest in the Euro Area if the euro is expected to appreciate by more than 3 percent. If, for example, the euro appreciates by 6 percent against the dollar, then the American financial investor will be better off investing only in the Euro Area countries since the rate of return from this investment is 10 percent (4% + 6%). This is higher than the 7 percent rate of return in the US. Lastly, if the rate of appreciation of the euro versus the dollar is exactly 3 percent, then the uncovered interest rate parity condition is met and the US investor will be indifferent whether to purchase the US or the Euro Area security.

## Testing the Uncovered Interest Rate Parity Condition

Figure 7.3 illustrates time plots for the 1-month, 3-month, and 1-year US Treasury bill interest rates along with the sum of the corresponding equivalent maturity Euro Area interbank deposit interest rates and the expected percent appreciation (depreciation) of the euro during the same period that the two assets are held. For uncovered interest rate parity to hold, the time plots of the two variables of Equation (1) (the return rates) must move close to one another. According to these graphs, uncovered interest rate parity does not hold well. However, there is some loose co-movement of the US interest rates with the Euro Area expected rates of return. The plot of the Euro Area expected rate of return fluctuates widely around the time plot of the US interest rate, which is relatively stable. According to Figure 7.3, the longer the maturity of the interest-bearing asset, the larger the deviations of the two time plots from each other. This can be attributed to exchange rate fluctuations, which increase with time. Many empirical studies in the literature involving various pairs of currencies have found that the uncovered interest rate parity condition does not hold.[5] Various explanations are given as to why the uncovered interest parity condition does not hold. The most important reason is that financial investors often prefer domestic assets over foreign assets. This behavior of financial investors is known as home bias, and it has been observed with investors of many countries who prefer domestic assets to foreign assets for the purpose of avoiding foreign exchange risk.

## Covered Interest Rate Parity

Due to exchange rate risk, the rate of return on the foreign held assets is volatile, creating uncertainty for investors. Exchange rate risk arises because the exchange rate at the time of the conversion of the foreign earnings to domestic currency is expected to be different from what it was when the foreign assets were first purchased. Foreign financial investors for most major world currency investments have the option to avoid foreign exchange rate risk. They can eliminate foreign exchange risk by entering into a forward contract, which allows them to convert their foreign earnings at the end of the investment period into

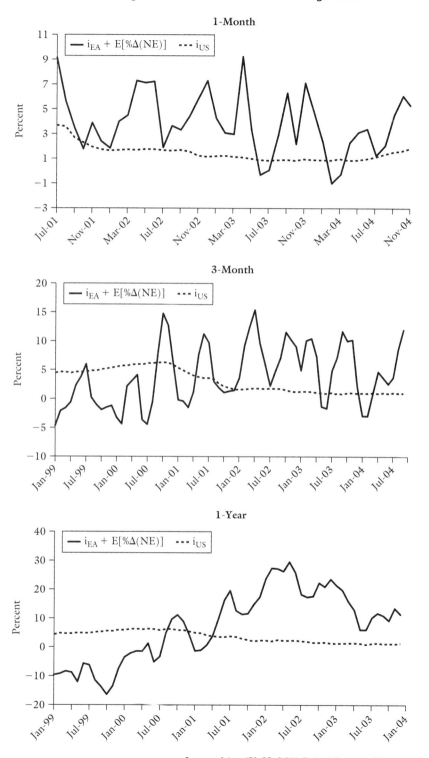

Figure 7.3  Uncovered Interest Rate Parity between the US and the Euro Area using the Nominal Dollar/Euro Exchange Rate

Source of data: IFS CD-ROM, Federal Reserve of St. Louis

domestic currency at an agreed upon exchange rate. This forward contract can be signed at the same time that the foreign assets are purchased. There is, nonetheless, a fee for this service that is usually provided by large banks that many foreign financial investors utilize extensively. Approximately half of all foreign exchange transactions take place in the forward market, facilitating merchants and financial investors who choose to hedge at some known cost (fee) and totally avoid foreign exchange rate risk. Many foreign financial investors take advantage of this option since they are attracted to foreign financial investments because of the higher interest rates and do not want to be exposed to foreign exchange risk.

With forward exchange rate contracts available, the interest rate parity condition given by Equation (1) is modified by replacing the expected change of the $NE_{S/\text{\euro}}$ exchange rate by the percent difference of the spot from the forward rates.[6] As a result, the foreign earnings of the American investor from the Euro Area are covered (guaranteed) with a forward contract. The foreign exchange risk is eliminated for the financial investor and shifted to the bank, which sold the forward contract. The interest rate parity condition in this case is called covered interest rate parity. The forward exchange rate (FE) is the best estimator for the expected future spot rate; thus, the difference between the forward and spot over the spot measures the expected appreciation (depreciation) of the exchange rate for the entire period that the foreign security is held by the investor. If, for example, the forward rate is less than the spot rate (FE < NE), then the dollar is expected to appreciate versus the euro. On the other hand, if the forward is greater than the spot (FE > NE), then the dollar is expected to depreciate in relation to the euro. If the two are equal, FE = NE, then the exchange rate is expected to remain unchanged.

$$i_{US} \approx i_{EA} + \frac{FE - NE}{NE} \qquad \text{Covered Interest Rate Parity} \qquad (2)$$

According to Equation (2), the American investor will be indifferent to investing in the US or in the Euro Area since the interest rate in the US is equal to the sum of the Euro Area interest rate and the rate of appreciation (depreciation) of the euro. If the interest rate parity condition does not hold, then intertemporal arbitrage will equate the rates of return among countries.[7] Since investors can avoid exchange rate risk with the use of forward contracts, covered interest rate parity is expected to hold better than the uncovered interest parity condition. Equation (2) can also be rewritten as follows:

$$i_{US} - i_{EA} \approx \frac{FE - NE}{NE}. \qquad (2a)$$

In this form, Equation (2a) states that the interest rate difference be-tween the US and the Euro Area, or the interest rate spread, must be equal to the expected rate of appreciation (depreciation) of the euro, which is the forward premium or discount. For example, if the interest differential is positive, i.e., if the US interest rate is higher than the Euro Area interest rate, then the forward rate should exceed the spot rate. This implies that the dollar is expected to depreciate in relation to the euro for the covered interest parity condition to hold. In other words, countries with observed higher interest rates should expect a depreciation of their currencies in the near future.

## Testing the Covered Interest Parity Condition

Figure 7.4 illustrates the covered interest parity condition for the US and the Euro Area. In Figure 7.4, the 1-month, 3-month, and 1-year US Treasury bill interest rates are utilized for the US, while the corre-sponding rates for the Euro Area are the interbank rates. The longer the maturity of the foreign and domestic held securities, the stronger the covered interest rate parity condition holds. This is supported by Figure 7.4, which shows a closer co-movement in the 1-year time plots than the 1-month and 3-month time plots. Figure 7.4 provides evi-dence that the existence of forward contracts reduces deviations in the rates of return in financial investments among countries more for the longer periods than for the shorter periods.[8]

Figure 7.5 illustrates the covered interest rate parity condition be-tween the UK and the Euro Area for the period from January 1999 to January 2004 for 1-month, 3-month, and 1-year maturity interbank short-term interest rates. According to this graph, the covered interest parity condition between the Euro Area and the UK holds remarkably well for the 1-year interbank rate but not as well for the 1-month and 3-month maturity interbank interest rates.

Many studies that have examined the covered interest rate parity condition have found strong evidence that supports the covered in-terest rate parity condition using data from various countries. The conclusion is that the presence of sufficient arbitrage leads to equal-ization of the rates of return for securities held in two different currencies provided the currencies are freely traded and forward con-tracts exist.

The covered interest parity condition was found empirically to hold almost perfectly for foreign currencies held in the same bank. Foreign currencies deposited in a foreign bank are called eurocurrencies. The eurocurrency market is well developed. Large banks in many countries hold and trade large amounts of eurocurrencies. The above discussion

Figure 7.4　Covered Interest Rate Parity between the US and the Euro Area
using the Dollar/Euro Nominal and Forward Exchange Rates

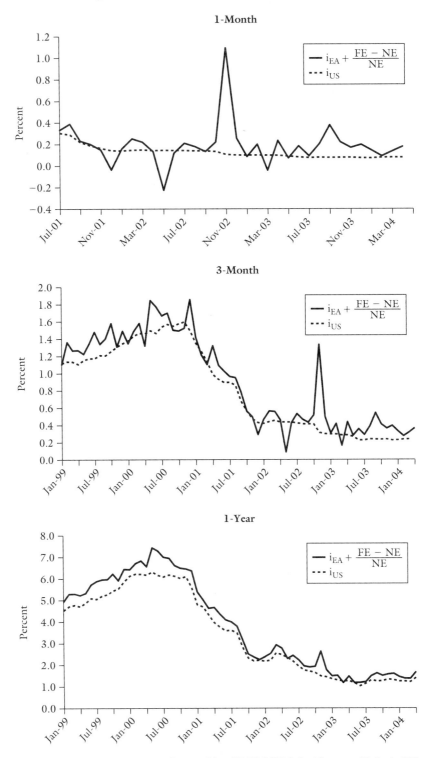

Source of data: IFS CD-ROM, Federal Reserve of St. Louis, ECB

Figure 7.5  Covered Interest Rate Parity between the UK and the Euro Area using the Pound/Euro Nominal and Forward Exchange Rates

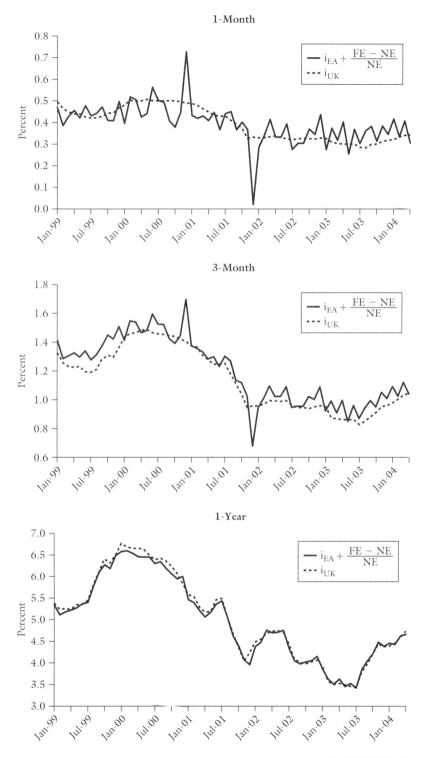

Source of data: IFS CD-ROM, BOE, ECB

suggests that covered interest rate parity holds well unlike the uncovered interest rate parity condition, which did not hold mainly because of insufficient arbitrage.

## Real Interest Rate Parity

Uncovered and covered interest rate parity conditions are meaningful propositions from the point of view of a rational investor whose objective is to maximize profit for a portfolio consisting of domestic and foreign assets. The uncovered and the covered interest rate parity conditions were expressed in terms of nominal interest and exchange rates. An alternative proposition is the real interest rate parity condition, which is stated in terms of the real interest rates and the real exchange rates. These two variables were introduced in previous chapters. A financial investor should be interested in the real interest rate and the real rate of return rather than the nominal rates.

The real interest rate is defined by Fisher's equation shown below in Equation (3).[9]

$$\text{(a)} \ \ i_{US} = r_{US} + \pi^e_{US} \qquad \text{(b)} \ \ i_{EA} = r_{EA} + \pi^e_{EA} \qquad (3)$$

The above two equations state that the nominal interest rates in the US and the Euro Area are equal to the real interest rates, $r_{US}$ and $r_{EA}$, plus the expected inflation rates, $\pi^e_{US}$ and $\pi^e_{EA}$, in the US and the Euro Area, respectively. Subtracting 3b from 3a gives Equation (4).

$$i_{US} - i_{EA} = r_{US} - r_{EA} + (\pi^e_{US} - \pi^e_{EA}) \qquad (4)$$

The left-hand side of Equation (4), according to uncovered interest rate parity, is equal to the expected appreciation (depreciation) of the nominal exchange rate, $E[\%\Delta(NE)]$. The nominal exchange rate (NE) (defined in terms of dollars per euro $\$/€$) is given by $NE = RE(P_{US}/P_{EA})$, where RE is the real exchange rate and $P_{US}$ and $P_{EA}$ are the respective price levels of the US and the Euro Area. This definition of the NE was introduced in a different form in Chapter Five. First, take the percent change of the NE equation shown above and then substitute the right-hand side of this equation into (4). After rearranging, Equation (5) is derived.

$$r_{US} - r_{EA} \approx E[\Delta\%(RE)] \qquad \text{Real Interest Rate Parity} \qquad (5)$$

Equation (5) is the real interest parity condition that relates the real interest rates with the expected appreciation (depreciation) of the real exchange rate. Specifically, it states that the real interest rate difference between the US and the Euro Area is equal to the real expected appreciation (depreciation) of the euro. Equation (5) can be rewritten as follows:

$$r_{US} \approx r_{EA} + E[\%\Delta(RE)] \tag{5a}$$

In this form, Equation (5a) states that real interest rate parity holds when the real rates of return of the US and the Euro Area are approximately equal. More precisely, real interest rate parity states that the real US interest rate is equal to the real Euro Area rate plus the real expected appreciation or depreciation of the euro. If real interest rates between countries are equal, the real exchange rates will remain unchanged. Real interest rates, however, differ among countries. US and Euro Area real interest rates also differ, implying a varying real exchange rate. This is exactly what was shown in Chapter Five where the real dollar-euro exchange rate was illustrated in Figure 5.4.

## Testing the Real Interest Rate Parity

In Figure 7.6, the time plot of the real US interest rate is shown together with the sum of the Euro Area real interest rate and the real appreciation (depreciation) of the euro. The latter is the real expected rate of return from investing in the Euro Area. If empirical evidence indicates that the two expected rates of return move closely, then this will provide strong support for real interest rate parity. The graphs in Figure 7.6, however, suggest that the real interest rate parity condition does not hold well though the real rates of return are loosely related as indicated by the time plots. Numerous studies have found that the real interest parity condition does not hold closely. The main reason that real interest rate parity does not hold is the same reason the uncovered interest rate parity condition does not hold. The reason for this is insufficient arbitrage since foreign investors avoid exposure to foreign exchange risk by preferring assets denominated in domestic currencies. Financial investors do not perceive securities denominated in domestic and foreign currencies as perfect substitutes.

For the real interest rate parity condition to hold, there must be sufficient arbitrage and willingness of foreign investors to become exposed to two types of risks. The first is the foreign exchange risk occurring when an investor converts the foreign earnings at the end of the period to domestic currency. The other risk is the real interest rate risk, which depends on the expected rate of inflation. Real interest rate parity does not hold closely in the short-run because of insufficient capital movements that fail to equalize the real rates of return between domestic and foreign investments.

Figure 7.6    Real Interest Rate Parity using the Real Dollar/Euro Exchange
Rate

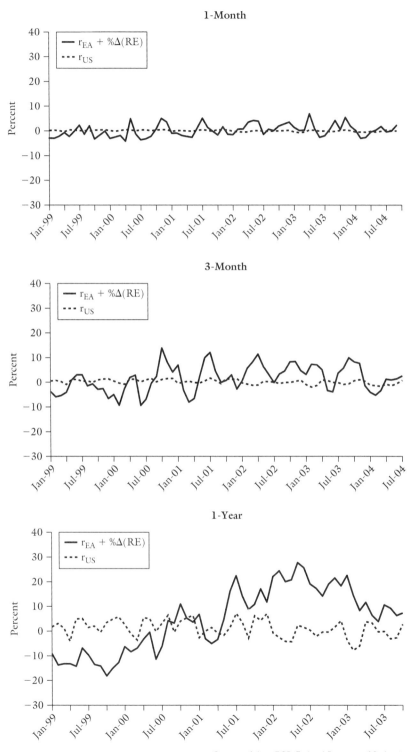

Source of data: ECB, Federal Reserve of St. Louis

Real interest rate parity may also fail due to factors operating in the long-run. Long-run factors affecting the real exchange rate involve domestic and foreign demand and supply shifts of goods and services in the two countries. For example, if Euro Area countries' preferences for US products increase, the dollar will appreciate, but if the Euro Area demand for US products decrease, the dollar will depreciate.

# The Term Structure of Interest Rates and Exchange Rate Expectations

Interest rates of identical debt instruments such as bonds issued in the same country can differ if they are issued for different maturity periods. The relationship of interest rates for identical securities in terms of risk, liquidity, and taxation with different maturity dates is known as the term structure of interest rates. A curve joining the points at which various interest rates of different maturities are observed is known as the yield curve. The yield curve describes the term structure of interest rates.[10] In particular, the slope of the yield curves provides valuable information for forecasting. Yield curves are utilized extensively by economists and financial analysts to predict future short-run interest rate movements.

In international finance, the term structure of interest rates can help forecast the expected exchange rate change of a currency. This can be accomplished by comparing the interest rates of two similar securities such as bonds, Treasury bills, or any other debt instruments of the same maturity in two countries.

According to the uncovered interest rate parity condition, the expected appreciation (depreciation) of a currency during a certain period is equal to the nominal interest rate difference of the two securities of the same maturity held for the same time period. Based on the uncovered interest rate parity condition, it can be determined which currency of the two countries will be expected to appreciate (depreciate). In Figure 7.7, the 1-month, 3-month, 6-month, and 12-month Treasury bill rates for the US and the Euro Area interbank deposit rates are plotted for January of each year from 1999 to 2004, respectively.

In January 1999, all four US interest rates were above the corresponding Euro Area interest rates, with the difference between the two yield curves increasing slightly. The interpretation of this graph is that, in January 1999, the high interest rate currency (the dollar) was expected to depreciate at a mildly increasing rate. From the adjacent graph for January 2000, shown to the right, the US interest rates were higher than the Euro Area interest rates of the same

Figure 7.7    Short-Term Interest Rates for the US and the Euro Area

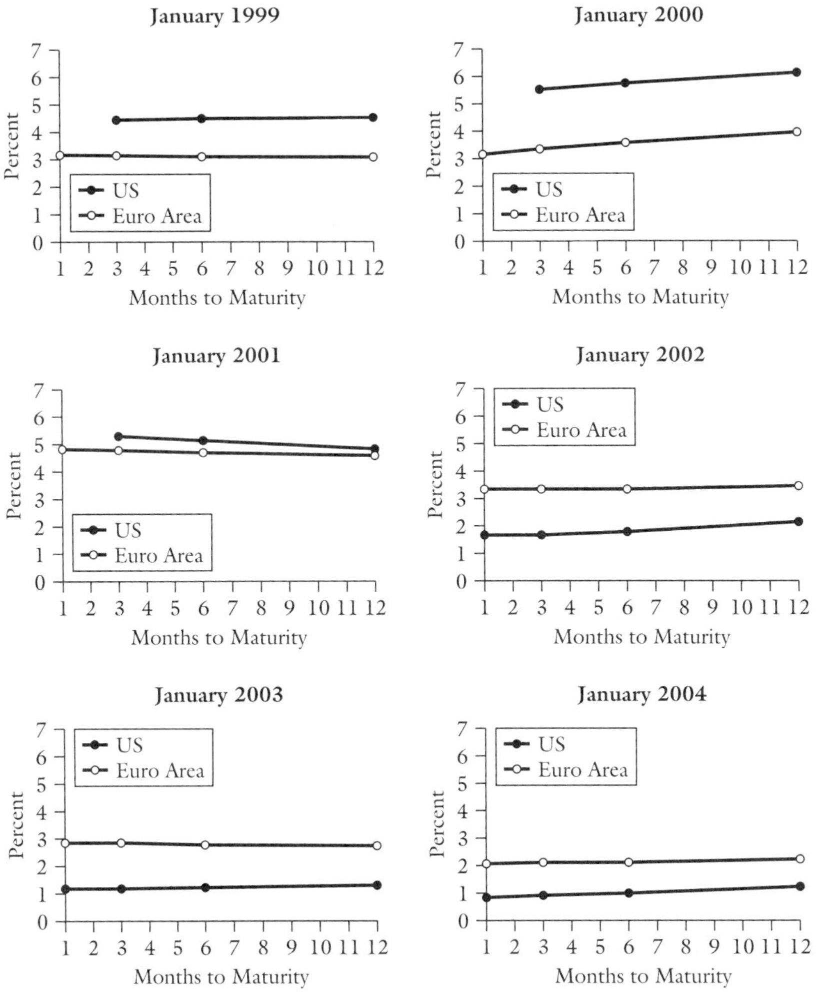

January 1999

January 2000

January 2001

January 2002

January 2003

January 2004

Source: Federal Reserve of St. Louis, ECB

maturities observed in January 1999. This implies that the dollar was expected to depreciate by a greater percentage than it was expected to depreciate in 1999. The expected percentage depreciation was, nonetheless, constant since the two yield curves were parallel. In January 2001, the US and Euro Area interest rates were converging and ended up close to each other. This is particularly evident for the 12-month maturity interest rates. The implication of this graph is that the US dollar was not expected to depreciate further against the euro.

The forecasted direction of the exchange rate during the first three-year period, 1999–2001, was correct since the euro appreciated in the subsequent three-year period. According to interest rate parity, when combined with the term structure theory, the higher US interest rates helped one form the correct expectations that the dollar was going to depreciate. Still, the depreciation of the dollar did not begin until the end of this three-year period. When the interest rates converged, expectations of further depreciation of the dollar reversed at the end of 2001. The data of Figure 7.7 speak eloquently of this forecast.

Indeed, in January 2002, all four US interest rates were below the Euro Area interest rates for the first time and continued to be lower in January 2003 and January 2004. Nevertheless, the gap between the two yield curves became smaller in January 2004. This development in the US and Euro Area interest rates implies that the high interest rate currency (the euro), in this case, is expected to depreciate. The rate of expected depreciation is slow, implying that the value of the euro will be, for some time, above the rate predicted by interest rate parity. The forecasts of the euro exchange rate based on the interest rate parity condition, in combination with the term structure theory shown in Figure 7.7, were correct. The euro has been appreciating during the three-year period since January 2002 (see Figure 5.1 of Chapter Five). It has been in an upward appreciating trend against the dollar, surpassing its introductory value of $1.168. During the entire period, starting January 2002, the euro was expected to depreciate and the interest rate gap between the US and the Euro Area would close. This might be more likely to occur because, for the first time after four years, the Fed began raising the federal funds rate on June 30, 2004. The Fed continued raising the federal funds rate, which on February 2, 2005, reached 2.5 percent, above the ECB's 2 percent repo rate. The increasing CA deficit sends an opposite signal that the euro can further appreciate and reach new highs against the dollar. If such an expectation prevails, it would probably be picked up by the January 2005 term structure of interest rates.

# The Long Run Purchasing Power Parity (PPP)

## The Law of One Price

Assume that a popular computer software product sells in the US for $120, and the dollar-euro nominal exchange rate is equal to $1.20/1€. If transportation, insurance, and any other costs associated with buying, selling, and shipping this product across the Atlantic are assumed to be zero, then the same product must sell for €100 ($120/[1.2$/1€] = €100) in the Euro Area.[11] The computer software should sell for €100 in the Euro Area because the price in the US should equal the nominal exchange rate multiplied by the Euro Area computer software price. Any other price under free trade cannot be sustained for long. Let us assume that the computer software is sold for €130 in the Euro Area countries. In this case, any merchant can buy one unit of this software from the US for €100 or $120 and sell it in the Euro Area to earn €30, or $36, profit. With this kind of profit per unit, it is certain that transatlantic trade for this software will thrive. It is, therefore, certain that many merchants will be eager to purchase this software from the US and sell it in the Euro Area countries. As long as the US price is lower than the Euro Area price, there will be room for profitable arbitrage. Trade would have taken place in the opposite direction if the Euro Area price was lower than the US price. Ultimately, the US and the Euro Area prices will be equalized and any further transatlantic trade of this commodity will cease. Perfect arbitrage between two countries will equalize prices of identical commodities. This relation is known as the law of one price.

Economists, long ago, tried to generalize the relation of the law of one price to larger bundles of goods and services produced among two countries. They even tried to generalize the law of one price to all goods and services of the entire economies.

## Absolute Purchasing Power Parity

To generalize the law of one price to all goods and services of a country, a measure of the overall price level is necessary. Economists often employ price indices such as the GDP deflator, the producer price index (PPI), and the consumer price index (CPI).

If the law of one price is to be generalized for two entire economies, Equation (6) must be satisfied. This relation is well known in economics and is called absolute purchasing power parity.

$$NE_{\$/€} = \frac{P_{US}}{P_{EA}} \qquad \text{Absolute Purchasing Power Parity} \qquad (6)$$

Absolute PPP states that the nominal exchange rate, NE, must be equal to the ratio of the two countries' price levels.[12] For the absolute PPP to hold, it is necessary that all opportunities for profitable arbitrage between the two countries first be exhausted. Figure 7.8 illustrates absolute PPP graphically for the Euro Area in relation to the US, Japan, and the UK. The time plots of the respective nominal exchange rates of the $/€, ¥/€, and the £/€, along with the corresponding price

## Figure 7.8   Absolute Purchasing Power Parity (Based on CPI)

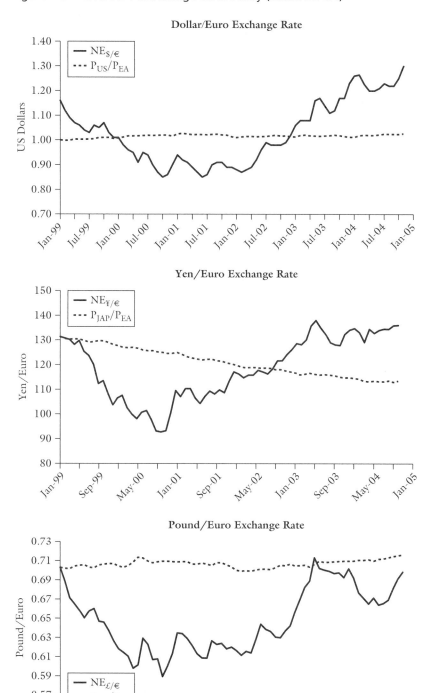

ratios $P_{US}/P_{EA}$, $P_{JAP}/P_{EA}$, and $P_{UK}/P_{EA}$ are illustrated in three different graphs. The value of the three price ratios at any point in time indicate what the nominal exchange rate should have been if absolute PPP held.

Figure 7.8 shows that absolute PPP holds poorly. This finding is expected because many studies for several different pairs of currencies have found that absolute PPP does not hold closely. There are many reasons why so many empirical studies have failed to provide support for absolute PPP. One of the most important reasons is that many commodities and services are not traded. For non-tradable commodities and services, there is no reason for their prices to converge. It is trade and arbitrage that lead to price convergence. For example, few Americans, if any, will go to Mexico to have a haircut because haircut prices are cheaper in Mexico.

A few authors included only tradable goods in their studies of PPP. These studies, unsurprisingly, found that PPP holds better than in studies that included all goods and services.

Other reasons why absolute PPP does not hold include the existence of transportation and insurance costs, trade barriers, and differing taxes among countries. Absolute PPP, nevertheless, holds better for long periods of 100 years or more and for countries experiencing high inflation. Two reasons cause such findings. First, exchange rates change because of shocks occurring in economies, such as change in productivity, change in relative demands of products, change in weather conditions and other reasons. These kinds of shocks change the relative prices of commodities and services between two economies and, in the short-run, affect the exchange rate randomly. The second reason that contributes to changes in exchange rates is a change in a country's price level. Economic and other shocks are random and in the long-run, their effects on the exchange rates tend to cancel out. In the long-run, a change in the price levels is the most important variable affecting nominal exchange rates. Consequently, a country experiencing higher increases in its overall price level in relation to another country will observe its currency depreciating in the long-run.

If absolute PPP performs poorly, a question arises: Why do economists insist on continuing with new studies on PPP? Though PPP holds poorly, PPP can be used as a benchmark to determine if a currency is overvalued or undervalued. After all, PPP is thought of as a long-run equilibrium condition for the exchange rate and indicates the expected direction of the exchange rate. In this way, PPP is useful.

Figure 7.8 illustrates absolute PPP for the Euro Area in relation to the US, Japan, and the UK. Though the euro has been in existence for a short period, useful information can be drawn from these three graphs. According to the upper part of Figure 7.8, after January 2003, the euro was overvalued since the euro values indicated by the nominal exchange rate were higher than those implied by PPP versus the dollar. According to the same graph, the euro was introduced at a higher value in relation to the US dollar than implied by the PPP on January 4, 1999. It was, therefore, overvalued during the first year, but the euro was undervalued the following two years. Similar scenarios can be presented for the yen-euro and pound-euro exchange rates. These two graphs show that the euro in mid-2004 was overvalued against the yen but undervalued against the pound sterling. It was, however, introduced at parity equal to what was implied by PPP against both of these currencies, as this can be seen from the two graphs since the two time plots coincided in January 1999. The euro was undervalued against the yen and the pound for relatively long periods after its introduction.

## Relative Purchasing Power Parity

By taking the percentage change of the variables from both sides of Equation (6), the absolute PPP can be rewritten as follows:

$$\%\Delta(NE) = \%\Delta P_{US} - \%\Delta P_{EA} = \pi_{US} - \pi_{EA} \qquad \text{Relative PPP} \qquad (7)$$

In this form, the PPP theory is called relative PPP. It states that the percent change in the nominal exchange rate is equal to the difference in the inflation rates of the US and the Euro Area.[13] For example, if US inflation is higher than inflation in the Euro Area countries, then a depreciation of the dollar will be expected. On the other hand, if inflation in the Euro Area is higher than inflation in the US, then the euro will depreciate according to relative PPP theory. Figure 7.9 portrays the relative PPP of the Euro Area with respect to the US, Japan, and the UK. According to Figure 7.9, relative PPP performs better than absolute PPP. This is not surprising as other studies have found similar results.

As absolute PPP was found to hold better with annual data rather than monthly data, the same is true for relative PPP. For longer intervals, such as years, the influence of inflation on exchange rates is more evident. Both theories hold better in the long-run rather than in the short-run.

## Figure 7.9 Relative Purchasing Power Parity (Based on CPI)

### Dollar/Euro Exchange Rate

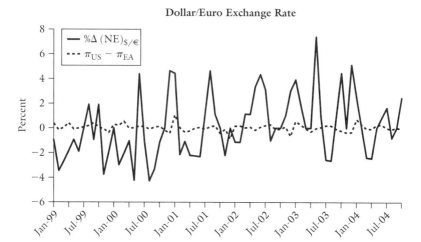

### Yen/Euro Exchange Rate

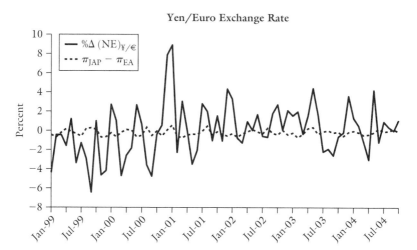

### Pound/Euro Exchange Rate

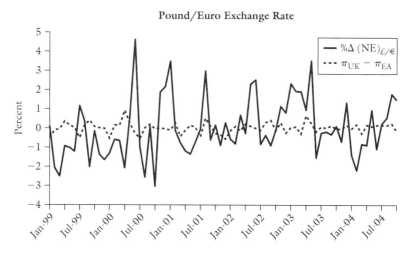

Source of data: IFS CD-ROM, ECB

Note: $\pi_{US}$ and $\pi_{EA}$ represent inflation rates for the US and the Euro Area, respectively, and NE stands for the nominal exchange rate.

## Big Mac Index

Different authors have relied on various price indices to test PPP's validity. A few such price indices that are utilized to test the PPP theory are the CPI, the PPI, the GDP deflator, and the export price index. In the summer of 1986, the British magazine *The Economist,* published an unexpected price index to test PPP. The price index was the price of the McDonald's Big Mac hamburger, which is sold in many cities around the world. It is an unusual index based on one good and has been calculated and reported every year since 1986 for several major world currencies. The purpose of the construction of this index is dual: to test the law of one price and to test whether the PPP holds based on the Big Mac price comparisons. It was first introduced by *The Economist* as a joke to tease international economists who were struggling with PPP since the Swedish economist Gustav Cassel popularized the PPP theory after World War I. In Table 7.1 on the next page, the US and the Euro Area Big Mac prices are presented for 1999–2004. These data are utilized to calculate the implied PPP of the dollars-euro exchange rate that is compared with the actual dollars-euro exchange rate to determine whether the euro is overvalued or undervalued in each of these six years.

In Column 1, the price of the Big Mac is reported for each of the six years, 1999–2004, in euros. In column 2, the price of the Big Mac in dollars is reported. The actual $/1€ exchange rate appears in Column 3. In Column 4, the ratio of Column 2 to Column 1 is reported. This is the implied PPP $/1€ exchange rate or, more precisely, the $/1€ exchange rate based on the law of one price. These PPP implied $/1€ exchange rates are compared with the actual exchange rates reported in Column 3. In Column 5, the overvaluation (undervaluation) of the euro in relation to the dollar is reported. According to these results, the euro was overvalued the first year by approximately 12 percent, it was undervalued for three years by 5, 11, and 5 percent, respectively; in 2003, it became overvalued by 10 percent. Should the Big Mac index be taken seriously? According to *The Economist,* the answer is yes. The Big Mac index has predicted overvalued (undervalued) currencies. For the euro, many economists predicted that it was

introduced below its long-run equilibrium value and they expected it to appreciate. The Big Mac index, however, suggested
that when the euro was introduced, it was overvalued and
was expected to depreciate. This indeed happened for the
next three years. Whether the euro is overvalued or undervalued based on the Big Mac index, the results are similar to
the absolute PPP results shown in Figure 7.8. The Big Mac
index, therefore, according to The Economist, is not a laughing
matter.

Table 7.1

## Big Mac PPP Index

| | Big Mac Price | | (3) Actual | (4) | (5) Over (+)/ Under (−) |
| | (1) in Euros | (2) in US Dollars | Exchange Rate 1 Euro = | Implied PPP | Valuation against the Dollar, % |
|---|---|---|---|---|---|
| 1999 | €2.52 | $2.43 | $1.08 | 0.96 | +12 |
| 2000 | €2.56 | $2.51 | $0.93 | 0.98 | −5 |
| 2001 | €2.57 | $2.54 | $0.88 | 0.99 | −11 |
| 2002 | €2.67 | $2.49 | $0.89 | 0.93 | −5 |
| 2003 | €2.71 | $2.71 | $1.10 | 1 | +10 |
| 2004 | €2.65 | $2.90 | $1.24 | 1.09 | +13 |

Source: © The Economist Newspaper Limited, London, April 1 1999, April 27 2000,
April 19 2001, April 25 2002, April 24 2003, March 27 2004.

# Asset Approach to Exchange Rate Determination

The traditional approach to exchange rate determination is based
on the conviction that the exchange rate continuously adjusts to balance the goods and services trade account. Persistent deficits cause a
depreciation of the exchange rate since they affect capital flows due
to the increased demand for foreign currency to finance the country's chronic deficits. The depreciation of the currency triggers the
corrective mechanism in this case since it discourages imports and

encourages exports of goods and services. Similarly, a persistent trade surplus leads to an appreciation of the country's currency that corrects the trade imbalance. More recent theories of exchange rate determination have shifted the focus from the flows of funds to finance trade imbalances to the supply and demand of stocks of domestic and foreign financial assets.

The asset approach to exchange rate determination theory consists mainly of two dominant theories: the monetary approach to the exchange rate (MAER) determination and the portfolio balance approach to exchange rate (PBAER) determination. Both of these models will be discussed in this section.

## The Monetary Approach to Exchange Rate (MAER) Determination

The MAER was developed in the early seventies. According to the MAER, the supply and demand of money determines exchange rates. The MAER assumes that domestic and foreign currencies are perfect substitutes. If one country, for example, experiences excess money demand, this will trigger an inflow of a foreign currency into that country. Similarly, an excess supply will be corrected by an outflow of the domestic currency abroad.

Money supplies are controlled by central banks, aiming to attain certain macroeconomic objectives such as price stability and economic growth.

Money demand refers to the money balances that individuals and businesses desire to hold during a certain time period. What factors influence the amounts of money individuals and firms desire to hold in terms of cash and checking account balances? Two economic variables have been identified to affect money demand ($M^d$): the real GDP or real national income ($Y$) and the nominal interest rate ($i$). If national income rises, firms and individuals will need to hold larger money balances to carry out their transactions of buying more goods and services. This relation can be generalized by stating that money demand is positively related to real national income. If the interest rate rises, however, firms and individuals will choose to hold smaller amounts of cash and smaller money balances in their checking deposits. This decision is based on the interest rate, which is the opportunity cost for holding cash balances since cash balances do not pay interest to their holders.[14] By holding cash instead of interest-bearing securities, individuals and firms forego the interest they would have received if they were holding bonds. Consequently, money demand is negatively related to the rate of interest. Equilibrium in the money market, for example, in the US and the Euro Area can be written as follows:

$$M^s_{US} = M^d_{US}(\overset{+}{Y}_{US}, \overset{-}{i}_{US}) \tag{8a}$$

$$M^s_{EA} = M^d_{EA}(\overset{+}{Y}_{EA}, \overset{-}{i}_{EA}) \tag{8b}$$

Where $M^s_{US}$, $M^d_{US}$, $M^s_{EA}$, and $M^d_{EA}$ are money supply and money demand in the US and the Euro Area, respectively. Similarly, $Y_{US}$, $i_{US}$, $Y_{EA}$, and $i_{EA}$ are real GDPs and nominal interest rates in the US and the Euro Area, respectively. A plus (minus) sign above a variable (argument) denotes a positive (negative) relation of this variable with the money demand.

A money demand function based on the quantity theory of money assumes money demand balances to be proportional to the level of nominal GDP. Nominal GDP is equal to $P \cdot Y$, where $P$ is the price level and $Y$ is the real GDP as defined above.

Based on the quantity theory of money equations, Equations (9a) and (9b) indicate that the US and the Euro Area money markets are in equilibrium. The left-hand sides of Equations (9a) and (9b) are the money supplies of the US and the Euro Area. The right-hand sides of (9a) and (9b) are the money demands of the US and the Euro Area, respectively. $k_{US}$ and $k_{EA}$ denote the proportions of nominal national incomes of the US and the Euro Area held as money demand balances.

$$M^s_{US} = k_{US} \cdot P_{US} \cdot Y_{US} \tag{9a}$$

$$M^s_{EA} = k_{EA} \cdot P_{EA} \cdot Y_{EA} \tag{9b}$$

Dividing Equation (9a) by Equation (9b) and rearranging terms gives Equation (10).

$$\frac{P_{US}}{P_{EA}} = \frac{k_{EA}}{k_{US}} \cdot \frac{M^s_{US}}{M^s_{EA}} \cdot \frac{Y_{EA}}{Y_{US}} \tag{10}$$

Equation (10) states that the Euro Area to US price level ratio depends on the ratio of the proportionality money demand factors, $k_{EA}/k_{US}$, the ratio on the money supplies, $M^s_{US}/M^s_{EA}$, and the ratio of real national incomes $Y_{EA}/Y_{US}$. If one assumes that PPP holds, then Equation (10) can be rewritten below as follows:

$$\text{NE}_{\$/\€} = \frac{P_{US}}{P_{EA}} = \frac{k_{EA}}{k_{US}} \cdot \frac{M^s_{US}}{M^s_{EA}} \cdot \frac{Y_{EA}}{Y_{US}} \tag{11}$$

Equation (11) links the dollar-euro exchange rate with the money supplies, the real GDPs, and the proportionality parameters from the two money demand equations. It is interesting to allow any of the right-hand variables to change and observe the partial effect of this variable on the exchange rate. This is a static exercise and it need not be the final effect on the exchange rate since other variables cannot be held constant during any period. If the money supplies in the US and the Euro Area grow at the same rate, assuming all other variables are held constant, the exchange rate will remain unchanged. Any disproportional growth, however, in the money supplies will affect the exchange rate. For example, if the US money supply increases faster than the Euro Area money supply, the euro will appreciate versus the dollar.

This is a strong result that has been verified empirically with many pairs of currencies. Countries that pursued expansionary monetary policies by maintaining higher growth rates of their money supplies in relation to other countries end up with higher inflation rates and depreciating currencies. In the US and Euro Area case, the money supply growth data do not indicate that the relative growth rates of the money supplies affected the exchange rate. The most important reason for this is that money supply growth rates between the US and the Euro Area did not differ by much. It is possible that the effects of changes in money supplies on the exchange rate may take place through an indirect process by affecting interest rates or income first.

The MAER model predicts that real GDP growth in the Euro Area higher than that of the US causes an appreciation of the euro versus the US dollar. A proportional increase in the $Y_{EA}$ and $Y_{US}$, according to Equation (11), leaves the $N_{\$/\epsilon}$ exchange rate unchanged. If, however, the $Y_{EA}$ income grows at a slower rate than $Y_{US}$, the euro will depreciate. The explanation of the above result is that an increase in $Y_{EA}$ increases money demand in the Euro Area, which causes a rise in the Euro Area interest rate that triggers capital inflows into the Euro Area and a euro appreciation.

Lastly, if the ratio of the proportionality parameters $k_{EA}/k_{US}$ increases, the euro will appreciate and vice versa. An increase in the $k_{EA}/k_{US}$ arises because $k_{EA}$ increases or $k_{US}$ decreases, which implies that money demand in the Euro Area increases relative to US money demand. A relative increase in the Euro Area money demand will increase capital inflows and lead to an appreciation of the euro. A depreciation of the euro will take place when the $k_{EA}/k_{US}$ ratio declines.[15]

## The Portfolio Balance Approach to Exchange Rate (PBAER) Determination

The MAER determination proved to be useful because it could predict the effect of an expansionary (contractionary) policy on exchange rate movement. The MAER determination failed, however, to predict the exchange rates during the flexible exchange rate period after 1973. Many economists pointed out the oversimplification of the MAER theory, which focuses on money supplies and demands ignores all other assets such as bonds and stocks, and suppresses the goods market. The MAER determination model is improved with the introduction of bonds to the model. This modified model is known as the PBAER determination. A major assumption of this model is that domestic and foreign assets are imperfect substitutes. The portfolio balance model of exchange rate determination focuses on relative changes in the supplies and demands of money and bonds in both countries. It is considered to be an improvement to the MAER theory. However, this model is rather complicated and will not be introduced here to explain the euro exchange rate.

## Forecasting the Euro Exchange Rate

With so much supporting theoretical and empirical work on exchange rates, one would tend to believe forecasting the euro exchange rate would be an easy task. Accurate short-term forecasting of the euro for periods less than a year, like forecasting for any other freely traded currency, is almost an impossible task.

Short-term forecasting of the euro or of any other currency is difficult because unexpected changes in exchange rates are influenced by news; i.e., the occurrence of unexpected events. Since such events are unknown a priori, the forecaster cannot incorporate them in a model to forecast the exchange rate. Short-term exchange rate forecasting is also difficult because of a phenomenon known in the exchange rate literature as overshooting (Dornbusch, 1976). Overshooting occurs because the exchange rate responds to a shock much stronger than would have been necessary to converge to its long-run equilibrium value. This happens because exchange rates as a rule are more responsive and volatile than prices are to news and surprises.

In the long-run, however, the PPP theory can predict the direction of the exchange rate, but such knowledge cannot help someone profit by speculating in the foreign exchange market. The reason is that, though one may know the correct direction that the exchange rate should follow, he or she does not know when the turning point will take place for an overvalued or undervalued currency. Holding on to an undervalued currency can turn out to be very expensive—many professional and amateur investors lost a lot of money since expectations failed to materialize for a long time. The vast majority of economists agree that in the short-run, the exchange rate path is a "random walk process," which means the exchange rate, at any point in time, can move in any possible direction.

## SUMMARY

This chapter examined whether existing exchange rate determination theories could explain the bilateral exchange rate of the euro in relation to three other currencies. The focus was mostly on the dollar-euro exchange rate since the US dollar is by far the most important currency in the foreign exchange market. Approximately 90 percent of all foreign exchange transactions involve US dollars. The yen-euro and UK pound-euro exchange rates were examined for the same purpose. Prior to introducing any exchange rate theory, time plots of nominal and real US and Euro Area interest rates were presented and studied. Interest rates are considered to be the most important variable influencing exchange rates. Indeed, these graphs prove the expectations correct. During the period that US short-term and long-term interest rates were higher than the Euro Area interest rates, the dollar was appreciating. When the Euro Area interest rates were higher than the US interest rates, the euro was appreciating. Knowledge of two countries' interest rates makes prediction of the direction of the exchange rate possible and accurate.

In the case of the US and Euro Area, nominal and real interest rates yield the same results. In general, however, from the point of view of the financial investor, the real interest rate matters. Specifically, the real after-tax rate of return is what attracts foreign capital inflows.

Interest rate parity is derived by assuming free capital mobility and is based on a typical international investor's optimizing behavior, aiming to maximize profit. According to the uncovered interest rate parity, the difference of two countries' interest rates must equal the expected appreciation of a country's currency with the lowest interest rate. The uncovered interest rate parity does not hold closely in the case of the dollar and the euro, nor does it hold closely for the euro in relation to the yen or the pound sterling. An important reason that interest rate parity does not hold is insufficient arbitrage between domestic and foreign financial assets.

Uncovered interest rate parity can be stated in terms of real interest rates and real exchange rates. In this version, the investor equates the real rates of return among the domestic and the foreign currency-denominated assets. This real interest rate parity holds poorly for insufficient arbitrage similar to the uncovered interest rate parity. Both of these theories do not hold closely due to the unwillingness of the investors to be exposed to foreign exchange rate risk. If the exchange rate risk could be avoided, then the interest rate parity should hold. Indeed, forward contracts allow the foreign investor to avoid foreign exchange risk for a small fee. Under such a situation, interest rate parity is called covered interest rate parity and is found to hold well, especially with annual data, as was shown in the case of the Euro Area in relation to the US and the UK.

Combining interest rate parity with the term structure of interest rates theory can provide useful information as to which currencies are expected to appreciate and depreciate. Such information, however, may not be useful in the short-run because it may take years for an overvalued or undervalued currency to be corrected. The combination of the two theories proved useful in recognizing when the euro (dollar) was overvalued (undervalued) as it was shown in Figure 7.7.

Similarly, absolute and relative PPP versions can provide useful information regarding overvalued (undervalued) currencies for the long run. Even for the dollar-euro exchange rate, PPP allowed one to determine when a currency was overvalued or undervalued despite the short life of the euro.

According to the MAER determination, which was developed in the 1970s, the money supplies and demands in the two countries determine the relative price levels and the exchange rate. This theory links domestic and foreign money supplies, real GDPs to domestic and foreign prices and to exchange rates.

Lastly, with so many theoretical advances in the area of exchange rate determination, one may think that forecasting exchange rates will be an easy task. Unfortunately, short-run exchange rate forecasting is difficult because exchange rates are affected by unexpected events. It is difficult to forecast exchange rates in the short-run because they often overreact to a given shock and move away from their long-run equilibrium values. This phenomenon is known in the literature of the exchange rates as overshooting.

## Essay Questions

1. Exchange rates are influenced by many variables. One important variable is the interest rate. Discuss the effects of the nominal and the real US and Euro Area interest rates on the nominal dollar-euro exchange rate.

2. Describe the uncovered interest rate parity and the covered interest rate parity theories. Which of the two theories holds better in reference to the dollar per euro exchange rate according to data presented in the chapter?

3. What do economists mean when they refer to term structure of interest rates? How can the theory of term structure of interest

rates be employed in combination with the interest rate parity condition to forecast the direction of the foreign exchange rate? According to the data presented in Figure 7.7 on the short-term US and Euro Area interest rates, could one form a fairly accurate forecast on the direction of the euro exchange rate during the 1999–2004 period?

4. What is the law of one price theory? Discuss the absolute and relative purchasing power theories. Are these two theories accurate in general? Can these theories be useful in predicting the dollar-euro exchange rate?

5. Many agree that forecasting economic variables such as exchange rates, in general, is a difficult task. If you were asked to predict the dollar-euro exchange for the next year, what would be your forecast? You may want to provide a forecast interval, i.e., a lower and a higher value for the dollar-euro exchange rate. It is important to explain what led you to your forecast. Your explanation may include an exchange rate theory along with economic news and other relevant information that, in your opinion, will be important.

6. Explain the meaning of the expression "exchange rate overshooting." Is this concept useful in explaining exchange rate volatility?

# c h a p t e r  8

# The Euro Area Enlargement Challenge

## Introduction

As a result of the April 16, 2003, Accession Treaty of Athens, ten new countries joined the European Union on May 1, 2004. This latest enlargement of the EU was the most significant of any previous expansions. Eight Central and Eastern European Countries (CEECs) along with two Mediterranean island countries (Cyprus and Malta) joined the EU: Estonia, Hungary, Latvia, Lithuania, Poland, the Slovak Republic, Slovenia, and the Czech Republic. The ten new EU countries signed the Accession Treaty in Athens, Greece, at an informal EU Council meeting that was accompanied by ceremonial celebrations and great publicity. This newest enlargement resulted in a substantial increase of the total EU population from 381 to 455 million, constituting a total increase of approximately 20 percent. In contrast to population, the increase in the combined Gross Domestic Product (GDP) was a little less than 10 percent because most of these countries were poorer than the former EU15 member states.

### Some Basic Statistics

Table 8.1 reports data on the 25 European countries that formed the EU25 on May 1, 2004. This group of the EU25 countries is larger than the US or Japan in terms of population and is only third to China and India, the two largest countries in the world with populations of over a billion each. In reference to GDP, the EU25 is approximately the same size as the US, but three times larger than Japan, measured in terms of 2003 Purchasing Power Parity (PPP) euros.[1] The real per capita GDP of the EU25 was lower than the real per capita GDPs of Japan and the US, with the per capita GDP of the US being equal to €34,100 in 2003. Nevertheless, the EU25 and the US each accounted for approximately a quarter of the world's total trade and income. Therefore, Table 8.1 shows that the EU25 is one of the most economically important regional trade blocs in the world, matching the US in terms of GDP.

Table 8.1

| Some Comparative Statistics (2003) | | | |
|---|---|---|---|
| | **Population (millions)** | **GDP (PPP €, trillions)** | **GDP per Capita (PPP €, thousands)** |
| **EU10 (New)** | 74 | 0.87 | 13.3 |
| **Euro Area (EU12)** | 308.7 | 7.3 | 23.5 |
| **EU15** | 381 | 9.2 | 24.1 |
| **EU25** | 455 | 10.1 | 21.1 |
| **US** | 291 | 9.9 | 34.1 |
| **Japan** | 128 | 3.2 | 25.1 |
| | | | Source: ECB Statistics Pocket Book |

Increased economic integration in the EU25 is expected to promote economic growth and prosperity for all EU members, particularly for the new EU10 countries. Trade of the EU10 was redirected toward the EU countries before these countries joined the EU in May 1 2004. The new EU10 countries began attracting foreign investment prior to the accession, mainly from the larger, neighboring EU members. This occurred as the new EU10 countries began undergoing major structural changes to transform their nations into internationally competitive market economies. This last EU enlargement resulted in increased benefits due to trade liberalization that began prior to the accession of the new EU10 countries to the EU. Exports from the EU10 to the EU15 countries account for 67 percent of their total exports. Similarly, the share of imports of the EU10 coming from the EU15 is 60 percent. Both of these trade shares have increased substantially since 1990. After the collapse of the Berlin Wall, many Eastern European countries decided to adopt low corporate tax rates. With the exception of Ireland, which has the lowest corporate income tax rate in the entire EU25, all the EU15 countries have much higher corporate income tax rates than the new CEECs and Cyprus.[2] Low corporate tax rates among the CEECs and a well-educated, low-wage, labor force attract substantial foreign direct investment (FDI) in these countries.

## EU10 Country Profiles

Table 8.2 provides some basic summary statistics and information for each of the EU10 countries in reference to area, population, GDP, FDI per capita, capital city, and currency. The largest of the EU10

Table 8.2

## Country Profiles (2003)
## New EU10 Countries

### Czech Republic

| | |
|---|---|
| Area | 78,864 sq km |
| Population | 10.2 million |
| GDP (PPP $) | $160.96 billion |
| Capital | Prague |
| Currency | Czech Crown |
| FDI per capita ($)* | $3,709 |

### Estonia

| | |
|---|---|
| Area | 45,227 sq km |
| Population | 1.4 million |
| GDP (PPP $) | $17.22 billion |
| Capital | Talinn |
| Currency | Estonian Crown |
| FDI per capita ($)* | $2,362 |

### Hungary

| | |
|---|---|
| Area | 93,036 sq km |
| Population | 10.1 million |
| GDP (PPP $) | $140.39 billion |
| Capital | Budapest |
| Currency | Hungarian Forint |
| FDI per capita ($)* | $2,089 |

### Latvia

| | |
|---|---|
| Area | 64,590 sq km |
| Population | 2.5 million |
| GDP (PPP $) | $25.25 billion |
| Capital | Riga |
| Currency | Lat |
| FDI per capita ($)* | $1,435 |

### Lithuania

| | |
|---|---|
| Area | 65,301 sq km |
| Population | 3.7 million |
| GDP (PPP $) | $41.44 billion |
| Capital | Vilnius |
| Currency | Lita |
| FDI per capita ($)* | $1,163 |

### Poland

| | |
|---|---|
| Area | 312,683 sq km |
| Population | 38.5 million |
| GDP (PPP $) | $423.5 billion |
| Capital | Warsaw |
| Currency | Zloty |
| FDI per capita ($)* | $1,105 |

### Slovak Republic

| | |
|---|---|
| Area | 49,040 sq km |
| Population | 5.4 million |
| GDP (PPP $) | $72.09 billion |
| Capital | Bratislava |
| Currency | Slovak Crown |
| FDI per capita ($)* | $1,873 |

### Slovenia

| | |
|---|---|
| Area | 20,270 sq km |
| Population | 2 million |
| GDP (PPP $) | $36.6 billion |
| Capital | Ljubljana |
| Currency | Tolar |
| FDI per capita ($)* | $1,646 |

Table 8.2 *Continued*

| Cyprus** | | Malta | |
|---|---|---|---|
| Area | 9251 sq km | Area | 320 sq km |
| Population | 751,500 | Population | 381,600 |
| GDP (PPP $) | $12.02 billion | GDP (PPP $) | $6.75 billion |
| Capital | Nicosia | Capital | Valletta |
| Currency | Cyprus Pound | Currency | Maltese Lira |

Source: IFS CD-ROM, ECB, IMF World Economic Outlook,
www.nationmaster.com, *Financial Times*

*cumulative net inflow, 1989–2002

**Includes the Southern Greek part of the island, which is the only one recognized
by the UN. The UN plan to unite the divided island after the 1974 invasion
by Turkey was rejected by the Greek Cypriot voters in a referendum
prior to the accession to the EU on May 1, 2004.

countries is Poland in terms of area, population, and real GDP. Poland has approximately half of the EU10 population (38.5 million), followed by Hungary and the Czech Republic, each having populations nearly one third of Poland. Both countries have achieved a higher standard of living than Poland. The wealthiest EU10 countries are Slovenia, Malta, Cyprus, and the Czech Republic (see Figure 8.1). The Czech Republic and Estonia received larger FDI per capita cumulative net inflows for the years 1989–2002 than all the other CEECs.

The bar chart in Figure 8.1 depicts the real per capita GDP of each of the EU25 countries for the year 2003, expressed in PPP US dollars. Figure 8.1 shows that the per capita GDP of the EU15 countries in 2003, on average, was nearly double the per capita GDP of the new EU10 countries. This is the largest disparity in the standards of living between the EU member countries and any other accession group that had joined the EU in the past.

This gap in the real per capita GDP is expected to close. According to an economic convergence theory based on the neo-classical growth model publicized by Robert Solow (1956) and others, poor countries are expected to grow faster and catch up with the rich countries.[3] An alternative economic theory, known as endogenous growth, predicts economic divergence between rich and poor countries. According to such models, divergence takes place because rich countries develop and adopt advanced technologies and invest heavily in human capital.[4]

Figure 8.1   GDP per capita 2003 (PPP $)

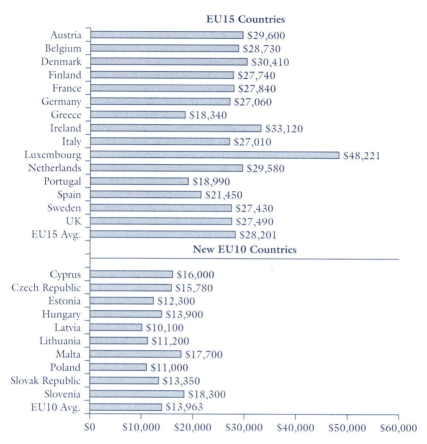

Source: www.nationmaster.com

The eight new CEECs are rich in culture and history and share a common European heritage with the EU15 members. For many people in the CEECs, joining the EU was like a European reunification after gaining their independence and freedom from the Soviet Union. This became possible only after the collapse of the Berlin Wall in 1989 and the fall of the communist regime in the Soviet Union.[5] After living under centrally planned economies for approximately 45 years, the people of the eight CEECs had to rediscover themselves by reintroducing privatization in their economies. After the introduction of the free market system, the road to prosperity was possible, but steep, long, and painful. Many structural and institutional changes had to be introduced and adopted, including the transfer of state-owned assets and property to individuals and private firms. Property rights had to be redefined and granted to private citizens and firms because the notion of private property under the communist regimes was limited.

After the fall of the communist regimes, it was necessary for consumers and businesses to become familiar with daily activities, such as shopping for a good deal and learning how to manage and operate a firm. Such routine activities of free market economies were practically unknown to the people and the newly established companies of these countries. These countries became known as transition economies due to the many structural changes and reforms that these states had to undergo before becoming similar to modern democratic and free market economies. During this period, all CEECs and previous Soviet republics' economies suffered a sharp reduction in the standards of living while experiencing high unemployment rates. After 2000, most of the CEECs have been able to attain equivalent real per capita GDP levels to those they had achieved prior to the collapse of communism.

Following the fall of the communist regimes, all eight CEECs experienced prolonged recessions that lasted, depending on the country, from two to six years. According to the upper part of Figure 8.2, these countries are still suffering from high unemployment rates. Two countries, Poland and the Slovak Republic, have experienced unemployment rates of more than fifteen percent during the 2001–2003 period and four other countries recorded unemployment rates higher than ten percent.

The lower part of Figure 8.2 shows the real per capita GDP growth rates of the new EU10 countries. According to this graph, the EU10 countries' economies grew at an average rate of 4.1 percent in 2003, a rate much higher than the average growth rates of the EU15 countries, which was only 1 percent during the same year. In contrast to the new EU10, the former EU15 countries grew at lower rates during the years 2001 and 2002. Unemployment and real GDP growth rates for each of the EU15 countries are presented in Figure 8.3. A higher real GDP growth rate for the new EU10 countries in comparison to the former EU15 countries is necessary to achieve real convergence in the EU. Many economists believe that it may take many years for these countries to attain real economic convergence with the EU15 countries.

The slow growth in the EU15 countries is almost certain to have had a negative impact on the terms of the accession for the ten new countries. For example, the new EU10 countries will receive less aid from the various EU structural funds in relation to the funding received by previous accession groups. The EU10 countries will also receive lower agricultural subsidies than the EU15 countries during the present and next EU budget plans. Similarly, all EU15 countries, with the exception of the UK and Ireland, have essentially closed their borders to potential migrant workers from the new EU10 members.

In 2004, relatively high unemployment rates, particularly among the large EU states, and slow real economic growth have caused

Figure 8.2

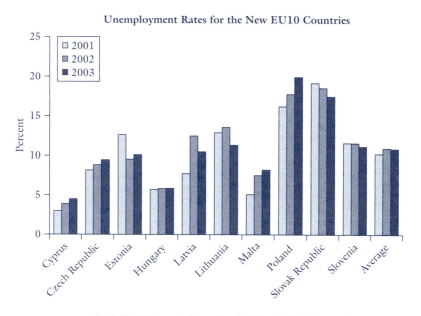

Unemployment Rates for the New EU10 Countries

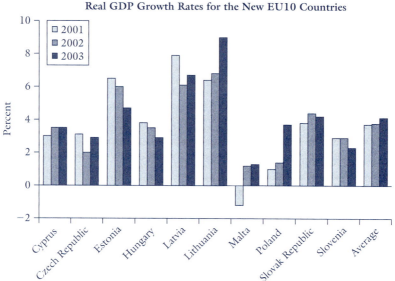

Real GDP Growth Rates for the New EU10 Countries

Source: IFS CD-ROM; IMF World Economic Outlook

dissatisfaction and a decline in the popularity of the EU in almost all 25 EU countries.

This last EU expansion was the most difficult one, requiring major preparations by the EU10 countries to integrate their economies with the EU. This difficulty is attributed to two main factors. The first factor is the adverse economic conditions in the EU15 existing during the time of the accession negotiations. The second factor is the necessary

Figure 8.3

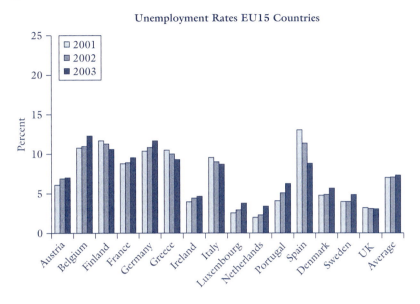

Unemployment Rates EU15 Countries

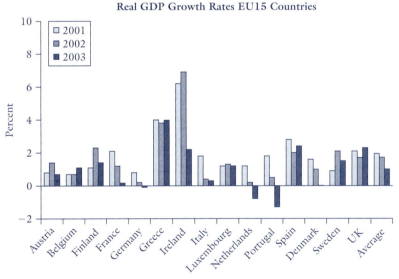

Real GDP Growth Rates EU15 Countries

Source: IMF World Economic Outlook, ECB, IFS CD-ROM

major structural, legal, administrative, and financial changes and reforms that the CEECs had to undertake to become compatible with
the EU15 market economies.

To integrate the new EU10 countries, the EU must adopt a constitution. This EU Constitution will facilitate the EU decision-making
process by minimizing indecision due to possible vote-blocking coali-
tions in the EU Council.

Conflicts between the new EU members and a few of the larger former EU15 members had begun prior to the official admission date of the new EU10 member countries. One major conflict arose when Spain and Poland refused to go along with the proposed vote allocation among the EU member states in the Council. Poland and Spain argued that the proposed vote allocation favored larger countries, such as France and Germany. It seems that this dispute has been resolved. The EU Constitution was approved by all EU25 governments that signed the historic Treaty of Rome on October 29, 2004. The EU Constitution will still have to be approved in national referenda by several EU countries in order to be adopted and become effective.

### Warnings to New EU10 Countries

In the fall of 2004, Germany and France launched a campaign aiming to convince their EU partners to harmonize corporate taxes in the EU. An average corporate income tax rate of 21.5 percent in the new EU10 versus 31.5 percent for the former EU15 provides, according to Germany and France, a competitive advantage for the new EU10 countries, attracting companies east at the expense of former EU15 members. Nicolas Sarkozy, the former finance minister of France, initiated an official complaint and suggested the EU reduce regional aid to EU10 countries unless they agreed to corporate tax harmonization in the EU. The EU Commission, however, was unmoved and refused to take any action against the new EU countries. Furthermore, two EU commissioners suggested that the EU15 members' response to this situation could be a reduction of their own corporate tax rates.

On October 11, 2004, the new EU monetary affairs commissioner, Joaquin Almunia, warned the poorest of the EU countries about their excess deficit to GDP ratios. He cautioned that these countries risked losing their aid from the Cohesion Fund. Such funding can only be received by countries having per capita GDPs below 90 percent of the EU average. Cohesion funds finance big transportation and environmental projects. Spain, Greece, and Portugal, and all of the EU10 countries, qualify for cohesion funds. It would be ironic if this threat is implemented because the large EU countries, France and Germany, have violated the deficit rule for at least two consecutive years and will go unpunished because both are too wealthy to qualify for cohesion funds.

In the biannual Convergence Report, Jean-Claude Trichet, the president of the ECB, gave another warning to the new EU10 countries for not making sufficient progress in their road to gaining membership in the EMU and falling behind. He expressed concerns about the rising debt to GDP ratios and large deficit to GDP ratios, above the 3 percent Maastricht limit in six EU10 countries. Rising inflation was an additional issue of major concern.

Sources: Jenkins, P. and G. Parker. "ECB Warns New EU Members Over Progress Toward euro," *Financial Times;* October 21, 2004.

Parker, G. "Sarkozy Fires Parting Shot At Low-Tax Eastern Europe," *Financial Times;* September 10, 2004.

Parker, G. "Poor EU Nations' Aid 'at risk if they break rules,'" *Financial Times;* October 12, 2004.

Parker, G. "Four EU Countries 'risk deficit breach,'" *Financial Times;* October 22, 2004.

After obtaining EU membership, the next step for the new EU10 countries is the adoption of the euro as their own currency. As a matter of fact, membership to the EMU is almost certain because these countries, according to the Accession Treaty of Athens, do not have an opt-out clause from EMU membership as Denmark and the UK have.[6] As long as these countries remain in the EU, they will have to join the EMU, but the exact date of their entry to the EMU and the adoption of the euro is unknown.

## The Road to EMU

Prior to joining the EMU, the new EU10 countries must meet the five Maastricht convergence criteria. All EU10 countries will be evaluated according to the same procedure that was employed to determine membership of the original EMU member countries. When a country meets the Maastricht convergence criteria, it is said to have achieved nominal convergence, permitting it to receive an entry ticket to the EMU and adopt the euro.

The candidate EMU countries must officially apply for membership and submit economic data regarding nominal convergence along with other information as specified by the Maastricht Treaty. The EU Commission and the ECB must evaluate each application and respond to the EU Council with a detailed report in reference to the performance of the countries on the Maastricht criteria and provide a recommendation pertaining to the qualification of each country for EMU membership. This is the same procedure that was applied to the original 12 members that established the EMU.

Nominal convergence can be attained when all EU countries co-ordinate monetary and fiscal policies leading to convergence in the following macroeconomic variables: inflation rates, long-term interest rates, government deficit and national debt to GDP ratios. In addition, each candidate EMU country must obtain membership to the modi-fied Exchange Rate Mechanism (ERM II) for at least two years prior to the adoption of the euro.

The ERM II was introduced with the establishment of the EMU in 1999. This was done to provide a set of rules that guide and adminis-ter monetary and exchange rate policies for those EU countries that are members of the ERM II but have not joined the EMU. Once new members join the EU, they are not obligated to join the EMU at the same time. They will have to join when they qualify and apply for EMU membership. For this purpose, the central bank governors of the EU10 began attending the ECB Governing Council bi-monthly meet-ings in 2003 as non-voting members.[7] All candidate EMU countries that declared their intention to seek membership to EMU must join and remain members of the ERM II for at least two years without any major exchange rate problems.

Excessive exchange rate volatility must be avoided. Exchange rate fluctuation of each ERM II member country's currency versus the euro or another ERM II currency cannot exceed the ±15 percent ref-erence band limits. Each ERM II member country's currency cannot be devalued against the euro or against any ERM II member country's currency when the devaluation is initiated by the candidate country. Lastly, a crucial requirement of all candidate EMU countries prior to the adoption of the euro is the rendering of independence to their cen-tral banks from the executive branch of the government. Central bank independence is essential in preventing governments from interfering with the price stability objective of the ECB.

## Empirical Performance of the EU10 Countries in Reference to the Five Maastricht Convergence Criteria

For the rest of this chapter, the performance of the EU10 countries will be evaluated with reference to each of the five Maastricht con-vergence criteria. This evaluation will help one to form an opinion whether each of the EU10 countries has satisfied the Maastricht convergence criteria or has been making progress toward meeting them in the future.

Prior to presenting historical data for every EU10 country pertinent to the Maastricht convergence criteria, each of the following subsections will begin with a short explanation of the particular Maastricht criterion in italics. Each explanation will be followed by three different graphs that will demonstrate the performance of each of the EU10 countries with respect to each of the five Maastricht convergence criteria.

The first graph is a bar chart demonstrating the performance of each country during the three or four most recent years in relation to each of the five Maastricht convergence criteria. The second graph is a time plot of the coefficient of variation (CV) of the particular variable for each Maastricht criterion. The CV is a measure of relative convergence/divergence of a set of values for a particular variable that is calculated and often plotted for a given time interval.[8] Four different CVs were calculated for every Maastricht criterion, each of them corresponding to EU10, Euro Area (EU12), EU15, and EU25 countries. The third graph is a time plot showing the historical performance of each of the EU10 countries in relation to other EU10 countries and in relation to the Maastricht reference value, which is indicated by an interval or a shaded area. If an EU10 country meets this Maastricht criterion, then the time plot of this particular variable for this country falls within the interval or the shaded area corresponding to this Maastricht criterion.

## Inflation Rate

*In the year prior to the examination, a candidate EMU country must have an inflation rate of no more than 1.5 percentage points above the average inflation rate of the three EU25 countries with the lowest inflation rates.[9]*

Many economists are convinced that inflation is the most important Maastricht convergence criterion. In their view, if this criterion is met, all other Maastricht criteria will subsequently be satisfied and, thus, become redundant.

A candidate country that intends to join an existing monetary union must coordinate its monetary and fiscal policies with those of the monetary union countries to achieve nominal convergence. Price stability is essential to candidate countries pursuing membership to a monetary union for many reasons. Many studies have found that economic growth and price stability are closely associated. On the other hand,

Figure 8.4

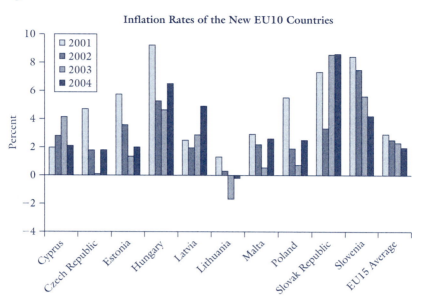

Inflation Rates of the New EU10 Countries

the lack of price stability causes volatility in interest and exchange rates, sudden massive capital flows, and frequent exchange rate crises. Price instability causes distortion in the domestic economy by affecting relative prices of goods and services and leading to misallocation of resources.

The detrimental and destabilizing effects of inflation on the domestic economy, international trade, and the foreign exchange markets are well known. For this reason, inflation is the first and most important Maastricht criterion that must be met by a candidate country to qualify for EMU membership.

Figure 8.4 shows the inflation rate of each of the new EU10 countries along with the EU15 average inflation rate for the years 2001–2004.[10] The calculation of the inflation rate is based on the arithmetic average of the 12 monthly Harmonized Indices of Consumer Prices (HICPs). According to this graph, inflation in 2003 declined in seven of the EU10 countries and increased in only three.[11] The opposite occurred in 2004 when inflation increased in seven countries.

Figure 8.5 depicts the CV for the inflation rates of the EU10, the Euro Area (EU12), the EU15, and the EU25 countries. According to these four CVs, the EU15 and the Euro Area countries achieved convergence in the rates of inflation until 2001. The remaining EU groups attained convergence in the rates of inflation until 1998 and divergence between 1998–1999. From 1999, convergence was repeated for

Figure 8.5

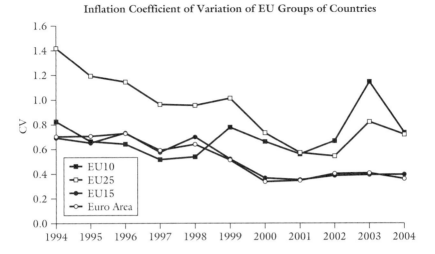

the EU10 and EU25 with a disruption (divergence) in 2001 and 2002. The CVs of Figure 8.5 support the view that the EMU contributed to substantial convergence in inflation rates of the Euro Area countries. The CV of the EU15 and the Euro Area increased only slightly after 2001, while the CV of the EU10 increased sharply during the period 2001–2003. Because the EU10 countries constitute a subset of the EU25 countries, an increase in the EU10 CV is responsible for the rise in the CV of the EU25. As a result, divergence in the inflation rates among the new EU10 countries caused divergence of the inflation rates of the EU25 member countries. In 2004, the CVs of the EU10 and EU25 have declined, indicating that the inflation rates of these two groups began converging.

In Figure 8.6, the inflation time plots of each EU10 countries are presented in groups of two or three in relation to the Maastricht inflation criterion (shown as a shaded area). This graph allows one to determine if a candidate EMU country met the Maastricht inflation criterion, during any of the years 1997–2004, by observing the country's historical inflation performance. If the inflation rate time plot declines, this implies that the country is making progress toward meeting the inflation Maastricht criterion. The inflation time plots show that a few EU10 countries qualify for EMU membership with respect to inflation, and others are moving in the correct direction. The inflation rate time paths of Hungary, Slovenia, Latvia, and the Slovak Republic deviated from the Maastricht reference values denoted by the shaded area. The three graphs show that these four EU10 countries, as of 2004, are not meeting the Maastricht inflation criterion.

Figure 8.6    Inflation Rates of the New EU10 Countries

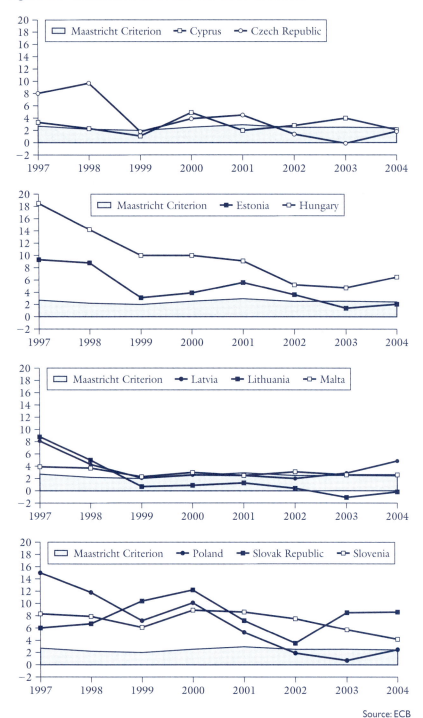

Source: ECB

Inflation differences are present among the new EU10 countries (see Figure 8.4) and among the Euro Area and the EU15 countries. In the Euro Area, for example, some countries that grew faster than others tended to have higher inflation rates. This was the case for Ireland and Greece in 2000–2004; the opposite was true for low growth countries, such as Germany. Another reason for the inflation differentials among EU countries is differing structures of the economies, such as trade openness and financial markets. For example, the increase in oil prices during 2004 affected EU countries' annual inflation rates differently.

Another source of inflation differences among countries is attributed to what is known as the Balassa-Samuelson (BS) effect. This arises because in some countries, prices in the non-tradable sector increase faster than in the tradable sector. The BS effect is observed in emerging economies. The most competitive sector of these economies is the tradable sector because it competes in the international economy. Productivity increases in the tradable sector cause wage increases in that sector and, as a consequence, wages in the non-tradable sector in this economy increase. Prices in the tradable sector, however, cannot increase as fast as in the non-tradable sector due to international competition. In the non-tradable sector, wage increases that are not matched by labor productivity cause inflation. As a result, inflation of the entire country increases. Countries with large non-tradable sectors, such as the new EU10 countries, can expect to experience greater inflation than countries with smaller non-tradable sectors. Most of the EU15 countries, particularly the most developed ones, do not have large non-tradable sectors and, as a result, inflation due to the BS effect should be small or absent.

The EU10 countries, because of the catching-up effect (for real convergence), are expected to have higher inflation than the EU15 countries. If the new EU10 countries continue to grow faster than the former EU15, then these countries will experience higher inflation rates. The EU10 countries cannot prevent inflation attributed to the catching-up effect. They can, nonetheless, keep inflation from rising when inflation is attributed to the BS effect. This can be achieved by adopting labor policies that promote flexible labor markets, resulting in sectoral wage increases, according to labor productivity in the particular sector.

## Long-Term Interest Rate

*In the year prior to the examination, a candidate EMU country must have a long-term interest rate of no more than 2 percentage points above*

Figure 8.7

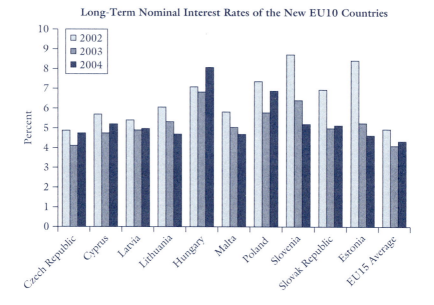

Long-Term Nominal Interest Rates of the New EU10 Countries

*the average interest rate of the three EU25 countries with the lowest inflation rates.*

The long-term interest rate is measured by the 10-year government bond yield. Long-term bond yields are related to expected inflation. If a country is expected to be confronted with high inflation in the future, financial investors will not be interested in buying the country's bonds unless the interest rate on the long-term bond is increased accordingly to include an inflation premium. The ECB, in cooperation with the national central banks (NCBs) of the EU10 and the EU Commission, has defined and made available harmonized long-term interest rates for nine of the EU10 countries. For Estonia, a temporary interest rate indicator is published until a better interest rate indicator replaces it.

Figure 8.7 portrays the long-term interest rates for the period 2002–2004 for all EU10 countries.[12,13] The graph shows that all EU10 countries have experienced difficulty in reducing their long-term interest rates. For some countries, the long-term interest rate declined during the period 2001–2004. For a few others, it increased. Poland and Hungary had the highest long-term interest rates among the EU10 countries in 2004.

In Figure 8.8, the time plots for the CVs of the EU10, the Euro Area, the EU15, and the EU25 are presented. The CVs of the EU15

Figure 8.8

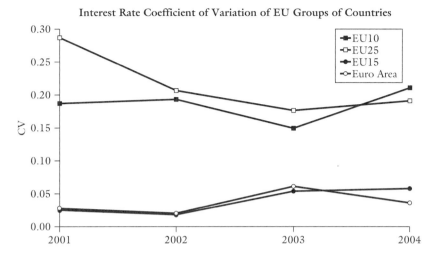

Interest Rate Coefficient of Variation of EU Groups of Countries

and the Euro Area are lower than the CVs of the EU10 and the EU25. This indicates evidence of more convergence in the interest rates of these two EU groups of countries than in the new EU10 or the EU25. This finding implies that interest rate convergence in the Euro Area was the result of the Single Monetary Policy for the Euro Area.

Lastly, in Figure 8.9, the time plots of the interest rates for the period 2001–2004 are shown for two or three countries together along with the Maastricht convergence reference criterion, which is indicated as a shaded area. As seen in Figure 8.9, the long-term interest rate plots in eight EU10 countries fell within the shaded area. Consequently, eight of the EU10 countries met the Maastricht interest rate criterion, but Poland and Hungary did not. A substantial reduction in interest rates took place once it became certain that the EU10 countries were going to join the EU. This phenomenon was observed in previous EU expansions. Spain, Greece, Italy, and Portugal reduced their inflation and interest rates substantially prior to joining the EU. When it became certain that the four Southern European countries would join the EMU, all their interest rates declined. The inflation and long-term interest rate experience of the Mediterranean countries are expected to be repeated by the EU10 countries. This borrowed price credibility from the existing EU members will be the greatest benefit to the EU10 countries from joining the EU and the EMU.

Figure 8.9   Long Term Nominal Interest Rates of the New EU10 Countries

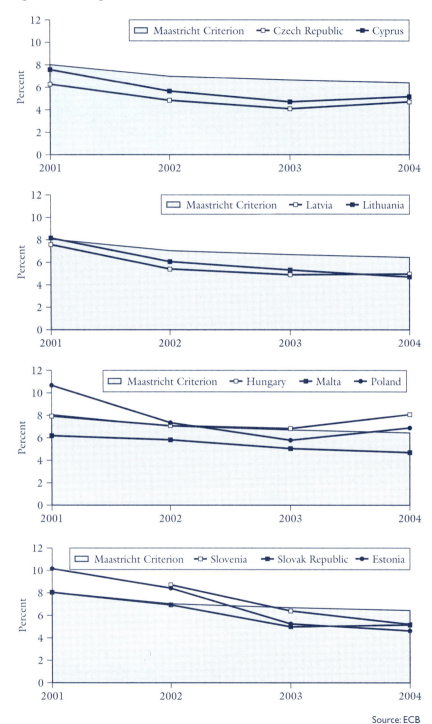

Source: ECB

# The Two Fiscal Maastricht Criteria

In addition to the inflation and the long-term interest rate, two additional Maastricht criteria deal exclusively with fiscal discipline. The two fiscal Maastricht criteria are the government deficit and the government debt to GDP ratios.

## Government Deficit to GDP Ratio

*In the year prior to the examination, a candidate EMU country must have a deficit to GDP ratio equal to or less than 3 percent.*

Figure 8.10 indicates that during the years 2001–2003, six EU10 countries exceeded the 3 percent maximum government deficit to GDP ratio allowed by the Maastricht Treaty. These countries are the Czech Republic, Cyprus, Hungary, Malta, Poland, and the Slovak Republic. The highest government deficit to GDP ratio was that of the Czech Republic, which in 2003 was above 12 percent. Because of the high deficit, the Czech Republic decided to postpone the adoption of the euro until 2010. On the other extreme, among the countries that respected the 3 percent maximum government deficit to GDP ratio was Estonia, which generated only surpluses during 2001–2003. Latvia, Lithuania, and Slovenia maintained deficits below 3 percent.

Figure 8.10 implies that most of the EU10 countries have no other choice but to adopt contractionary fiscal policies in the next few years

Figure 8.10

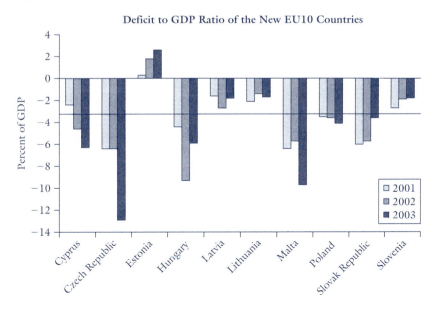

Deficit to GDP Ratio of the New EU10 Countries

Figure 8.11

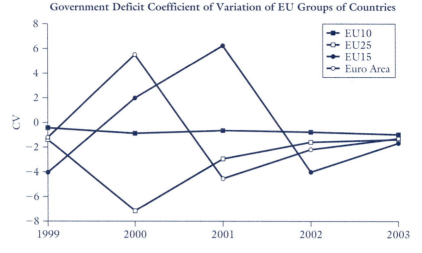

Government Deficit Coefficient of Variation of EU Groups of Countries

as they prepare their way to ensure membership to the EMU. EU countries can pursue fiscal discipline by cutting government expenditures, increasing taxes, or some combination of these two policies. Both of these policies are unpopular and already caused social distress in the CEECs.

Figure 8.11 portrays the CVs of the government deficit to GDP ratio for the EU10, the EU15, the Euro Area (EU12), and the EU25 countries. The CVs of all EU groups indicate a high degree of volatility during the period 1999–2003. Starting in 2001, however, the CVs of all groups began converging toward zero, suggesting relative convergence in the government deficit to GDP ratios within each EU group of countries.[14]

Even after the formation of the EMU and the adoption of the euro, a few Euro Area countries violated the government deficit to GDP ratio Maastricht criterion. The first country to violate the deficit to GDP ratio was Portugal in 2001, but after imposing strong austerity measures, Portugal reduced its deficit to GDP ratio below 3 percent in 2002 and 2003. The most troublesome news came from the two largest EU countries, France and Germany. These two countries violated the 3 percent Maastricht limit for two consecutive years, 2002 and 2003, and repeatedly defied the EU Commission's recommendations to reduce their deficit to GDP ratios. In the spring of 2004, the French and German finance ministers convinced their counterpart EU15 ministers in the ECOFIN not to allow the EU Commission to exercise its authority to impose penalties on these two countries. This decision of the ECOFIN practically killed the

Stability and Growth Pact (SGP), and it left the Euro Area countries divided and distrusting each other. In a fall 2004 meeting of the finance ministers (ECOFIN), it was decided that the SGP would be modified to give more weight to economic growth than to price stability.

Even more shocking news regarding the Maastricht rules, which were designed to be the pillars of the EMU and the euro, came in September of 2004 when the Greek government admitted that its predecessor had underreported the actual deficit to GDP ratio during 1999–2002 by excluding certain defense expenditures from the annual budgets. This accusation, however, was denied by the representatives of the previous Greek government. They suggested that they were correct to amortize and spread expenditures of less than $10 billion on military aircraft, which Greece had not yet received from the US for several years. In October 2004, an investigation by the EU Commission found that Greece had violated the Maastricht deficit rule, and it would take Greece to court.

With such an unsettling record regarding the government deficit to GDP ratio in the Euro Area, it is almost impossible for one to expect that the new EU10 countries will eagerly comply with this Maastricht requirement. Figure 8.12 shows the historical performance of the EU10 countries in relation to the deficit to GDP Maastricht criterion of 3 percent during the pre-membership period of 1999–2003. The deficit to GDP time paths of the EU10 countries are reported in groups of two or three on each time plot along with the Maastricht reference value of 3 percent, shown as a shaded area. According to these graphs, as of 2003, four countries met the 3 percent Maastricht limit, two countries approached it, and four countries deviated from it.

## Government Debt to GDP Ratio

*In the year prior to the examination, a candidate EMU country's government debt to GDP ratio must not exceed 60 percent.*

The fourth Maastricht criterion upon which the new EU10 countries will be evaluated is the government debt to GDP ratio. The debt to GDP ratio of a country is related to the country's annual budget deficits. The EU countries and most developed countries finance their annual deficits by issuing debt (government bonds). In other words, the accumulated deficits of all past years give rise to a country's public outstanding debt. Similarly, a country's annual governmental budget surpluses can result in a reduction of a country's public debt to GDP ratio since surpluses allow the country to buy back (retire) some of its outstanding public debt.

Figure 8.12   Government Deficit to GDP Ratios of the New EU10
Countries

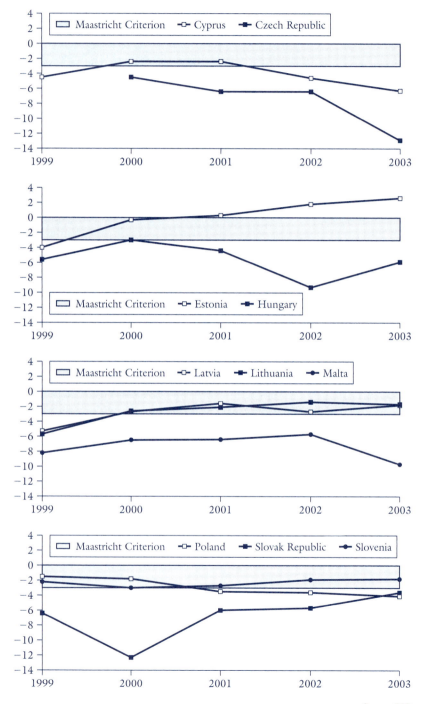

Figure 8.13

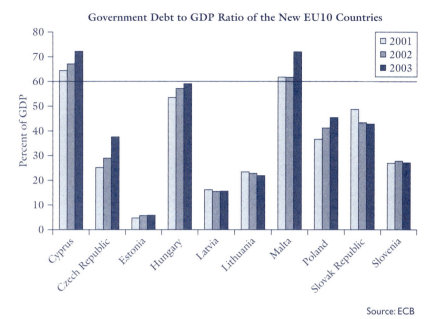

Source: ECB

Figure 8.13 shows that Cyprus and Malta violated the government debt to GDP ratio criterion. All other EU10 countries, with the exception of Hungary, which was approaching the 60 percent Maastricht reference limit value, attained low government debt to GDP ratios. Latvia, Lithuania, the Slovak Republic, and Slovenia stabilized their public debt to GDP ratios. All the remaining EU10 countries' government debt to GDP ratios were generally lower than that of the former EU15 countries.[15] Furthermore, though only two EU10 countries surpassed the Maastricht government debt to GDP criterion, six Euro Area countries had violated this fiscal criterion. Of the six Euro Area countries that exceeded the 60 percent Maastricht limit, Belgium, Italy, and Greece accumulated over 100 percent government debt to GDP ratios.[16] Reducing the government debt to GDP ratio to the 60 percent Maastricht level has turned out to be impossible for these three countries.

In Figure 8.14, the CVs of the EU10, the EU15, the Euro Area and the EU25 are shown as time plots. The CV of the EU10 began rising after 2002. This is evidence of a small increase in the divergence of the government debt to GDP ratios of the EU10 countries. The CVs of the other three EU groups remained flat, indicating that government debt to GDP ratios' dispersion within each of the groups of countries remained unchanged.

Figure 8.14

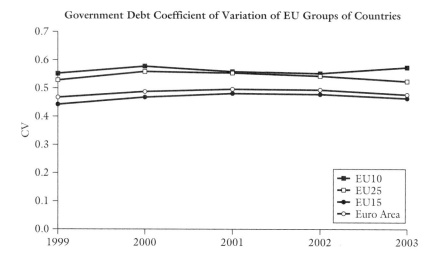

Lastly, Figure 8.15 depicts the performance of the EU10 countries in reference to the government debt to GDP ratio for the period 1999–2003 in comparison to the 60 percent Maastricht criterion as well as the EU25 average government debt to GDP ratio. According to these graphs, only the debt to GDP ratios of Cyprus and Malta surpassed the 60 percent Maastricht reference criterion, and Hungary exceeded the EU25 unweighted average. The relatively low government debt to GDP ratios for most of the EU10 countries is a positive characteristic of these economies. As discussed in Chapter Three, highly indebted countries have trouble reducing their national debt to GDP ratio. During recession periods, national debt to GDP ratios increase because countries are inclined to adopt expansionary fiscal policies that generate larger budget deficits. In addition, during periods of recession, GDP declines, causing the government debt to GDP ratio to increase more rapidly.[17]

## Examining Government Deficit and Debt to GDP Ratios Together

The scatter diagram of Figure 8.16 portrays the performance of the EU10 countries with reference to both fiscal criteria for the years 2000 and 2003. The government debt to GDP ratio is shown along the horizontal axis, and the government budget surplus (deficit) to GDP ratio is depicted along the vertical axis. The years 2000 and 2003 were chosen to ascertain whether the EU10 countries made progress in reference to the two fiscal Maastricht criteria prior to their accession to

Figure 8.15   Government Debt to GDP Ratios for the New EU10 Countries

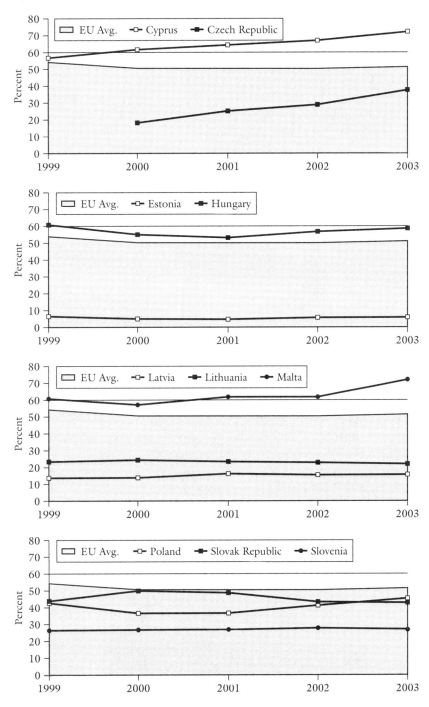

Source: ECB

Figure 8.16

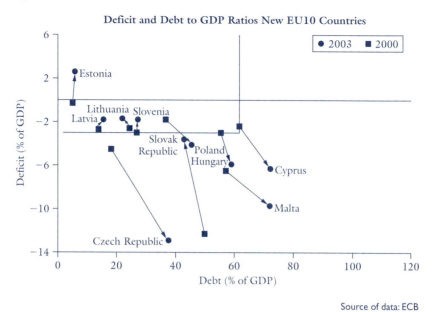

Source of data: ECB

the EU. In Figure 8.16, two points correspond to each EU10 country. The coordinates of the initial points represent each country's government deficit and government debt ratios in the year 2000. Similarly, the coordinates of each final point, where the head of the arrow ends, are the government deficit and debt ratios of each EU10 country in 2003. The rectangle formed, starting from the origin in the fourth quadrant with coordinates (60, −3), includes all points that correspond to countries that meet both Maastricht fiscal criteria. If a final point lies within or above the rectangle, then this displays that the country met both fiscal criteria. The further a country's final point is located from the rectangle, the more the candidate EMU country violates both fiscal Maastricht criteria. If an arrow points towards the rectangle, then this is an indication that a candidate EMU country is making progress in meeting the two fiscal Maastricht convergence criteria.

In Figure 8.16, four countries' final points are located above or inside the rectangle: Estonia, Latvia, Lithuania, and Slovenia. If 2003 were the year of the evaluation for membership to EMU, then these four countries would have qualified for EMU membership based on the two fiscal Maastricht criteria. For the Slovak Republic, the final point is located close to the rectangle, and the arrow indicates that this country is moving closer to meeting the Maastricht fiscal criteria. Consequently, if the Slovak Republic persists in pursuing the convergence process, then this country could soon meet the two fiscal criteria.

Lastly, for the remaining five countries, the coordinates of the final points fall outside the rectangle and the arrows point away from it.

This implies that the performance of these five countries, in reference to the two fiscal Maastricht convergence criteria, is worsening. Malta and Cyprus are the only two countries that have not met the government debt to GDP Maastricht criterion. Both of these Mediterranean countries are smaller than the remaining Euro Area countries. Consequently, their large debt to GDP ratios are so small that they cannot affect Euro Area interest rates. One must be reminded that the two fiscal criteria were adopted to protect the Euro Area from high inflation countries. Inflation can be caused by persistent deficit spending and by relatively high interest rates on government bonds as a result of high risk premia. High risk premia on government bonds are caused by countries' heavy indebtness, i.e., relatively high debt to GDP ratios.

The overall fiscal situation of the EU10 countries requires corrective policies. Some EU10 countries diverge from the Maastricht reference values, primarily due to the violation of high deficits. Because it is easier for countries to reduce their deficits than to reduce large public debt to GDP ratios, fiscal stability in the new EU10 countries can be attained if EU10 countries pursue fiscal discipline within the next few years. All EU10 countries, however, must be vigilant to assure continuous fiscal stability, particularly as they move closer toward adopting the euro. Fiscal consolidation is recommended to most of the EU10 countries to attain sustainable price and fiscal stability. For a few CEECs, deficit reduction may become more difficult because most countries have sold (privatized) almost all state assets and, as a result, state revenues from this source have practically dried up. Almost all CEECs governments that adopted austerity programs to comply with the Maastricht criteria suffered major political setbacks as these programs became unpopular with their citizens in 2004.

## Exchange Rate

*Each EMU candidate country must join the ERM II and respect the normal band of ±15 percent for the last two years prior to the examination.*

In January 1999, with the establishment of the EMU, the ERM was modified and launched as the ERM II. The principal role of the ERM II was to create a framework and a set of rules to administer the exchange rate relations of the euro with the currencies of EU countries that joined the ERM II but did not adopt the euro.[18]

According to a multilateral agreement between the ECB, the Euro Area countries, Denmark, and the new EU10 countries, the exchange rate policy of new EU10 members will be a matter of common interest. This means that the new EU10 countries will have to pursue exchange rate stability as long as this policy does not conflict with price stability, which is the ultimate objective of the ECB.

The new EU10 countries joined the EU on May 1, 2004, with a derogation. This means that these countries entered the EU without adopting the euro. All EU10 Countries will eventually join the EMU. Before joining the EMU these countries must undertake all the appropriate measures and policies to transform their economies into efficient market economies and achieve nominal convergence by meeting the Maastricht convergence criteria.

The Treaty provides that all the new EU10 countries must join the ERM II and remain members for at least two years before they can adopt the euro. An EU10 member state can request ERM II membership when convinced that it has achieved sufficient nominal and real convergence that will enable the country to maintain exchange rate stability. Prior to joining the ERM II, the central exchange rate versus the euro and all other ERM II currencies must be agreed upon by all the signatory parties of the agreement. The central rates are jointly decided by the ECB and all the other central banks of those EU countries that are members of the ERM II or are candidate members applying for admission to ERM II. The ERM II is, therefore, a multilateral arrangement of fixed, central, but adjustable exchange rates with central band limits of $\pm 15$ percent.

Prior to joining the ERM II, the EU10 countries may maintain or adopt different types of exchange rate strategies, provided such strategies are compatible with their decision of joining the Euro Area. The new EU10 countries cannot, for example, peg their currencies to any currency other than the euro. The EU10 countries cannot adopt the euro as their national currency on their own (by euroization) without first joining the ERM II for at least two years.[19] Once an EU10 country becomes a member of the ERM II upon agreement with the ECB and other ERM II non-Euro Area countries, the country is periodically allowed to realign its currency. After joining the ERM II, the EU10 countries can expect to utilize the short-term financing facilities of the ECB to stabilize their currencies. Intervention in the margin to support the central rates is unlimited unless such activity conflicts with the ECB's principal objective, which is price stability.

Figure 8.17 portrays exchange rate indices of the EU10 countries against the euro for 2001–2003. The year 2000 was chosen to be the base year and, as such, is set to 100 for all EU10 countries. Consequently, it is not shown in the bar chart of Figure 8.17.[20] The exchange rate indices of the other years, 2001–2003, indicate changes from the base year. According to this figure, none of the EU10 countries violated the $\pm 15$ percent band. Most of the new EU10 countries violated the older normal band of $\pm 2.25$ percent, which is no longer applicable since it was abolished by the EU Council in August 1993, after the exchange rate crisis of the EMS.

Figure 8.17

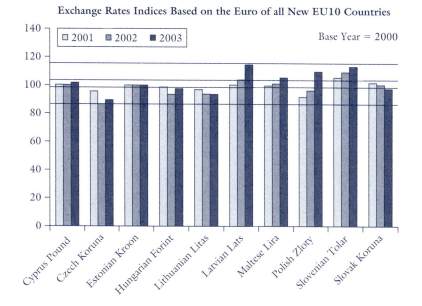

Figure 8.18

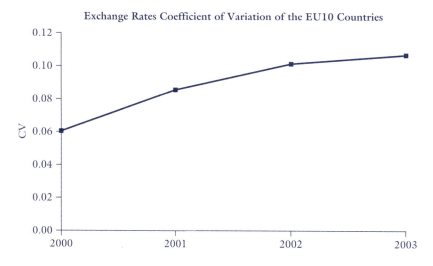

Figure 8.18 shows the CV of the EU10 exchange rates in relation to the euro (based on the constructed indices) for 2000–2003. Figure 8.18 suggests increased variability in the exchange rates of the EU10 countries. The rate of change in the exchange rate variability, however, declines. This means the EU10 exchange rates may soon stabilize.

The Governing Council of the ECB has adopted an official policy position regarding all exchange rate issues of the new EU10 countries.[21] In this document, the ECB offers detailed guidelines on how the EU10 countries should proceed with their ultimate objective to join the EMU and adopt the euro. According to the ECB official position, each EU10 country must consider its own special circumstances before it decides to seek admission to the ERM II. The Governing Council recommends that the EU10 countries must not hurry to join the ERM II unless they have first achieved substantial convergence and introduced flexibility in their economies. This could be attained by adopting the appropriate macroeconomic policies and by undergoing significant structural and institutional changes, including market and trade liberalization. The 1992–1993 exchange rate crisis of the EMS that shook the ERM was such a fresh memory in the minds of the ECB officials and other EU national monetary authorities that they were determined to avoid catastrophic speculative attacks on ERM II countries' currencies. As a result, premature fixing of the exchange rate of the EU10 countries' currencies to the euro was discouraged by the ECB to avoid an exchange rate crisis.

## Three EU10 Countries Have Joined the ERM II

According to the ECB policy position on exchange rate issues, the ERM II membership will be decided according to the performance of each country considered independently on its own merits. Four EU10 countries made substantial progress in many areas and came closer to adopting the euro in 2003. On June 27, 2004, three of these four countries gained membership to the ERM II, while a fourth country announced that it would fix its currency to the euro on January 1, 2005. The three countries that joined the ERM II are Estonia, Lithuania, and Slovenia. The fourth country that accelerated its course to joining the EMU is Latvia, which fixed its currency to the euro at the rate of 1€ = .702804 Latvian lats on January 1, 2005. Three of the four countries that made significant progress toward joining the EMU are former Soviet Union republics: Lithuania, Estonia, and Latvia.

The three former Soviet republics were anxious to break away from Russia economically and develop closer ties to Western economies. The three countries' economies began integrating rapidly with their Scandinavian neighbors and Germany by opening up trade and inviting foreign investment. After dropping the ruble, all three countries pegged their new currencies. Estonia pegged its kroon to the Deutsche mark (later to the euro). Lithuania first pegged its litas to the US dollar (and on February 2002 to the euro). Latvia's lat was pegged to the IMF's Special Drawing Right (SDR) but was pegged to the euro on January 1, 2005.

As one of the former Yugoslavia's six republics, Slovenia enjoyed greater economic freedom than the three Baltic, ex-Soviet states and is more developed than all of the new EU10 countries. This is reflected by Slovenia's real per capita GDP. Slovenia chose to move in the fast lane toward the adoption of the euro. Slovenia, unlike Estonia, Lithuania, and Latvia, never pegged its currency, the tolar, to any currency but employed a managed floating system.

On June 27, 2004, the president of the ECB, the finance ministers, and the central bank governors of the Euro Area countries and of Denmark agreed to accept Estonia, Lithuania, and Slovenia into the ERM II, following requests from the governments of the three countries. This is an important historic event for these three countries because in a short period of only two years from the day of the agreement, they could adopt the euro. For these three countries, EU membership, along with the admission to the ERM II, provides assurance of political stability and hope for economic advancement. In the June 27, 2004 agreement, the central exchange rates with respect to the euro were set along with the compulsory intervention rates of ±15 percent for each of the three currencies, which are shown below in Table 8.3.

Estonia and Lithuania both had their currencies fixed to the dollar and were administered by currency board arrangements (CBAs).[22] Both countries were asked to keep the CBAs in place. This put the responsibility on the two countries' CBAs and not on the ECB to maintain their exchange rates of their currencies fixed to the euro.

In Figure 8.19, the nominal exchange rates of the EU10 countries are shown in relation to the euro. The exchange rate of the Estonian

Table 8.3

| Euro Central Rates and Compulsory Intervention Rates for Three EU10 Countries Participating in ERM II | | |
|---|---|---|
| **Country and Currency** | | **EUR 1 =** |
| **Estonia** | Upper rate = 115 | 17.9936 |
| **Estonian kroon** | Central rate = 100 | 15.6466 |
| | Lower rate = 85 | 13.2996 |
| **Lithuania** | Upper rate = 115 | 3.97072 |
| **Lithuanian litas** | Central rate = 100 | 3.4528 |
| | Lower rate = 85 | 2.93488 |
| **Slovenia** | Upper rate = 115 | 275.586 |
| **Slovenian tolar** | Central rate = 100 | 239.64 |
| | Lower rate = 85 | 203.694 |

Source: ECB

## Figure 8.19　Nominal Euro Exchange Rates of the EU10 Countries' Currencies

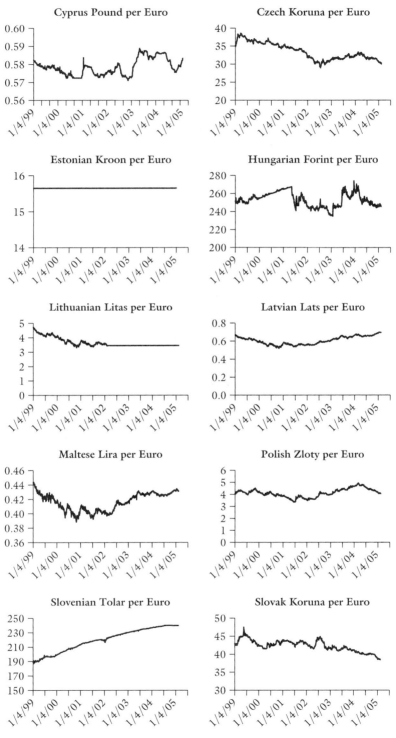

Source: ECB

kroon and the Lithuanian lita, which are fixed with respect to the euro (the lita after 2002), are shown as straight horizontal lines. The Slovenian tolar, on the other hand, is not fixed. Figure 8.19 shows that the tolar has been depreciating since 1999. The depreciation of the tolar is likely to be attributed to the relatively higher inflation rate of Slovenia in comparison to the average Euro Area inflation rate.

Table 8.4 below provides a summary of the performance of all EU10 countries in reference to all five Maastricht convergence criteria. According to Table 8.4, two countries, Estonia and Lithuania, met four Maastricht convergence criteria in 2003. Slovenia only met three Maastricht criteria as it fell short on meeting the inflation rate criterion. On June 28, 2004, three countries joined the ERM II. Thus, in the middle of 2004, Estonia and Lithuania met all five Maastricht convergence criteria, while Slovenia met four. Though most of the EU10 countries did not meet the inflation criterion, eight of the EU10 countries met the interest rate Maastricht criterion.[23] The relationship between inflation rates and long-term interest rates is similar to the relationship between the government deficit and the government debt to GDP ratios. Regarding the two fiscal convergence criteria, most EU10 countries, though they did not meet the deficit to GDP ratio, did meet the government debt to GDP ratio.

In addition to meeting the five Maastricht convergence criteria, each EMU candidate country, prior to the adoption of the euro, is legally obligated to render its central bank fully independent. A few years ago, EU10 countries began the legal process of rendering independence to their central banks. As of October 2004, none of the EU10 countries has yet rendered their central banks completely independent by meeting all legal requirements of the treaty.[24] Despite the legislative shortcomings, the NCBs act independently from their national governments in their role in the implementation of monetary policy. Many studies have found that central bank independence is one of the most important and necessary factors ensuring price stability.

An interesting question that arises is, what will be the impact of the Euro Area enlargement on the EMU and the ECB monetary policy? Achieving an optimal monetary policy for an enlarged EMU of 25 members or more is expected to be a true challenge. On July 29, 2004, the vice president of the ECB, Lucas Papademos, elaborated on some of the upcoming EMU challenges.[25] He presumed that the enlarged EMU would be characterized by asymmetries and, consequently, the single ECB monetary policy will have asymmetric effects. The vice president of the ECB was optimistic for the future of the EMU since many of the new EU10 countries have efficient economies. In addition, new EU10 countries will have sufficient time to pursue nominal

Table 8.4

## Maastricht Convergence Criteria Checklist for the New EU10 Countries

| Country | Inflation Rate | | Long Term Interest Rate | | Government Deficit/GDP | | Government Debt/GDP | | ERM II Member | | Total | |
|---|---|---|---|---|---|---|---|---|---|---|---|---|
| | 2002 | 2003 | 2002 | 2003 | 2002 | 2003 | 2002 | 2003 | 2002 | 2003 | 2002 | 2003 |
| Cyprus | N | N | Y | Y | N | N | N | N | N | N | 1 | 1 |
| Czech Republic | Y | Y | Y | Y | N | N | Y | Y | N | N | 3 | 3 |
| Estonia | N | Y | N | Y | Y | Y | Y | Y | N | N | 2 | 4 |
| Hungary | N | N | Y | Y | N | N | Y | Y | N | N | 2 | 2 |
| Latvia | Y | N | Y | Y | Y | Y | Y | Y | N | N | 4 | 3 |
| Lithuania | Y | Y | Y | Y | Y | Y | Y | Y | N | N | 4 | 4 |
| Malta | N | N | Y | Y | N | N | N | N | N | N | 1 | 1 |
| Poland | Y | Y | N | Y | N | N | Y | Y | N | N | 2 | 3 |
| Slovak Republic | N | N | Y | Y | N | N | Y | Y | N | N | 2 | 2 |
| Slovenia | N | N | N | Y | Y | Y | Y | Y | N | N | 2 | 3 |

and real convergence prior to adopting the euro and, as a result, most of the asymmetric shocks will become less significant or be eliminated. In addition, the ECB has a plan for the governance of the Eurosystem for an expanded EMU. For these reasons, Lucas Papademos' view of a future, enlarged EMU is optimistic.

## SUMMARY

On May 1, 2004, the EU accepted ten new member countries. Eight of them are CEECs and two are Mediterranean island countries. This was the largest and most challenging expansion of the EU.

With this expansion, the EU became much larger in terms of population, but poorer in terms of real per capita income. The latest expansion is challenging and promising as the new countries are already off to a good start. They began liberalizing their economies, attracting foreign investment mainly from their neighboring EU countries, while introducing many structural changes, aiming to transform their countries to efficient, modern free market economies.

As members of the EU, new EU10 countries are entitled to apply for membership to the EMU when they are qualified to do so. In this chapter, the progress of each of these countries in terms of nominal convergence was evaluated. To assess the EU10 countries' nominal convergence, the performance of each country in terms of all the Maastricht convergence criteria was reported.

The performance of each of the ten countries in reference to inflation, long-term interest rate, government deficit and government debt to GDP ratios, and the exchange rate was evaluated and reported. The results are encouraging. Two countries have met five Maastricht criteria and a third country has met four as of June 27, 2004. Membership to the ERM II is a prerequisite to joining the EMU. None of the ten countries has rendered full independence, according to the letter of the law, to their central bank, as it is required by the Maastricht Treaty. Though much has been accomplished in terms of nominal convergence, most of the EU10 countries need to continue to work toward their long-term objective of complete economic and monetary integration with the EU. On October 29, 2004, European leaders signed the European Union's first constitution. The EU Constitution was designed to make economic and monetary integration feasible and smoother for an enlarged EU.

Real convergence in standards of living, as measured by real per capita income, is not a requirement for the candidate countries to join the EMU. Real convergence in terms of institutional structures, legislative framework, infrastructure, investment, trade liberalization, and financial integration are necessary and important in achieving monetary integration and real economic convergence.

# Essay Questions

1. On May 1, 2004, ten new countries were admitted to the EU. Discuss the impact of this recent expansion on the EU. You can begin by referring to some basic economic statistics of the new EU10 countries in comparison to the former EU15. You may want to explain any structural differences that may still exist between the two groups of EU countries. Is this a problem in your opinion? Will this problem be eliminated? Explain. Compare the EU25 with the US and Japan in reference to some basic statistics such as population, GDP, and per capita GDP.

2. For an EU country to be allowed to join the EMU and adopt the euro, it must meet the five Maastricht convergence criteria. Discuss how the EU10 countries performed in terms of achieving price stability and convergence regarding the inflation criterion. Why is monetary stability (low inflation) such an important requirement for candidate EMU countries prior to joining the EMU?

3. A candidate EMU country may experience inflation attributed to two different sources. The first is due to the "catching-up effect." The second source of inflation is due to the Balassa-Samuelson effect. Explain both types of inflation thoroughly. Which of the two sources of inflation is unavoidable to the new EU10 countries? Explain.

4. The long-term interest rate is the second Maastricht convergence criterion. How have the EU10 countries performed with respect to this Maastricht convergence criterion? How is the reference value of the long-term interest rate calculated? Do you think that the long-term interest rate criterion is related to the other Maastricht convergence criteria? If yes, which ones? Why was the long term interest rate selected to be one of the Maastricht convergence criteria? Explain.

5. State and explain the two fiscal convergence criteria. Explain why fiscal discipline of the candidate EMU countries is important for the success of the EMU. How did the EU10 countries perform

in reference to the two fiscal criteria? Are the two fiscal criteria related to each other? Do you foresee any problems with the EU10 countries meeting these criteria? Explain.

6. State and explain the exchange rate Maastricht criterion. How did the EU10 countries perform regarding the exchange rate Maastricht convergence criterion? What is the ERM II? Have any EU10 countries joined the ERM II? If yes, which countries and how did they accomplish it?

# conclusion

# Looking Ahead: The Dollar and the Euro Relation

The performance of the euro since January is impressive and there is little doubt in anyone's mind that the euro is here to stay. Empirical evidence shows that the euro is rapidly becoming an international currency competing with the US dollar. The euro became more popular particularly after 2001 when the US dollar began depreciating in relation to the euro. Ultimately, the depreciation of the dollar will end. This depreciation has been caused by large current account (CA) deficits that, in 2004, approached 6 percent of GDP, and are considered by many economists as unsustainable. The depreciation of the dollar has also been caused by US government deficits and by low US private saving in relation to private investment.

The US is in need of capital inflows of approximately $2 billion a day to finance its CA deficit. This means that foreigners must be willing to lend money to the US. Lending to the US mainly requires that foreigners must be willing to purchase US government securities denominated in dollars. These securities will continue to lose value as long as the dollar depreciates. It is very likely that such foreign lenders will become more hesitant to invest in a currency that continuously loses value. The most important holders and buyers of dollars are South-East Asian central banks that have been determined to keep their currencies undervalued in order to help their export industries. It will be interesting to see for how long these South-East Asian central bankers will continue to accumulate US dollars.

It is highly unlikely that all Asian central banks, which all together hold $2.4 trillion in foreign reserves, will move simultaneously to diversify their portfolios away from US dollars. The US dollar, however, fell against several currencies after the exchange market misinterpreted an announcement made by the Central Bank of South Korea on February 22, 2005. The Bank of South Korea announced that it was going to "diversify the currencies it held by targeting higher yield investments". The next day the dollar recouped some of its losses after the central banks of Japan, Taiwan, and South Korea tried to calm the markets by assuring that they would not be selling dollars. As of the end of January 2005, Japan held the largest foreign reserves in the world at $841 billion, followed by China, which held $604 billion at the end of 2004. Taiwan and South Korea each hold substantial foreign reserves of approximately $243 billion and $200 billion respectively. It is evident that structural imbalances in the US CA cause the US dollar to overreact and to be sensitive to rumors (see *Financial Times*, February 23 and 24, 2005).

In the meantime, the US government seems unmoved to do anything drastic to stop further depreciation of the dollar. Some in the US government believe that the depreciating dollar is the only corrective tool to reduce US CA deficits. Such an approach, however, has proven to be totally unsuccessful in 2004. The US government announced measures to reduce government deficits starting in 2005 by initiating across-the-board reductions in governmental expenditures. Starting in June 2004, the Federal Reserve increased the federal funds rate five times in order to curtail price increases triggered by rising oil prices in the second half of 2004. The Fed announced its intention to continue raising its federal funds target rate and has already done so on February 2, 2005 to 2.5 percent. In contrast, the ECB kept its repo rate unchanged at 2 percent for twenty consecutive months into February 2005, as a response to the slow growth in the Euro Area.

Higher US interest rates are expected to cause capital inflows to the US and increase demand for dollars, leading to an appreciation of the dollar. The Fed, however, has moved cautiously so far, since higher interest rates can reduce growth and take the country into a recession. Higher US interest rates are expected to discourage consumption and increase private domestic US saving. Increased domestic saving can contribute to the appreciation of the dollar. Private saving is not expected to increase very rapidly, thus, the effect on the US dollar is expected to be small and gradual.

Joint intervention of the ECB with the US Fed does not seem likely in the near future. Joint intervention of the two central banks could have been very effective, but central bankers seem to agree with the US Treasury that exchange rates should be determined by market forces. This might be their view as long as the exchange rate does not move outside of some perceived tolerable limits. Many in the private sector expect the euro to trade as high as $1.40 or $1.50, starting in spring of 2005.

Paul De Grauwe, a Belgian economist and author on European monetary policy, suggested that a unilateral intervention by the ECB could reverse the rise of the euro. This can happen because the ECB theoretically has unlimited amounts of euros to purchase the necessary number of dollars to reverse the trend. Either unilateral or bilateral intervention will take place if the dollar-euro exchange rate approaches a value outside a perceived tolerable band by the two central banks. Only time will tell what exactly will happen with the dollar-euro exchange rate and if it will ever reach the tolerable band limits.

# The Role of the EU in a More Harmonious World

The EU began with six members in 1957 and has grown to 25 members in 2004. In 2007, the EU is expected to include two more countries, Romania and Bulgaria, and has decided to start accession negotiations with two other countries, Croatia and Turkey. Other European countries are also expected to apply for membership. Ukraine, which has gained freedom with the recent political triumph of Victor Yuschenko, has already expressed interest in joining the EU.

Some expressed concern that EU enlargement will weaken the integration process. Some Europeans believe that, with enlargement, the EU will become nothing more than a free trade area. This is something that the UK government always pursued because it was unwilling to delegate its sovereign authority to the EU (Brussels). On the other hand, some Central European governments like Belgium and Germany have campaigned for further integration (deepening). The EU followed a path somewhere in between these two extremes; therefore, it is highly unlikely for the EU to become the United States of Europe, or alternatively, to be reduced to a simple trading bloc.

There may be problems for the EU if any of the countries fail to ratify the new EU Constitution, which was approved by the EU leaders in Rome on October 29, 2004. If a rejection of the EU Constitution by the voters in any of the countries holding referenda occurs, it is certain that European integration will be set back. The EU has often become unpopular with its citizens, because EU decisions were taken by the national leaders without the consent of their constituency.

If the EU Constitution is approved, then the EU is expected to become more effective. The EU will have a president of the European Council and a foreign minister as representatives for the entire EU. The EU will also have a president of the Economics and Finance Council (ECOFIN) that will, along with the ECB, be responsible for the euro. All three new official positions will be 18-month appointments.

Will the EU ever be a challenge to the US for world leadership? It is difficult to answer this question, since the larger EU is more diverse and, thus, is unlikely that all EU countries will adopt and enforce common foreign and defense policies. The split of the EU countries over the

Iraq issue is an example indicating the difficulty of adopting common foreign and defense policies. Some predict that the EU will eventually evolve into at least two different groups and will result in a two-speed model of Europe. One group of countries, which is willing to delegate national authorities to a central supranational EU authority, will join a tighter group of integrated countries. This group is also expected to proceed with monetary integration. A second group of countries may also emerge, comprised of countries that might decide (at least for a few years) not to proceed with further integration.

The EU, however, seems to be capable of playing a positive role in promoting economic development, stability, and peace, not only for its members and neighboring countries, but for the entire world community as well. The EU will be able to pursue and achieve prosperity and peace provided that further integration is successful. Such a positive role for the EU will be crucial in promoting a balanced world economic and political system that is conducive to political and economic stability and affluence throughout the world.

The outcomes of the upcoming referenda of the EU Constitutional Treaty will most likely be the determining factors to point the direction of the EU's future. In my view, there is strength in unity and benefits to be gained through further EU integration, both deepening and widening (including new members). The EU is a model to be followed by other world continents. The next few years will be critical for the future of the EU and many challenges lie ahead. High unemployment rates in most countries along with disparity in the standards of living between new and old EU member countries will continue to create strenuous conditions for EU citizens and countries. Increased globalization and movements in factors of production such as labor immigration and capital outflows and outsourcing are threats to the relatively high standards of living in most former EU countries. Greater competition in product markets from developed and emerging economies, coupled with the persistent appreciation of the euro are additional problems for the EU and the Euro Area.

Ongoing and future structural changes of the EU economies promise future benefits that will arise from growth and development. Such benefits, however, come at high present costs and at the expense of workers and some of the weaker groups in the societies. Such groups include the unemployed and retirees, who have no bargaining power. In the last few years, businesses in EU countries under continuous threat of closing plants and of moving to other countries were able to reduce costs and increase profits at the expense of the workers. At least this was the case in Germany. Unless the cost of restructuring is borne by all groups of the European societies, the continuous decline in the standards of living of workers and other groups will lead to unrest and social upheaval.

It is imperative that Europe becomes innovative in creating a new socio-economic system that focuses on human values, the environment, and the prosperity of its people. It is evident that the EU cannot accomplish prosperity and social justice simultaneously on its own. It is in need of global cooperation. All countries together can successfully address global problems such as pollution, social dumping, and the violation of intellectual property rights. Such measures will promote efficiency in all national economies and fairness in international competition. An increase in international trade and specialization in production based on the countries' genuine comparative advantages will raise the standards of living throughout the world. Investment in human capital, such as education and training, will help the EU and all other countries in the world to raise their standards of living. Economic advancement of the EU need not be at the expense of another country. Global economic integration, as an extension of European integration, can be beneficial to the world community by promoting democracy, human rights, and advancing quality of life.

# Glossary*

**Bilateral procedure:** A procedure whereby the central bank deals directly with one or a few counterparties without making use of tender procedures. Bilateral procedures include operations executed through stock exchanges or market agents.

**Counterparty:** The opposite party in a financial transaction (e.g., any transaction with the central bank).

**Cross-border settlement:** A settlement that takes place in a country other than the country or countries in which one or both of the parties to the trade are located.

**Deposit facility:** A standing facility of the Eurosystem, which counterparties may use to make overnight deposits at an NCB, and which are remunerated at a pre-specified interest rate.

**Economic and Monetary Union (EMU):** The Treaty establishing the EC describes the process of achieving an EMU in three stages. Stage One of the EMU started in July 1990 and ended on December 31, 1993. It was mainly characterized by the dismantling of all internal barriers to the free movement of capital within the EU. Stage Two of the EMU began on January 1, 1994. It provided for, among other things, the establishment of the EMI, the prohibition of financing of the public sector by central banks and the avoidance of excessive deficits in public finances. Stage Three started on January 1, 1999, with the transfer of monetary competence to the Eurosystem, the irrevocable fixing of exchange rates between the currencies of the participating EU Member States, and the introduction of the euro.

**European Economic Area (EEA) countries:** The EU Member States and Iceland, Liechtenstein and Norway.

**Council of the European Union (EU Council):** A body made up of representatives of the governments of the Member States, normally the ministers responsible for the matters under consideration (therefore often referred to as the Council of Ministers). The EU Council meeting in the composition of the ministers of economics and finance is often referred to as the ECOFIN Council.

**Euro:** The name of the single European currency adopted by the European Council at its meeting in Madrid on 15 and 16 December 1995, to be used instead of the term ECU.

---

*Source: European Central Bank. http://www.ecb.int

**Euro Area:** The term by which the EU Member States which have adopted the euro as their single currency in accordance with the Treaty are collectively defined. The Euro area is often called Eurozone and rarely Euroland.

**Eurogroup:** An informal gathering of the ministers of economics and finance of the EU Member States participating in the euro area. At meetings of the Eurogroup, the ministers discuss issues connected with their shared responsibilities in respect of the single currency. The European Commission and the ECB are invited to take part in the meetings. The Eurogroup usually meets immediately before a normal ECOFIN meeting.

**European Central Bank (ECB):** Established on June 1, 1998, and located in Frankfurt am Main, the ECB has its own legal personality. It ensures that the tasks conferred upon the Eurosystem and the ESCB are implemented by its own activities or through the NCBs.

**European System of Central Banks (ESCB):** Refers to the ECB and the NCBs of the EU Member States. NCBs of Member States, which have not adopted the single currency in accordance with the Treaty, retain their powers in the field of monetary policy according to national law and are, thus, not involved in the conduct of the monetary policy of the Eurosystem.

**Eurosystem:** Comprises the ECB and the NCBs of the Member States of the euro area. The decision-making bodies of the Eurosystem are the Governing Council and the Executive Board of the ECB.

**Executive Board:** One of the decision-making bodies of the ECB. It comprises the President and the Vice president of the ECB and four other members.

**Fine-tuning operation:** A non-regular open market operation executed by the Eurosystem mainly to deal with unexpected liquidity fluctuations in the market.

**Fixed rate tender:** A tender procedure where the interest rate is specified in advance by the central bank and participating counterparties bid the amount of money they want to transact at the fixed interest rate.

**Foreign exchange swap:** The simultaneous spot purchase/sale and forward sale/purchase of one currency against another. The Eurosystem executes open market monetary policy operations in the form of foreign exchange swaps where the national central banks (or the ECB) buy (or sell) euro spot against a foreign currency and at the same time sell (or buy) it back in a forward transaction.

**General Council:** One of the decision-making bodies of the ECB. It comprises the President and the Vice president of the ECB and the governors of all 25 EU NCBs.

**Governing Council:** One of the decision-making bodies of the ECB. It comprises all the members of the Executive Board of the ECB and the governors of the national central banks of the EU Member States, which have adopted the euro.

**Longer-term refinancing operation:** A regular open market operation executed by the Eurosystem in the form of a reverse transaction. Longer-term refinancing operations are executed through monthly standard tenders and have a maturity of three months.

**M3:** The broad monetary aggregate M3 has been defined by the ECB as currency in circulation plus euro area residents' (other than central government) holdings of the following liabilities of euro area money issuing institutions: overnight deposits, deposits with an agreed maturity of up to two years, deposits redeemable at a period of notice of up to three months, repurchase agreements, money market fund shares/ units, and money market paper and debt securities with a maturity of up to two years.

**Main refinancing operation:** A regular open market operation executed by the Eurosystem in the form of a reverse transaction. Main refinancing operations are conducted through weekly standard tenders and normally have a maturity of two weeks.

**Marginal lending facility:** A standing facility of the Eurosystem, which counterparties may use to receive overnight credit from a national central bank at a pre-specified interest rate.

**Minimum reserve requirement:** The requirement for credit institutions to keep a deposit with the central bank. The minimum reserve requirement for an individual institution is calculated as a percentage of the money deposited by the (non-bank) customers of this institution.

**Open market operation:** An operation executed on the initiative of the central bank in the financial market. With regard to their aims, regularity and procedures, Eurosystem open market operations can be divided into four categories: main refinancing operations, long-term refinancing operations, fine-tuning operations, and structural operations. As for the instruments used, reverse transactions are the main open market instrument of the Eurosystem and can be employed in all four categories of operations. In addition, the issuance of debt certificates and outright transactions are available for structural operations, while outright transactions, foreign exchange swaps and the collection of fixed-term deposits are available for the conduct of fine-tuning operations.

**Outright transaction:** A transaction whereby assets are bought or sold up to their maturity (spot or forward).

**Repurchase agreement (repo):** An arrangement whereby an asset is sold while the seller simultaneously is obtaining the right and obligation to repurchase it at a specific price on a future date or on demand. Such an agreement is similar to collateralized borrowing, with the difference that the seller does not retain ownership of the securities. The Eurosystem uses repurchase agreements with a fixed maturity in its reverse transactions.

**Repurchase price:** The price at which the buyer is obliged to sell back assets to the seller in relation to a transaction under a repurchase agreement. The repurchase price equals the sum of the purchase price and the price differential corresponding to the interest on the extended liquidity over the maturity of the operation.

**Reserve account:** An account with the national central bank on which a counterparty's reserve holdings are maintained. The counterparties' settlement accounts with the national central banks may be used as reserve accounts.

**Reverse transaction:** An operation whereby the NCB buys or sells assets under a repurchase agreement or conducts credit operations against collateral.

**Real-Time Gross Settlement (RTGS) system:** A settlement system in which processing and settlement take place on an order-by-order basis (without netting) in real time (continuously). *See also* Trans-European Automated Real-time Gross Settlement Express Transfer (TARGET) system.

**Standard tender:** A tender procedure used by the Eurosystem in its regular open market operations. Standard tenders are carried out within a time frame of 24 hours. All counterparties fulfilling the general eligibility criteria are entitled to submit bids in standard tenders.

**Standing facility:** A central bank facility available to counterparties at their own initiative. The Eurosystem offers two overnight standing facilities: the marginal lending facility and the deposit facility.

**Structural operation:** An open market operation executed by the Eurosystem to adjust the structural liquidity position of the financial sector vis-à-vis the Eurosystem.

**Trans-European Automated Real-time Gross settlement Express Transfer (TARGET) system:** The real time gross settlement (RTGS) system for the euro. It is a decentralized system consisting of 15 national RTGS systems, the ECB payment mechanism, and the Interlinking mechanism.

**Tender procedure:** A procedure in which the central bank provides liquidity to or withdraws liquidity from the market on the basis of bids submitted by counterparties in competition with each other. The most competitive bids are satisfied with priority until the total amount of liquidity to be provided or withdrawn by the central bank is exhausted.

**Treaty establishing the European Community:** The Treaty, was signed in Rome on March 25, 1957, and entered into force on January 1, 1958. It established the European Economic Community (EEC) and is often referred to as the Treaty of Rome. The Treaty on European Union was signed in Maastricht (therefore often referred to as the Maastricht Treaty) on February 7, 1992, and entered into force on November 1, 1993. It amended the Treaty of Rome, which is officially called the Treaty establishing the European Community. The Treaty on European Union has since been amended by the Amsterdam Treaty, which was signed on October 2, 1997, and entered into force on May 1, 1999.

**Variable rate tender:** A tender procedure whereby the counterparties bid both the amount of money they want to transact with the central bank and the interest rate at which they want to enter into the transaction.

# Endnotes

## Chapter 1

[1] The remaining three from the former EU15 countries, UK, Denmark, and Sweden, have not yet adopted the euro but may join the Economic and Monetary Union (EMU) and adopt the euro in the future. The same applies to the ten new Central Eastern and Mediterranean European countries that joined the EU on May 1, 2004, or other candidate countries that may become members of the EU.

[2] BENELUX is comprised of the initial syllables of Belgium, Netherlands, and Luxembourg and stands for these three countries together.

[3] A customs union allows free trade among its members while keeping a common external tariff against non-member countries. A common market is a customs union, which also allows free trade on goods and services and free mobility of the factors of production, capital, and labor.

[4] These policies were the regional policy, the social policy, and the common agricultural policy (CAP). The latter was the most important in terms of expenditures, amounting to over 80 percent of the budget in the early years of the EEC. From the outset of the negotiations that led to the Treaty of Rome, it was agreed that agriculture was a special sector of the economy and required a different policy approach than the other sectors of the economy. From member state governments, the EEC took over the administration, financing, and implementation of all national agricultural programs under the CAP. This implied heavy protection through subsidization that for a long time became expensive for the EEC and a source of friction between the EEC and its trading partners.

[5] Treaty of Rome, Article 2.

[6] The Commission is the executive body responsible in safeguarding the treaties and administering the daily affairs of the EC. Initially, the European Parliament was an advisory body when the governments of the EC states appointed its members. The European Parliament evolved and became more important after its members were elected directly by the European people since 1979. The European Court of Justice is independent of the member state governments and has powers above the member state courts in areas pertinent to EEC competencies. Lastly, the Council of Ministers is the legislative body of the EEC (like the US Senate) introducing and passing laws. Unlike the US Senate, which includes only American citizens, the EEC Council is consisted of cabinet member representatives from each EEC state.

[7] Both organizations are located in Washington, D.C., and are the two main international monetary organizations established to facilitate the smooth functioning of the international monetary and exchange rate system.

[8] A summit is a meeting of the EC Council of Ministers at which national governments are represented by their heads of state (i.e., presidents, prime ministers). The Council of Ministers in such composition is called the European Council. Summits take place two or three times a year and receive great publicity. They are usually expected to resolve major issues that cannot be resolved by the regular EC Council of Ministers. It should be noted that the EC Council of Ministers is represented and comprised by those ministers according to the issues discussed. For example, if the topic of discussion is agriculture, the ministers of agriculture will meet, if the topic is education the ministers of education will convene, and so on.

[9] All three will be discussed in this chapter and the following chapters.

[10] The G10 countries are the G7: the United States, Germany, Japan, Britain, France, Italy, and Canada and three other European countries, Belgium, Sweden and Netherlands.

[11] The EUA was introduced in 1975 as an accounting unit, used mainly by the EC to maintain all its accounts with the member countries. The EUA was a market basket (weighted average) of the nine EC countries' currencies at that time and was introduced and adopted as a response to the unstable exchange rates of the 1970s. Originally, it was equal to one Special Drawing Right (SDR), the monetary accounting unit, used by the IMF. While the SDR remains a monetary accounting unit, the EUA's destiny was different. First, it was renamed as the ECU with more functions than the SDR and, on March 1, 2002, became a full-fledged currency, the euro, replacing the currencies of 12 EC countries.

[12] For example, once the exchange rates of the DM and FF in terms of ECU are known, by dividing the two rates, DM/1ECU and FF/1ECU, it is clear that the bilateral exchange rate between the two currencies can be obtained, i.e., DM/1FF or its inverse FF/ 1DM.

[13] A fourth facility was available that was recommended first by the Werner Plan. This was the short-term monetary support, which with the creation of the EMS was increased from 10 to 25 billion ECUs.

[14] See Peter Kenen *Economic and Monetary Union in Europe Moving Beyond the Maastricht* (1995) Chapter 1 for more information on the EMS. This point regarding the unlimited access of the credit lines is a crucial one. Whether central banks were willing to lend their own currency in unlimited amounts is debatable. This is particularly true for the Bundesbank during the 1992–1993 EMS exchange rate crisis period.

[15] The EMS countries agreed tacitly to follow a coordination of monetary policy.

[16] There are a few exceptions, such as Fratianni and Von Hagen (1990), who found that the policy reactions in the EMS, though asymmetrical, were bi-directional. This means that the central banks of the EMS countries and the Bundesbank were reacting to each other's policies.

[17] A simple model explaining the n-1 currency problem is presented in *Economics of Monetary Union*, by Paul De Grauwe (2000), Chapter 5, pp. 101–103.

[18] This was the opinion of the speculators and many prominent economists who were openly recommending the UK government devalue the pound, see Neal and Barbezat, 1997, for more information regarding the situation in the EMS before the 1992–1993 crisis (pp. 155).

[19] After 1987, all EMS central banks followed the Bundesbank to gain credibility on price stability. This arrangement was tacitly ratified by the Basle-Nyborg Agreement, which took place in September 1987. According to this agreement, central banks agreed to "use interest rate differentials to defend the stability of the EMS parity grid." Thus, all central banks followed the Bundesbank in setting interest rates while the Bundesbank agreed to be more accommodating in using EMCF credit lines for exchange rate intervention before the exchange rates reached the band limits.

[20] *The Politics and Economics of the European Union* (2001), Second Edition, pp. 293.

[21] See Paul De Grauwe, *Economics of Monetary Union* (2000), Chapter 5, for an elaborate discussion of this explanation.

[22] See Peter Kenen, *Economic and Monetary Union in Europe Moving Beyond the Maastricht* (1995), pp. 163–64, who quoted original writings of the President of the Bundesbank Otmar Emminger, translated by Eichengreen and Wypolz (1993), pp. 109. In this quote, the German government through its chancellor and the finance minister publicly provided assurances for the independence of the Bundesbank. In other words, if the need arose for the Bundesbank to intervene in the exchange market to support an EMS member's currency, the Bundesbank should be free not to do so if it decided that such a move threatens domestic price stability. On the other hand, the German government, in cooperation with the other EC central banks, should pursue a correction in the ERM with devaluations of weak currencies.

[23] Kenen (1995) mentions the example of North American Free Trade Agreement (NAFTA), particularly the cases of Canada and the US, which constitute an integrated market without a common currency.

[24] For a more detailed analysis, see Paul De Grauwe, *Economics of Monetary Union* (2000).

# Chapter 2

[1] Economists describe this phenomenon by stating that economic integration becomes endogenous in the calculation of the expected costs and benefits.

[2] In some monetary unions, the member countries maintain their national currencies but fix the exchange rates irrevocably. The EU was such a monetary union from January 1, 1999, to February 28, 2002. Similarly, Belgium and Luxembourg, prior to the formation of the EMU, had formed a monetary union with the exchange rate of their currencies fixed. In this case, it happened that one Belgian franc was equal to one Luxembourgish franc.

[3] Two types of asymmetric shocks exist: The first type of asymmetric shock affects the aggregate demand of the economy. An example of such a shock occurs when consumers' preferences suddenly shift away from the domestic goods in favor of the products of another country. The second type of asymmetric shock is related to the supply side of the economy. This usually occurs whenever there is a substantial reduction in the supply of certain products due to an abrupt decline in any of the production inputs, such as raw materials, oil, or labor. An example of such a shock is a national labor strike.

[4] Intra-industry trade exists when a country imports and exports the same types of products.

[5] See Artis and Zhang (1995) among other authors and the literature on the real business cycles theory, which recently attracted much attention by many economists, including Prescott and Kydland, who received the Nobel Prize in economics in 2004.

[6] For example, in the case of the US, it is estimated that this benefit amounts to 1 percent of its GDP. This benefit for the US arises because many other countries use the dollar for international transactions and for foreign reserves. More recently, a few countries even gave up their national currency and now exclusively use the US dollar for domestic transactions. The aim of this decision was price stabilization, an objective the central banks and the governments of these countries failed to accomplish with their own national currencies. This new international monetary arrangement is known as dollarization.

[7] Paul Krugman (1993) provides an opposite view.

[8] Not all Southern EU countries are less developed; France, for example, attained higher per capita income than the EU average. The southern EU countries, however, have attained higher growth rates than the more developed, Northern-central former EU15 countries leading to convergence in terms of real per capita GDP. See Yin, Zestos, and Michelis (2003), *Journal of Economic Integration,* March 2003.

[9] The real exchange rate is defined as the nominal exchange rate multiplied by the ratio of the foreign to domestic price levels.

[10] "Money illusion" of workers is said to take place when workers are fooled into believing that their real wages increased because their nominal wages increased; they do not realize that because of the increase in prices, real wages can remain constant or can even decline.

[11] EU workers in several industries especially after 2000 were forced to accept lower wages and benefits for the sake of saving their jobs.

[12] See "Strikes Expose Strains on German Collective Bargaining." *Financial Times,* May 8, 2002, p. 3

[13] "Eurozone Seeks Productivity Secret." *Financial Times,* May 7, 2002.

[14] "The Euro's Right Turn." *The Wall Street Journal,* April 26, 2002.

[15] Such positive effects on the economies of these countries are expected to strengthen the OCA regardless of whether these countries are members of the Euro Area or are EU candidate EMU countries.

[16] The price level is measured by the GDP deflator or the consumer price index (CPI).

# Chapter 3

[1] Though the initials for the EMU stand for Economic and Monetary Union, it is practical to refer to EMU as European monetary union since this is what most people usually understand when referring to EMU. The reason for this is that the Maastricht Treaty, more than anything else, established a European monetary union and it is mostly known for that. The Maastricht Treaty, besides the accomplishment of the monetary union, successfully promoted integration in a few other areas as well.

[2] The initials of EU will be used for the rest of the book, since this is how the EC is now referred.

[3] Examination here refers to the evaluation of the countries' performance in reference to the five Maastricht criteria by the EU Council upon the recommendation of the EU Commission and the European Monetary Institute (EMI).

[4] For many years, macroeconomists believed that a trade-off relation exists between inflation and unemployment in the short run. British economist A.W. Phillips (1958) introduced this relationship, and the curve depicting this relation was named after him. Evidence exists that this relation broke down for many countries after the 1973–1974 oil crisis. In the long run, the negative relation between inflation and unemployment does not exist.

[5] Such a requirement was based on empirical evidence that countries with independent central banks consistently outperformed countries with central banks subordinated to the government in fighting inflation; see Alesina, A. and Summers, L. (1993).

[6] Ireland's relatively higher inflation rate is not considered a problem since price increases in the last few years in Ireland have been the result of a booming economy at an exceptionally high growth rate for EU countries standards.

[7] *The European Economy,* Supplement A, p. 13, 1998.

[8] Greece did not have a 10-year bond, and thus, a short-term interest rate was used as a proxy.

[9] The Greek drachma entered the ERM in March 1998 after a 14.5 percent devaluation against all ERM currencies. Greece became a member of the EMU on January 1, 2001. The Danish kroner remained in the ERM for the required period of two years but Denmark decided to opt out from the EMU.

[10] Sweden held a referendum for the adoption of the euro in September 2003. The Swedes rejected the euro in this referendum. Sweden, however, has not completed legislation to ensure the independence of its central bank nor has joined the ERM. However, these two requirements will be necessary in case Sweden tries to join the EMU again. See G. Parker, "Sweden Not Ready to Join Euro says Brussels," *Financial Times,* May 22, 2002.

[11] Two countries chose not to join the EMU for political reasons rather than an inability to meet the Maastricht criteria: the UK and Denmark. Most of the countries, however, experienced difficulty meeting the government debt to GDP ratio Maastricht criterion, forcing the European Council to bend this criterion rather than postponing the launching of the EMU.

[12] See Buiter, et al., (1993).

[13] According to the Treaty that established the EU, the Commission is the institution responsible for the enforcement of the EU laws and the guardian of the treaties.

[14] G. Parker, (2002) "Italy urged not to renege on budget plan," July 9, p. 7.

[15] Guerrera, F. and G. Parker, "France warned not to flout euro rules." *Financial Times,* January 30, 2003.

# Chapter 4

[1] According to Protocol 1 (No. 18), on the statutes of the ESCB and the ECB, Chapter IX and in Article 45, the General Council is recognized as the third decision-making body of the ECB.

[2] Some similarities exist with the Central Bank of the US, the Federal Reserve System.

[3] See Arestis, et al., p. 71 (2001).

[4] According to Article 2 of the Treaty, "The Community shall have as its task to promote throughout the Community, a harmonious and balanced development of economic activities, sustainable and non-inflationary growth, respecting the environment, a high degree of convergence of economic performance, a high level of employment and of social protection, the raising of the standards of living and quality of life, and economic and social cohesion and solidarity among member states." For more information regarding the "Treaty establishing the European Community," see the Glossary.

[5] A majority of the German Parliament was sufficient to change the statutes of the Bundesbank. A change to the statutes of the ECB requires the revision of the Maastricht Treaty. This revision is considered unlikely since it requires unanimity by all EU25 member states. In the US, however, a revision of the statutes of the Federal Reserve requires only a majority vote of the US Congress.

[6] "The European System of Central Banks Current Position and Future Prospects." Keynote address delivered by Dr. Willem Duisenberg at a conference on European Economic and Monetary Union Markets and Politics under the Euro, London, 27 November 1998.

[7] Where $M$ is a measure of the money supply, $V$ is the velocity of money, $P$ is the aggregate price level of the economy, and $Q$ is the aggregate output (GDP). By taking the natural logarithms on both sides of the equation, we have $\ln MV = \ln PQ$, which can be written as $\ln M + \ln V = \ln P + \ln Q$, by using the laws of logarithms. Lastly, by differentiating both sides of the equation, we obtain $(dM/M) + (dV/V) = (dP/P) + (dQ/Q)$. These fractions represent the rate of growth of each variable. Monetarists, by assuming the money velocity constant, claim to be able to predict the effect of the rate of growth of the money supply on the rate of growth of the price level (i.e., the inflation rate) provided that the trend rate of the growth of output is known. The above analysis is known as the quantity theory of money. This analysis explains how the growth of money affects the price level according to monetarists. The ECB, based on the above equation, sets the rate of growth of the money supply to target the inflation rate. Presently, the ECB has targeted an annual inflation rate for the Euro Area to be within the range of 1 to 2 percent. The ECB pursues a monetary policy for the medium run. Thus, it does not respond to any short-run deviations of the targeted inflation values by interfering in mechanistic ways to correct such deviations from the medium run targeted values.

[8] The repo rate is the rate that the Euro Area commercial banks pay to the ECB when they borrow liquidity on a competitive basis.

[9] Banks constitute the largest number of all financial institutions required by the ECB to hold minimum reserves. For this reason, all such financial institutions are often referred to as banks. Other financial institutions that are not banks are required to hold reserves.

[10] Counterparty here refers to the opposite party in a financial transaction with the ECB. The term counterparty is the broadest description of all financial institutions involved in transactions with the ECB. For this and other definitions related to the Euro Area monetary policy, see the Glossary, Annex 2 in "The Single Monetary Policy in the Euro Area: General documentation on Eurosystem Monetary Policy Instruments and Procedures," http://www.ecb.int. A smaller glossary appears at the end of the book.

[11] Under the overnight repurchase agreement, the NCB (i.e., the creditor) receives ownership of the asset (government securities), and the borrowing financial institution (counterparty) is responsible for repurchasing the asset the next business day. The NCBs provide liquidity on the condition of a collateral. In this case, the borrowing party receives interest payments and maintains ownership of the asset.

[12] For the definitions of the above operations, see the Glossaries cited in footnote 10.

[13] Trichet, J.C. "The Euro after Two Years." *Journal of Common Market Studies,* Vol. 39, No. 1, pp. 1–13.

[14] Parker, G. and H. Simonian. "France and Germany Ordered to Curb Deficits." *Financial Times,* November 14, 2002.

[15] Mallet, V. "Paris May Join Berlin to Save Stability Pact." *Financial Times,* November 20, 2002.

[16] See ECB publication, The TARGET (Trans-European Real-time Gross settlement Express Transfers) System, http://www.ecb.int.

# Chapter 5

[1] The foreign exchange rate is also defined as the number of foreign currency units that a domestic currency unit can be traded for. This definition of the foreign exchange rate is the inverse of the one given in the text. Using this definition, the euros per dollar € = 1$ exchange rate is 0.7485, i.e., 1 dollar is worth and trades for 0.7485 euros.

[2] This was happening even though Sweden never officially joined the Exchange Rate Mechanism (ERM) II, which requires EMU candidate member countries to maintain a stable exchange rate versus the euro for at least two years within the wider band of ±15 percent prior to joining the EMU.

[3] Since nominal trade-weighted and nominal effective exchange rates (NEERs) are used in the literature interchangeably, the same practice will be followed here as well.

[4] Japan probably deliberately followed a contractionary monetary policy, creating chronic deflation and a real depreciation of the yen to boost exports and economic growth. However, a contractionary monetary policy can have a negative effect on national income since it tends to reduce domestic spending by reducing consumption and investment and, thus, national income. This is a countervailing force to the export growth that was pursued by the Japanese government.

[5] The twelve industrial and newly industrialized countries of the narrow group are: the United States, the United Kingdom, Japan, Switzerland, Sweden, South Korea, Hong Kong, Denmark, Singapore, Canada, Norway, and Australia.

The EER-23 includes, in addition to the twelve countries of the narrow group, the new EU10 countries and China.

The EER-42 includes, in addition to the EER-23: New Zealand, Algeria, Argentina, Brazil, Croatia, India, Indonesia, Israel, Malaysia, Mexico, Morocco, Philippines, Romania, Russia, South Africa, Taiwan, Thailand, Turkey, and Bulgaria.

# Chapter 6

[1] Of course, there are exceptions. A few people made billions of dollars in the foreign exchange market. One of them is the financier and philanthropist George Soros, who made billions at the expense of European governments during the 1992–1993 EMS exchange rate crisis.

[2] Instead of focusing on the euro market, one could have analyzed the dollar market since the euro and dollar markets are not two separate markets but the same one in which dollars are exchanged for euros and where the dollars-euro exchange rate is determined.

[3] Price and quantity demanded for any commodity according to the law of demand are negatively or inversely related. This means when the price of a commodity decreases, consumers are willing and able to buy more of this commodity. Similarly, when the price of a commodity increases, consumers are willing and can purchase less of this commodity.

[4] Some of the most important of these shift factors are changes in the consumers' income, changes in tastes and preferences, and changes in the prices of related goods known as complements and substitutes. Change in the good's price, however, is not a shift factor since the good's price appears on the vertical axis of the graph of the demand curve. Therefore, a change in price is a movement along the same demand curve and not a shift factor.

[5] In general, the supply curve for any commodity shifts when some variables known as shift factors change. These include all changes in the cost of production. The price of the commodity, however, is not a shift factor since a change in price of the commodity causes a change in the quantity supplied because this is a movement along the same supply curve. There is a difference between a change in supply and change in quantity supplied as there is a difference between change in demand and change in quantity demanded. This important distinction arises because, in this diagrammatic model of supply and demand, price is explicitly included and measured along the vertical axis.

[6] Over half of the world's output is produced by the US, the Euro Area, Japan, and China.

[7] The factors of production are land, labor, capital, and entrepreneurship. The respective payments to the factors of production are rent, wages and salaries, interest, and profit.

[8] The two deficits are often referred to as twin deficits and are usually unfavorably looked upon as negatively impacting the stability of the US economy.

[9] A few years ago, the financial account was called the capital account. Today, the IMF uses the term capital account to refer to a small account, which is part of the CA and pertains to some unilateral transfers, mainly of non-market activities.

[10] *People's Daily Online,* "China sets no target for forex reserve: official", March 8, 2004, http://english. people.com.cn/200403/08/eng20040308_136818.shtml. See also *Muzi News,* "China Foreign Exchange Reserves Hit Record," January 13, 2005, http://news.muzi.com/ll/English/1344873.shtml.

[11] Saving and investment data were unavailable for the Euro Area countries, thus we used the data for all 15 EU countries.

# Chapter 7

[1] For a more elaborate discussion on this topic, see Robert Carbaugh (2004), Chapter 13.

[2] The expected rate of inflation was measured by using the actual rate of inflation based on the GDP deflator.

[3] The exact form of Equation (1) is a little different but, for practical purposes in calculating the rates of return, is accurate when the $i_{FA}$ interest rate is not high.

[4] It is called uncovered interest parity because investors purchasing foreign assets do not sign a forward contract to assure that their earnings in the foreign country are converted back to a national currency at an agreed upon and known exchange rate. These investors do not hedge and, thus, are exposed to foreign exchange risk.

[5] The expected change in the nominal exchange rate of the utilized data for the construction of the time plots of the right-hand side variable of Equation (1) in Figure 7.2 is measured with the actual change in the exchange rate during the same period that the interest-bearing asset is held. For the actual exchange rate to be a good proxy for the expected exchange rate, it requires that expectations regarding future exchange rates to be correct. This may not always be a realistic assumption. Because expected exchange rates are unobservable, finding a better proxy for the expected exchange rate is difficult.

[6] The spot exchange rate is the nominal exchange rate denoted by (NE).

[7] Forward markets are the vehicle for intertemporal arbitrage by shifting currencies from the spot to the forward market and vice versa leading to the covered interest rate parity condition.

[8] This result is plausible because the longer the period foreign assets are held, the higher the probability will be that intertemporal arbitrage will equate the rates of return between assets held in the two currencies.

[9] Irving Fisher was an American economist who first introduced this relation between the nominal interest rate, the real interest rate, and the expected inflation rate in the 1930s.

[10] See Mishkin (2004), Chapter 6 for an elaborate discussion of the term structure of interest rates. The material in this section was motivated by Husted and Melvin (2004), Chapter 15.

[11] One could assume a license agreement to purchase this software allows buyers to download the software to their personal computer from the Internet.

[12] In this case, "countries" refers to the US and the Euro Area.

[13] Note the percent change in a country's price level ($\%\Delta P$) from year to year is the annual inflation rate, which is usually denoted by $\pi$.

[14] Some banks pay interest rates on checking accounts, but this interest is low.

[15] $k_{EA}$ and $k_{US}$ often change with time. These two parameters depend on customs and habits of each country's households and businesses. The two parameters indicate the desired proportion of money balances demanded for any level of nominal GDP.

# Chapter 8

[1] Using the PPP rates to convert monetary amounts expressed in different currencies into the same currency is a more accurate comparison than relying on nominal exchange rates because the PPP rates take into consideration the price differences among countries.

[2] Malta is an exception, because it has one of the highest corporate income tax rates in the Union.

[3] See for example Barro and Sala-i-Martin (1991, 1992, 1995) for convergence studies on real per capita GDP among regions and countries. Also see Yin, Zestos, and Michelis (2003) for a study on real per capita GDP convergence between the EU15 member countries, and Zestos and Yin (2004) for a study on global economic convergence.

[4] Romer (1986), Krugman and Venables (1996), and Ben-David and Loewy (2000) are good examples of representative endogenous growth models.

[5] Three CEEC countries, Latvia, Lithuania, and Estonia, were part of the Soviet Union.

[6] Sweden does not have an opt-out clause, but it intentionally remained outside the Exchange Rate Mechanism (ERM) in order not to fulfill this Maastricht convergence criterion and not qualify for adoption of the euro. Furthermore, in September 2003, the Swedes voted in a national referendum against adopting the euro.

[7] The central bank governors of the UK, Denmark, and Sweden, which are members of the EU but did not join the EMU, attend the ECB's Governing Council meetings as non-voting members.

[8] The CV is equal to the standard deviation (a measure of dispersion) of a set of numbers divided by the mean (average) of these numbers. The CV was calculated for as many years back as data were available. If the CV declines with time, this constitutes evidence of relative convergence. If the CV increases, this provides evidence of divergence.

[9] The examination year is the year when the decision is made by the EU institutions to determine whether a candidate EMU country qualifies for EMU membership. All EU10 countries are expected to join the EMU before 2010.

[10] The inflation rate for 2004 was calculated by taking the average of the 12 months prior to August 2004, i.e., the average of the 12 months from September 2003 to August 2004. This is how the EUROSTAT (The Statistical Agency of the EU) calculated and reported the 2004 inflation estimate in its *Convergence Report 2004* published by the ECB, October 2004.

[11] In 2003, inflation increased the most in the Slovak Republic (five percentage points) and declined (disinflation) the most in Lithuania and the Czech Republic (approximately −1.5 percentage points). Lithuania is the only country to record deflation of −1.1 percent in 2003 and −.2 percent in 2004.

[12] Since expected inflation is related to present inflation, high inflation countries usually have high long-term interest rates.

[13] The 2004 nominal long-term interest rate was calculated by creating a mean of the monthly annualized interest rates for the last twelve months. Since the last month of interest rate data is August 2004, the value of the long-term interest rate for 2004 was calculated by taking the average of the monthly interest rates from September 2003 to August 2004.

[14] This does not imply that the average deficit to GDP ratios or the dispersion of the deficit to GDP ratios among EU10 and EU15 countries are similar. As a matter of fact, they are not. The EU15 had lower average deficit to GDP ratios than the EU10 for every year during the period 1999–2003. The EU10, however, had lower standard deviations during the same period than the EU15, implying lower dispersion of the government deficit to GDP ratios within the new EU10 countries.

[15] The average debt to GDP ratio for the EU10 countries in 2003 was 40 percent, but it was 59 percent for the EU15 and 63 percent for the Euro Area. The reason for this large difference between the EU10 and the EU15 countries is the fact that the CEECs governments did not issue debt (bonds) prior to 1989. The government debt is a recent phenomenon for these countries that accumulated in the post-communism era.

[16] As a matter of fact, these three countries entered the EMU in 1999 with government debt to GDP ratios above the Maastricht limit. The EU governing institutions had to bend this Maastricht criterion to allow the three countries to become members of the EMU.

[17] This should be expected because a ratio increases faster when its numerator rises and its denominator decreases simultaneously.

[18] At that time (1999), there were two currencies in the ERM: the Danish krone and the Greek drachma. Since Greece joined the EMU in January 2001 and adopted the euro, the Danish krone remained the only currency in the ERM until the middle of 2004.

[19] A few countries, for example, have unilaterally adopted the US dollar as their national currency. Such an arrangement is called dollarization.

[20] Since the exchange rates of the EU10 countries are expressed as number of currency units per euro, an increase in the exchange rate indices (bars) in Figure 8.17 denotes a depreciation of that currency with respect to the euro and a decrease denotes an appreciation of the currency.

[21] See "Policy Position of the Governing Council of the European Central Bank on Exchange Rate Issues Relating to the Acceding Countries." December 18, 2003; www.ecb.int.

[22] A currency board is a country's monetary authority. A currency board issues notes and coins that are backed up by reserves of a foreign currency, which is called the reserve, or anchor, currency. The US dollar, the euro, and the UK pound serve as anchors since these are strong, internationally traded currencies. Since the local currency is backed with 100 percent reserves of their anchor currency, the exchange rate of such a currency board system is strictly fixed.

[23] In the middle of 2004, two new EU10 countries, Hungary and Poland, had exceeded the long-term interest rate Maastricht reference value.

[24] Some EU10 countries made substantial progress toward rendering full independence of their central banks. A few other EU10 countries, however, achieved less. Some countries will have to amend article(s) of their constitution to be able to render their central banks fully independent.

[25] Speech given by Lucas Papademos entitled "Monetary policy in an enlarged euro area", at the conference "Asymmetries in Trade and Currency Arrangements in the 21st Century", Deutsche Bundesbank, Frankfurt, Germany, July 29, 2004.

# Bibliography

Akerlof, G., W. Dickens, and G. Perry (1996). "The macro-economics of low inflation." *Brookings Papers on Economic Activity.*

Alesina, A. and L. H. Summers (1993). "Central bank independence and macroeconomic performance: some international evidence." *Journal of Money, Credit, and Banking.* Vol. 25, No. 2, pp. 151–162.

Appleyard, D. and A. Field, Jr. (2001). *International Economics.* 4th ed. New York: McGraw-Hill.

Arestis, P., A. Brown, and M. Sawyer (2001). *The Euro: Evolution and Prospects.* Edward Elgar Publishing; Northampton, MA.

Artis, M. J. and W. Zhang (1995). "International business cycles and the ERM: Is there a European business cycle?" *Papers.* 95/34. European Institute, Economics Department.

Atkins, R. and N. George (2004). "Can Sweden give Germany fertile ideas to revive its ailing economy?" *Financial Times.* October 20.

Baldwin, R., G. Bertola, and P. Seabright (2003). *EMU: Assessing the Impact of the Euro.* Blackwell Publishing.

Bank of England (2004). Monetary and financial statistics interactive database—interest and exchange rates data. Retrieved from the World Wide Web on July 2004: http://www.bankofengland.co.uk/Links/setframe.html.

Barro, R. J. (1991). "Economic growth in a cross-section of countries." *The Quarterly Journal of Economics.* 106 May, pp. 407–443.

Barro, R. J. and X. Sala-i-Martin (1992). "Convergence." *Journal of Political Economy.* 100 (2), pp. 223–251.

Barro, R. J. and X. Sala-i-Martin (1995). *Economic Growth.* New York: McGraw-Hill.

Bayoumi, T. and B. Eichengreen (1994). "One money or many? Analyzing the prospects for monetary unification in various parts of the world." *Princeton Studies in International Finance.* No. 76, Princeton University Press, Princeton.

Ben-David, D. and M. B. Loewy (2000). "Knowledge dissemination, capital accumulation, trade, and endogenous growth." *Oxford Economic Papers* (52) October, pp. 638–649.

Blitz, J., et al. (2002). "Eurozone gives thumbs up to new currency." *Financial Times.* January 5–6, 2002.

Brada, J. C. and Z. Drabek (1998). "Exchange rate regimes and the stability of trade policy in transition economies." World Trade Organization Economic Research and Analysis Division, Staff Working Paper ERAD-98-07.

Buerkle, T. (2004). "Europhoria." *Institutional Investor.* New York: May 14, p. 1.

Buiter, W., G. Corsetti, and N. Roubini (1993). "Excessive deficits: sense and nonsense in the Treaty of Maastricht." *Economic Policy,* 16: 57–100.

Buldorini, L., S. Makrydakis, and C. Thimann (Feb. 2002). "The effective exchange rates of the euro." *European Central Bank.* Occasional Paper Series No. 2.

Bureau of Economic Analysis (2004). U.S. economic accounts. U.S. Department of Commerce. Retrieved from the World Wide Web on July 2004: http://www.bea.gov.

Carbaugh, R. (2004). *International Economics.* 9th ed. Thomson South-Western; US.

Champion, M. (2002). "In Ireland, fears that investment may stall—need to fix infrastructure tops agenda of all parties ahead of Friday's election." *The Wall Street Journal.* May 16, p. A. 16.

Champion, M. (2003). "U.K. rejects adopting euro this year but may revisit issue next year." *The Wall Street Journal.* June 10, p. A. 16.

Commission Services (1999). "Summary of the 1998 convergence report, euro 1999 part 1: recommendation."

Committee of Governors of the Central Banks of the Member States of the European Economic Community (1979). "Texts concerning the European monetary system."

De Grauwe, P. (2000). *Economics of Monetary Union.* 4th ed. New York: Oxford Publishing Press.

De Grauwe, P. and G. P. Kouretas (2004). "Editorial." *Journal of Common Market Studies.* November, 42, 4, pp. 679–687. Blackwell Publishing.

"Delivering Lisbon—reforms for the enlarged union." (2004). *Commission of the European Communities to the Spring European Council.* Brussels, February 20.

Dieckhoefer, S. and B. Swint (September 9, 2004). "ECB urges 'vigilance' on inflation amid recovery, oil." *Bloomberg.com.* Retrieved from the World Wide Web on September 29, 2004 at www.bloomberg.com.

"DJ Finland, US lead world in economic competitiveness report." (2004). *FWN Select,* October 13.

Dornbusch, R. (1976). "Expectations and exchange rates dynamics." *Journal of Political Economy.* Vol. 84, pp. 1161–1176.

Duisenberg, W. F. (1998). The European System of Central Banks Current position and future prospects [Electronic version]. *European Central Bank.* November.

Duisenberg, W. F. (1999). Monetary policy in the Euro Area [Electronic version].

Duisenberg, W. F. (2002). International Research Forum on Monetary Policy [Electronic version]. *European Central Bank.* July.

EC Commission (1990). "One market, one money." *European Economy,* 44, October.

*Economist, The* (2004). "Big Maccurrencies." *The Economist.* Retrieved from the World Wide Web on July 2004: http://www.economist.com/markets/Bigmac/Index.cfm.

Editorial (2002). "The Euro's right turn." *The Wall Street Journal*. New York: April 26. A10.

Eichengreen, B. (1993). "European monetary unification." *Journal of Economic Literature*, 31: 1321–1354.

Europa (2004). "Exchange rates: ERM fluctuations." Eurostat Metadata in SDDS format: Summary methodology. Retrieved from the World Wide Web in November 2004: http://europa.eu.int/comm/eurostat/newcronos/reference/sdds/en/exint/ermfluc_sm.htm.

European Central Bank (2002). "The single monetary policy in the Euro Area: general documentation on Eurosystem Monetary Policy Instruments and Procedures." (2002) April.

European Central Bank (2003). "Enlargement of the European Union." *ECB Annual Report 2003*. 156–165.

European Central Bank (2003). "Policy position of the Governing Council of the European Central Bank on exchange rate issues relating to the acceding countries." December 18. Retrieved from the World Wide Web in January 2004 at www.ecb.int.

European Central Bank (2003). Developments in the euro area's international cost and price competitiveness. ECB Monthly Bulletin, August 2003 pp. 67–74. Retrieved from the World Wide Web on June 2004: http://www.ecb.int.

European Central Bank (2004). "Conventions and procedures for the exchange rate mechanism II (ERM II)." *ECB Monthly Bulletin July 2004*. p. 41–42.

European Central Bank (2004). *Convergence Report 2004*. October. Retrieved from the World Wide Web in October 2004: http://www.ecb.int.

European Central Bank (2004). Euro Area participating countries. Retrieved from the World Wide Web in November 24, 2004: http://www.ecb.int/bc/intro/html/map.en.html.

European Central Bank (2004). Euro Area statistics. *ECB Monthly Bulletin*. Retrieved from the World Wide Web on July 2004: http://www.ecb.int.

European Central Bank (2004). "Frequently asked questions: EU enlargement and Economic and Monetary Union (EMU)." Retrieved from the World Wide Web in July 2004 at www.ecb.int.

European Central Bank (2004). "Long-term interest rates for assessing convergence in the acceding countries." April 29 press release. Retrieved from the World Wide Web on September 29, 2004, at www.ecb.int.

European Central Bank (2004). Section 8.1: effective exchange rates. ECB Monthly Bulletin, January 2004. Retrieved from the World Wide Web on January 2004: http://www.ecb.int. *European Central Bank*. January.

European Commission (1998). "The euro: our currency—conversion rates." Retrieved from the World Wide Web in December 2004: http://europa.eu.int/comm/economy_finance/euro/transition/conversion_rates.htm.

European Commission (1998). *European Economy*. Spring, Supplement A. p. 13.

European Commission (2003). *European Economy*. Spring.

Frankel, J. (2004). "Real convergence and euro adoption in Central and Eastern Europe: trade and business cycle correlations and endogenous criteria for joining EMU." Paper for conference on euro Adoption in the Accession Countries—Opportunities and Challenges, Czech National Bank, Prague, February 2–3.

Fratianni, M., J. Von Hagen, and D. Salvatore (1990). *Macroeconomic Policy in Open Economies*. Westport, CT: Greenwood Publishing.

Frommel M. and L. Menkhoff (2001). "Risk reduction in the EMS? Evidence from trends in exchange rate properties." *Journal of Common Market Studies*. 39 (2), 285–306.

Gerber, J. (2005). *International Economics*. 3rd ed. New York: Pearson, Addison-Wesley.

Grant, J. (2001). "Greece, Finland begins historic euro cash launch." *World Reuters*. Retrieved from the World Wide Web in January 2002: wysiwyg://19//http:// dailynews.yahoo.com/h/nm/20011231/wl/euro_dc_5.html.

Gros, D. and N. Thygesen (1998). *European Monetary Integration from the European Monetary System to Economic and Monetary Union*. 2nd ed. New York: Addison Wesley Longman Limited.

Guerrera, F. and G. Parker (2003). "France warned not to flout euro rules." *Financial Times*. January 30.

Hefeker, C. (2004). "Monetary policy for a larger Europe." *Intereconomics*. Hamburg: July/August, Vol. 39, Iss. 4; p. 178.

Hochreiter E. and H. Wagner (2002). "The road to the euro—exchange rate arrangements in European transition economies." *Annals of the American Academy of Social and Political Science*. Edited by Tavlas G. and M. Ulan. Vol. 579, 168–182.

Husted, S. and M. Melvin (2004). *International Economics*. 6th ed. New York: Pearson, Addison-Wesley.

International Monetary Fund (2004). International Financial Statistics database and browser. December CD-ROM; Washington D.C.

International Monetary Fund (April 2002). World Economic Outlook: Recessions and Recoveries. Washington D.C.

International Monetary Fund (July 2004). International Financial Statistics database and browser. CD-ROM; Washington D.C.

International Monetary Fund (September 2004). International Financial Statistics database and browser. CD-ROM; Washington D.C.

Jones, R. A. (2001), *The Politics and Economics of the European Union: An Introductory Text*. 2nd ed. Cheltenham, UK: Edward Elgar.

Kenen, P. B. (1969). "The Theory of Optimum Currency Areas: An Eclectic View," in R.A. Mundell and A.K. Swoboda (eds). *Monetary Problems of the International Economy*. Chicago: University of Chicago Press, 41–61.

Kenen, P. B. (1995). *Economic and Monetary Union in Europe Moving Beyond the Maastricht*. New York: Cambridge University Press.

Kowalski, P. (2003). "Nominal and real convergence in alternative exchange rate regimes in transition countries: implications for the EMU accession," *Center for Social and Economic Research Studies & Analyses*, 270.

Krugman, P. (1991). *Geography and Trade*. Cambridge, MA: MIT Press.

Krugman, P. and M. Obstfeld (2003). *International Economics: Theory and Policy*. 6th ed. New York: Addison Wesley.

Leblond, P. (2004). "Completing the Maastricht contract." *Journal of Common Market Studies*. Vol. 43, No. 3, pp. 553–72.

"Lisbon Agenda" (2004). *EurActiv.com—EU News, Policy Positions & EU Actors online*. November 8. Retrieved from the World Wide Web on November 21, 2004: http://www.euractiv.com.

Mallet, V. (2002). "Paris may join Berlin to save Stability Pact." *Financial Times*. November 20.

Mallet, V. (2002). "Trial order jeopardises Trichet bid to lead." *Financial Times*. July 17.

Mann, C. L. (1999). Is the US trade deficit sustainable? Institute for International Economics, Washington, D.C.

Marinov, M. A. (2002). *Internationalization in Central and Eastern Europe*. Great Britain: Ashgate Publishing.

McKinnon, R. (1963). "Optimum currency areas." *American Economic Review*. 53, 207–222.

McKinnon, R. (2004). "Optimum currency areas and key currencies: Mundell I versus Mundell II." *Journal of Common Market Studies*. November, 42, 4, pp. 689–715. Blackwell Publishing.

Melvin, M. (2001). *International Money and Finance*. 6th ed. New York: Addison-Wesley.

Mishkin, F. (2004). *The Economics of Money, Banking, and Financial Markets*. 7th ed. New York: Pearson, Addison Wesley.

Molle, W. (2001). *The Economics of European Integration—Theory, Practice, Policy*. 4th ed. Great Britain: Ashgate Publishing.

Mundell, R. (1961). "A theory of optimum currency areas." *American Economic Review*. 51, 657–665.

Mundell, R. (1973a). "Uncommon arguments for common currencies." Johnson, H.G. and A.K. Swoboda (eds).

Mundell, R. (1973b). "A plan for a European currency." Johnson, H.G. and A.K. Swoboda (eds).

Neal, L. and D. Barbezat (1998). *The Economics of the European Union and the Economies of Europe*. New York: Oxford University Press.

OANDA, The Currency Site (2004). FXHistory: historical currency exchange rates. Retrieved from the World Wide Web on May 2004: http://www.oanda.com.

Pacific Exchange Rate Service (2004). Database retrieval system. University of British Columbia; Sauder School of Business. Retrieved from the World Wide Web on March 2004: http://fx.sauders.ubc.ca.

Padoa-Schioppa, T. (2000). *The Road to Monetary Union in Europe—The Emperor, the Kings, and the Genies.* Oxford University Press.

Papademos, L. (2003). "Policy challenges of euro area enlargement." Speech at the 37th Economic Policy Panel Meeting, Athens, April 11. *EMU: Assessing the Impact of the Euro.* Edited by Baldwin R. et al.

Papademos, L. (2004). "Monetary policy in an enlarged euro area." Speech at the Asymmetries in Trade and Currency Arrangements in the 21st Century conference. Deutsche Bundesbank, July 29.

Parker, G. (2002). "Sweden not ready to join euro says Brussels." *Financial Times.* May 22.

Parker, G. and H. Simonian (2002). "France and Germany ordered to curb deficits." *Financial Times.* November 14.

Pollard, P. S. (2003). "A look inside two central banks: the European Central Bank and the Federal Reserve." *Federal Reserve Bank of St. Louis Review.* January/February, pp. 11–30.

Pournarakis, M. (2002). "Exchange Rate Regimes and Economic Policy Dilemmas in the European Transition Economies." *Money and Finance in the Global Economy; Challenges and Opportunities for the 21st Century.* Edited by Kintis, A. et al. APF Press; Toronto, Canada.

Reinert, K. A. (2005). *Windows on the World Economy: An Introduction to International Economics.* Thomson South-Western; US.

"Rome pressure on stability pact." (2002). *Financial Times.* July 7.

Romer, P. M. (1986). "Increasing returns and long-run growth." *Journal of Political Economy.* 94 (5), pp. 1002–1037.

Rosenberg, M. (2003). *Exchange Rate Determination; Models and Strategies for Exchange Rate Forecasting.* New York: McGraw-Hill.

Sawyer, C. S. and R. L. Sprinkle (2003). *International Economics.* New Jersey: Prentice Hall.

*Single European Act.* (1986). Council of the European Communities. Treaty published by the Office for Official Publications of the European Communities.

Solow, R. M. (1956). "A contribution to the theory of economic growth." *Quarterly Journal of Economics.* LXX, pp. 65–94.

Thornhill, J. (2004). "Camdessus prescribes bitter pills for ailing French economy." *Financial Times.* October 20.

Traistaru, I., P. Nijkamp, and L. Resmini (ed.) (2003). *The emerging economic geography in EU accession countries.* Great Britain: Ashgate Publishing.

*Treaty establishing the European Economic Community and connected documents.* (1957). Treaty published by the Secretariat of the Interim Committee for the Common Market and EURATOM, Brussels.

Trichet, J. C. (2001). "The Euro after two years." *Journal of Common Market Studies.* 39 (1), 1–13.

Trichet, J. C. (2004). "EU enlargement: challenges and opportunities." Speech at the Europe's frontiers: EU enlargement-its implications and consequences conference. Lisbon, October 27. Retrieved from the World Wide Web in October 2004 at: http://www.ecb.int.

Tumpel-Gugerell, G. (2003). "The euro in central and eastern Europe." Opening remarks at the Panel Discussion Euro Finance Week, October 27. *European Central Bank* [Electronic Version]

Turner, D. (2002). "Eurozone seek productivity secret." *Financial Times.* May 7.

Van den Berg, H. (2004). *International Economics.* New York: McGraw Hill, Irwin.

Weale, M. (1999). "Monetary and fiscal policy in Euroland." *Journal of Common Market Studies.* 37 (1), 153–62.

Williamson, H. (2002). "Strikes expose strains on German collective bargaining." *Financial Times.* May 8.

World Bank (2002). *Transition—The first ten years: analysis and lessons for Eastern Europe and the former Soviet Union.* Washington, D.C.

Wyplosz, C. (ed). (2001). *The Impact of EMU on Europe and the Developing Countries.* New York; Oxford University Press.

Yarbrough, B. and R. Yarbrough (2003). *The World Economy: Trade and Finance.* 6th ed. Thomson South-Western; US.

Yin, L., L. Michelis, and G. Zestos (2003). "Economic convergence in the European Union." *Journal of Economic Integration.* 18 (1), March, pp. 188–213.

Yusuf, S. et al. (eds). (2000). *Entering the 21st Century: World Development Report 1999/2000.* World Bank. New York: Oxford University Press.

Zestos, G. and L. Yin (2004). "Global Economic Convergence." Working Paper. pp. 1–52.

Zoubir, Y. and F. S. Lhabitant (2003). *Doing business in emerging Europe.* Great Britain: Palgrave Macmillan.

# Index